Continue the pattern by coloring squares in each row.

In the space beside each row, write the number of squares you colored in that row.

What do you notice about those numbers?

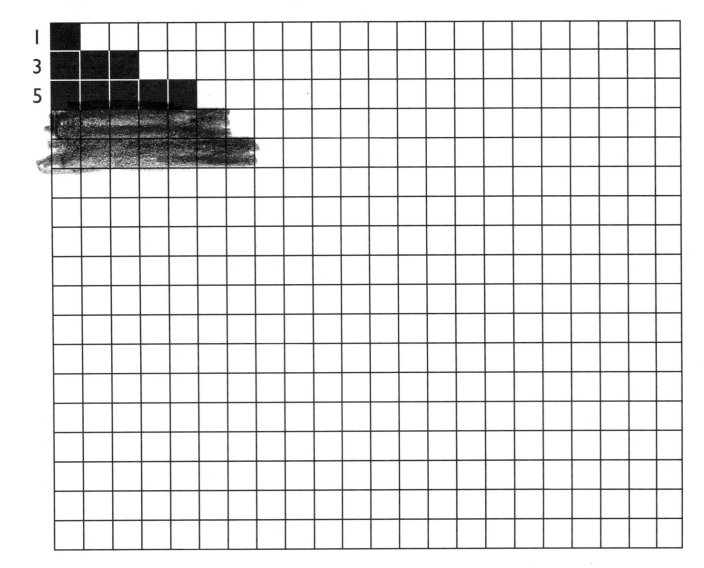

Use the 4 dominoes with the least number of dots and the 4 dominoes with the greatest number of dots. Cover the rectangle. Each side must have the same number of dots.

Hint: Dominoes with the greatest number of dots should be in the center of each line.

Write an equation for each side.

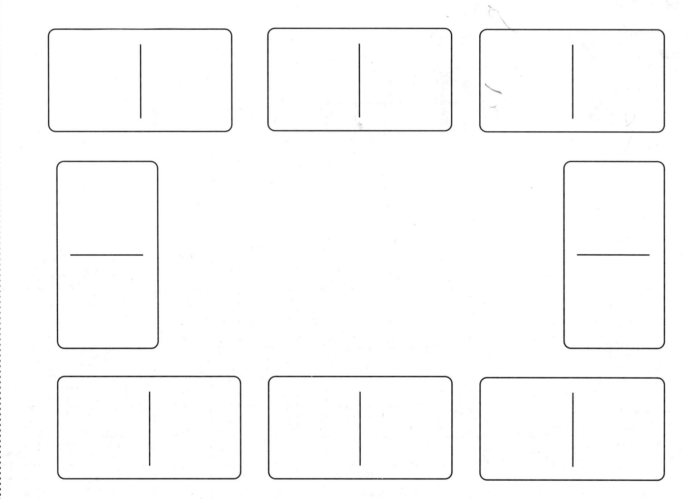

Using 2 colors, find different ways to make 8 using addition. Color in the squares and record the equation next to its grid.

$6 + 2 = 8$ 4. $12 + 10 = 22$ 5. $8 + 14 = 22$ 6. $9 + 13 = 22$ 7. $16 + 6 = 22$

9. $8 + 14 = 22$
8. $15 + 7 = 22$
10. $5 + 17 = 22$
11. $4 + 18 = 22$
12. $3 + 19 = 22$
13. $2 + 20 = 22$
14. $18 + 4 = 22$
15. $22 + 0 = 22$
16. $7 + 4 + 11 = 22$
17. $4 + 9 + 9 = 22$

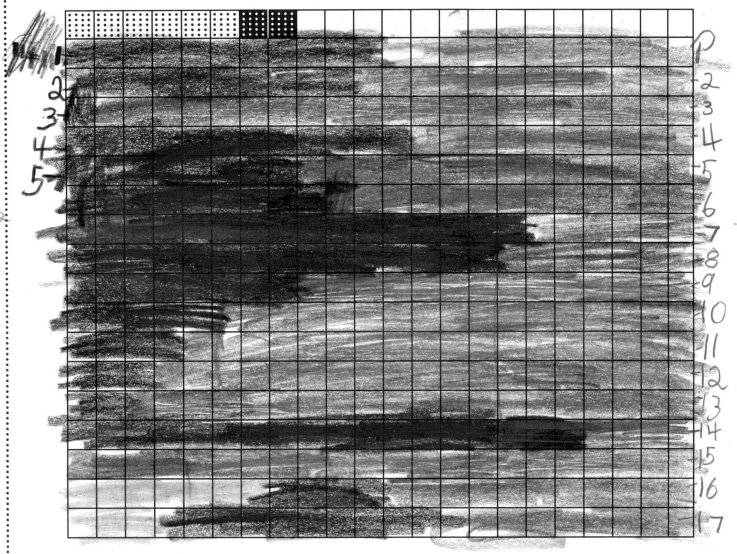

Use these dominoes:

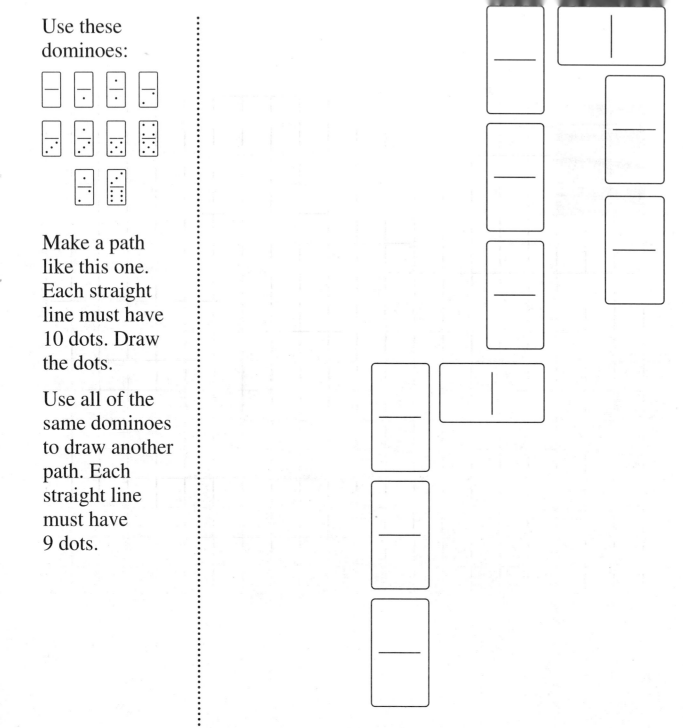

Make a path
like this one.
Each straight
line must have
10 dots. Draw
the dots.

Use all of the
same dominoes
to draw another
path. Each
straight line
must have
9 dots.

Using 1 color, find different ways to make 12 using multiplication. Color in the squares and record each equation next to its grid.

How many ways can you find?

4 x 3 = 12

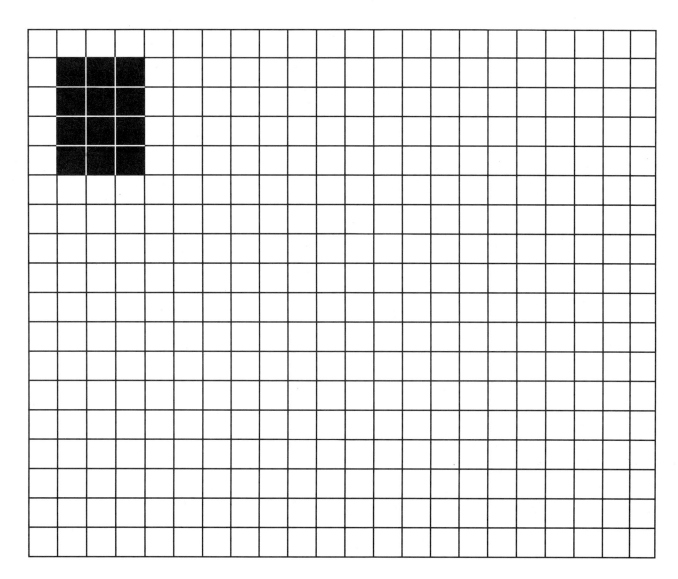

Use these
dominoes:

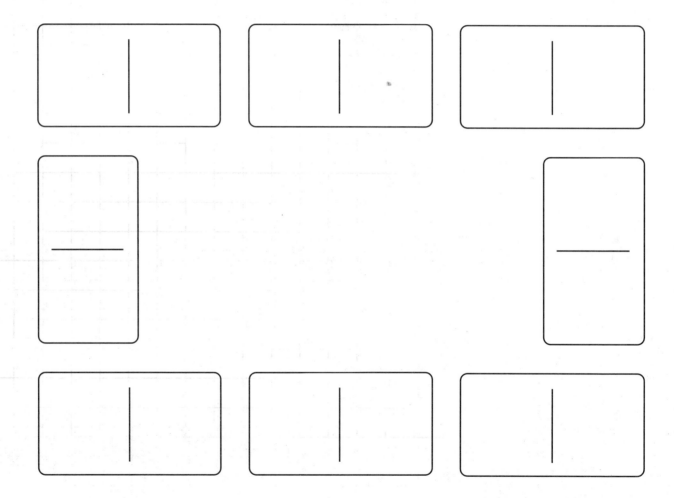

Cover the
square. Each
side must have
20 dots. Draw
the dots.

Write an
equation for
each side.

Continue the pattern by coloring squares in each row.

In the space beside each row, write the number of squares you colored in that row.

What do you notice about those numbers?

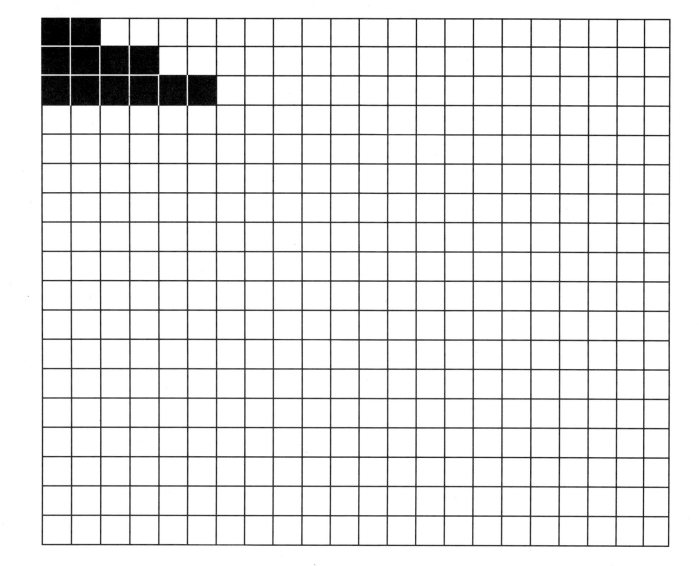

Use these dominoes:

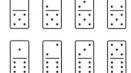

Make a path like this one. Each straight line must have 20 dots. Draw the dots.

Use all of the same dominoes to draw another path. Each straight line must have 16 dots.

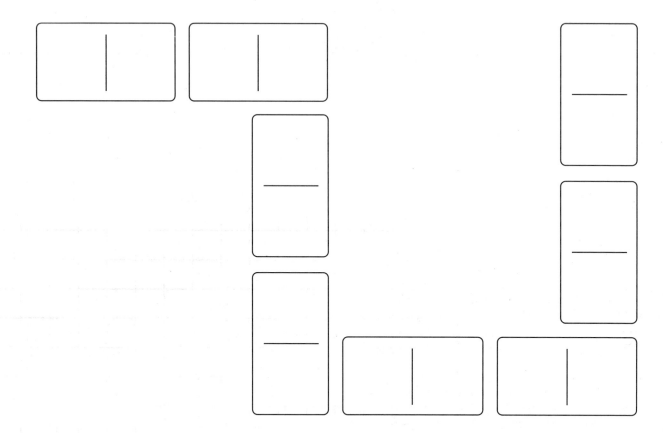

Continue the pattern by coloring the squares in each row.

In the space beside each row, write the number of squares you colored in that row.

What do you notice about the numbers you just wrote?

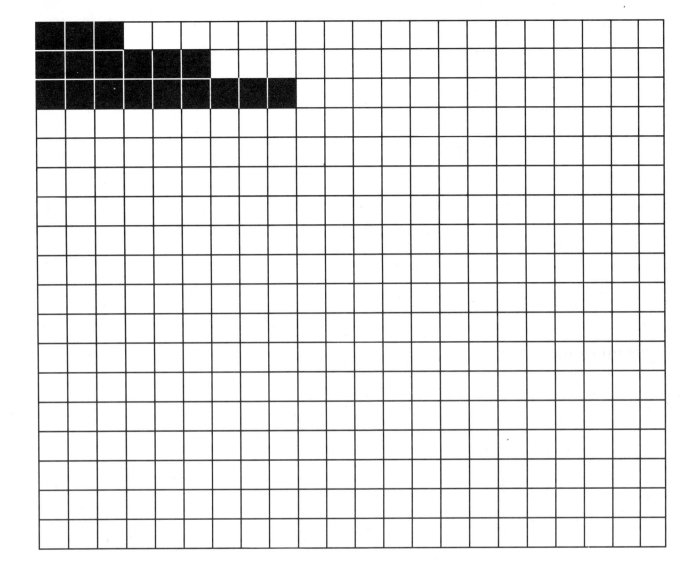

Use these
dominoes:

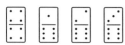

Cover the
square. Each
side must have
17 dots. Draw
the dots.

Write an
equation for
each side.

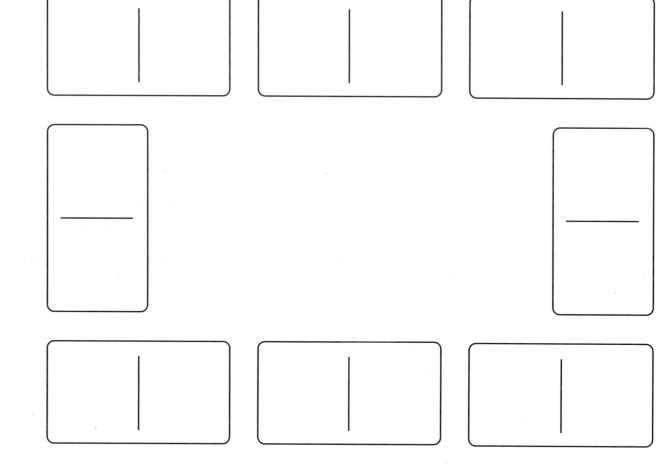

Continue the pattern by coloring in 4 more in each row.

In the space beside each row, write the number of squares you colored in that row.

What do you notice about the numbers?

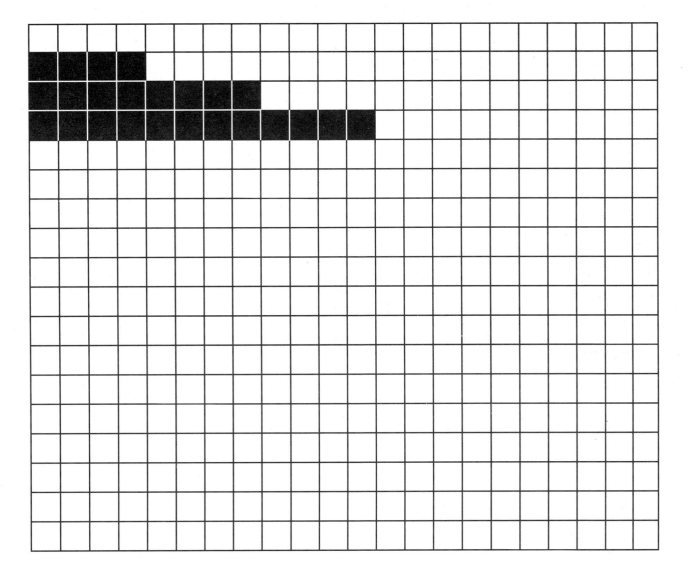

Use these
dominoes:

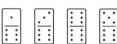

Make a path
like this one.
Each straight
line must have
23 dots. Draw
the dots.

Remove
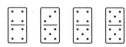 and 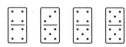 .
Use the rest of
the dominoes
to draw another
path. Each
straight line
must have
18 dots.

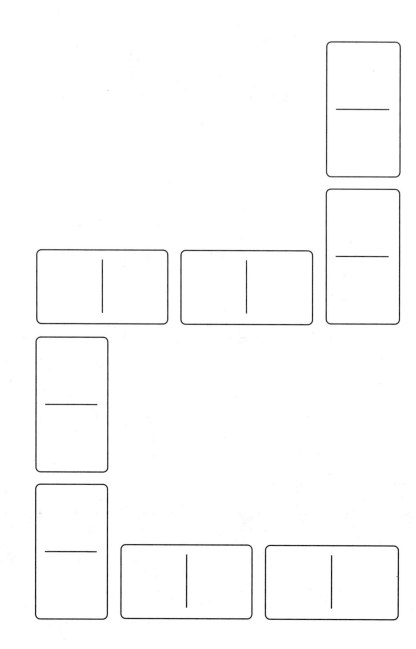

Color 3 rows
of 3 squares red.
Color 1 row of
9 squares blue.
Color 9 rows of
1 square green.

What do you
notice about the
squares you just
colored?

Record your
findings using
addition. Write
the equation
next to its grid.

$3 + 3 + 3 = 9$

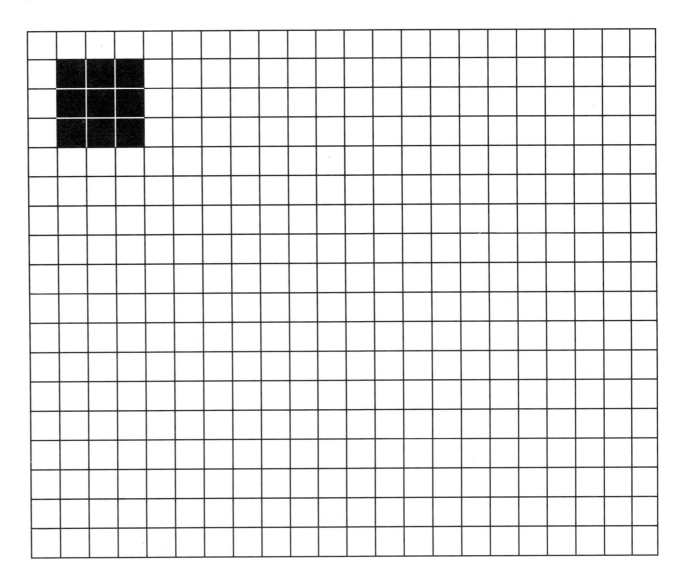

Use these
dominoes:

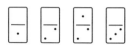
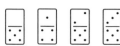

Cover the
square. Each
side must have
11 dots. Draw
the dots.

Write an
equation for
each side.

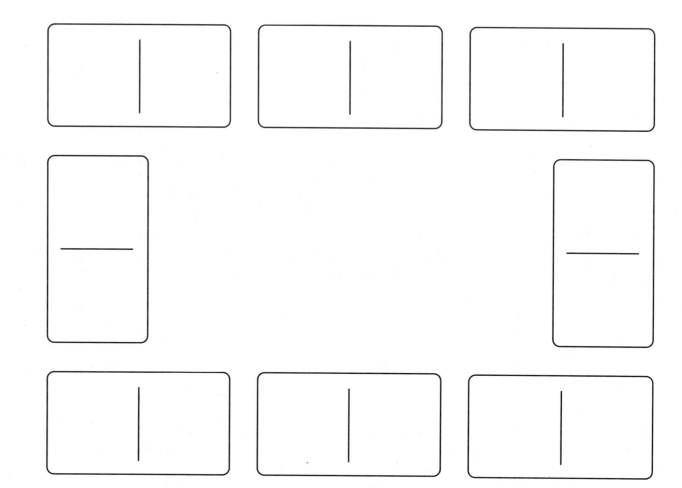

Using 2 colors, find different ways to make the sum equal 9. Color in the squares and record each equation next to its grid.

How many can you find?

$2 + 7 = 9$

Use these dominoes:

Make a path like this one. Each straight line must have 15 dots. Draw the dots.

Remove and . Use the rest of the dominoes to draw another path. Each straight line must have 17 dots.

Using 2 colors, find different ways to make the sum equal 10. Color in the squares and record each equation next to its grid.

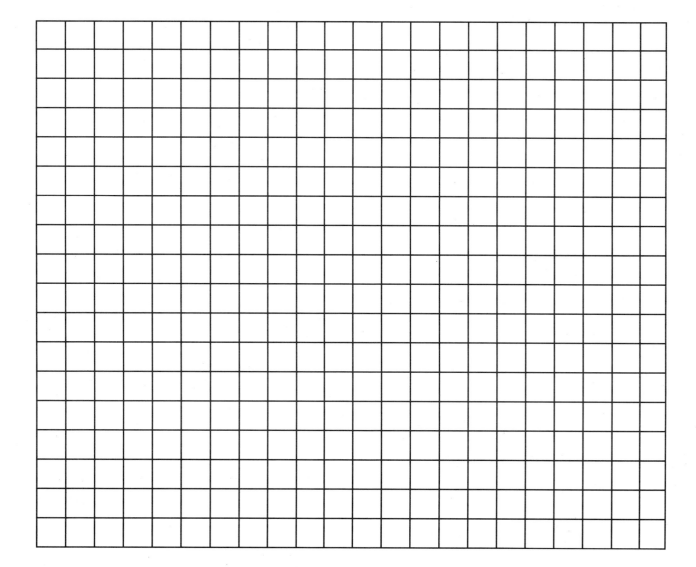

Use these dominoes:

Cover the square. Each side must have 10 dots. Draw the dots.

Write an equation for each side.

Using 1 color, find different ways to make the product equal 14. Color in the squares and record each equation next to its grid.

How many ways can you find?

$2 \times 7 = 14$

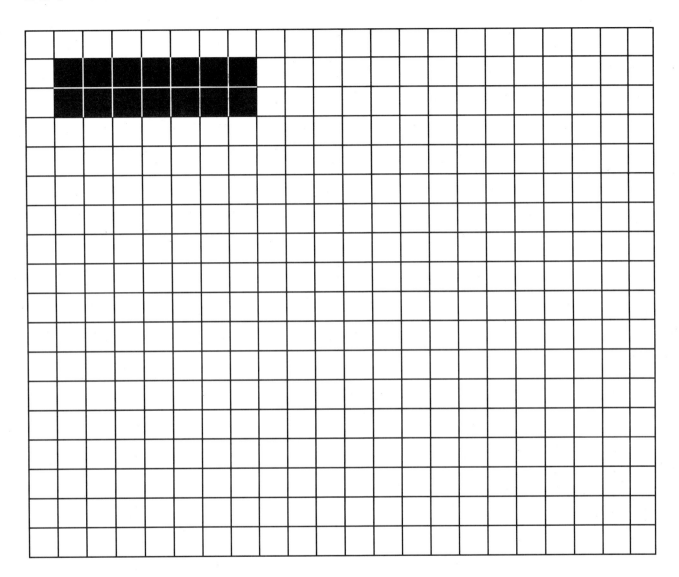

Use these
dominoes:

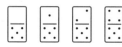

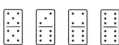

Make a path
like this one.
Each straight
line must have
21 dots. Draw
the dots.

Remove [.|:.].
Use the rest of
the dominoes
to draw another
path. Each
straight line
must have
15 dots.

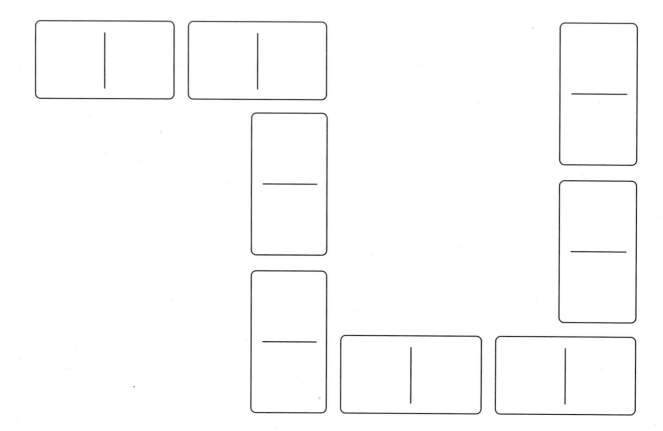

Using 1 color, find different ways to make the product equal 15. Color in the squares and record the equation next to its grid.

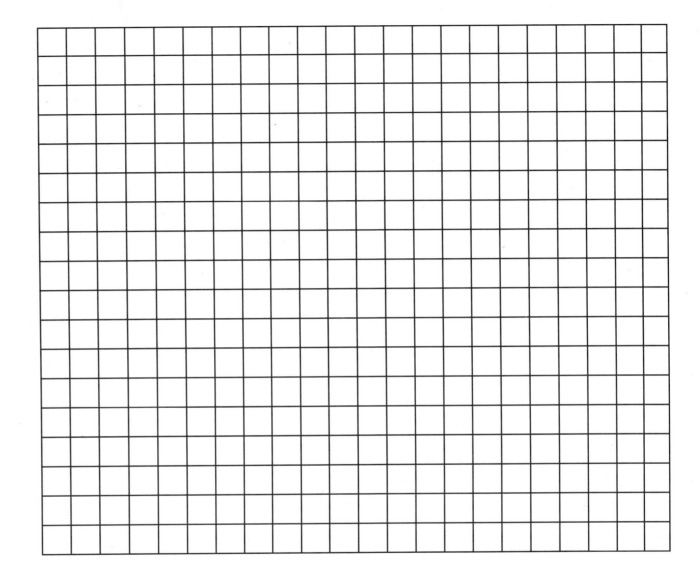

Use these
dominoes:

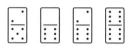

Cover the
square. Each
side must have
14 dots. Draw
the dots.

Write an
equation for
each side.

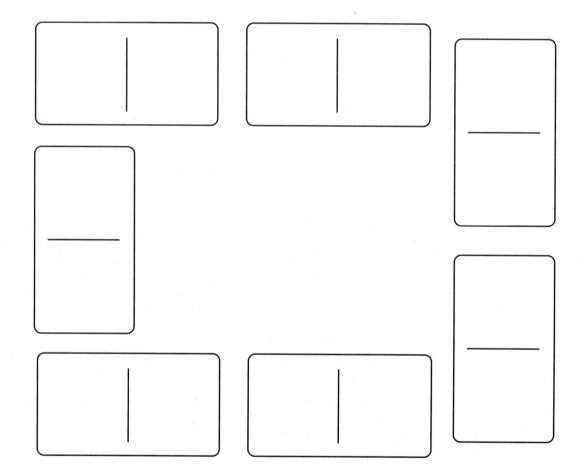

Using 1 color, find different ways to make the product equal 18. Record each equation next to its grid.

How many ways can you find?

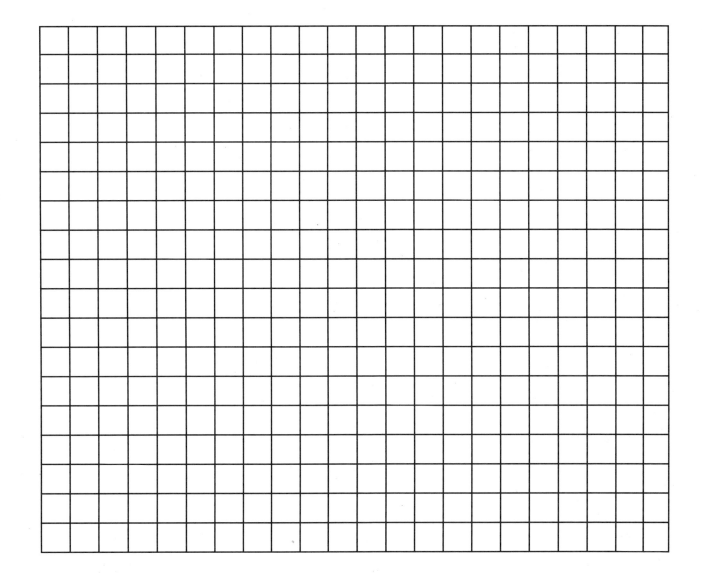

Use these
dominoes:

Make a path
like this one.
Each straight
line must
have the same
number of
dots. Draw
the dots.

Use all of the
same dominoes
to draw another
path. Each
straight line
must have
5 dots.

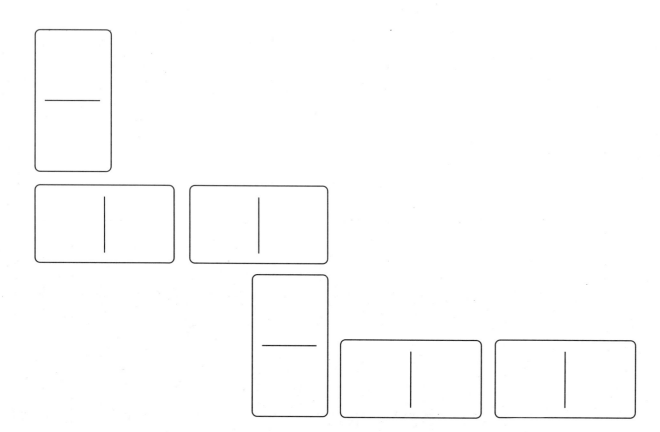

Color in the
first 5 squares
in the top row.

Continue the
pattern by
coloring 5 more
in each row.

In the space
beside each
row, write the
number of
squares you
colored in
that row.

What do you
notice about
the numbers?

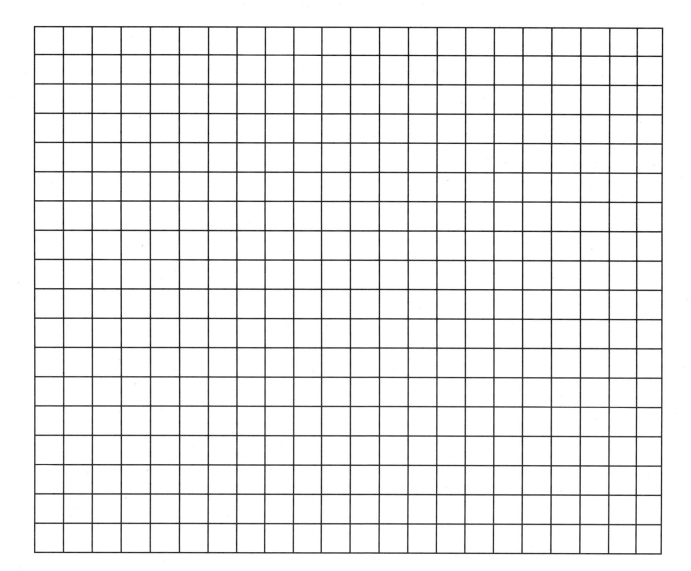

Use these
dominoes:

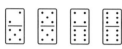

Cover the
square. Each
side must have
17 dots. Draw
the dots.

Write an
equation for
each side.

Color 6 rows of 5 squares red. Color 5 rows of 6 squares blue. Color 3 rows of 10 squares green. Color 10 rows of 3 squares yellow. Color 2 rows of 15 squares pink. Color 15 rows of 2 squares orange.

In the space beside each group, write the number of squares you colored in that grid.

What do you notice about those numbers?

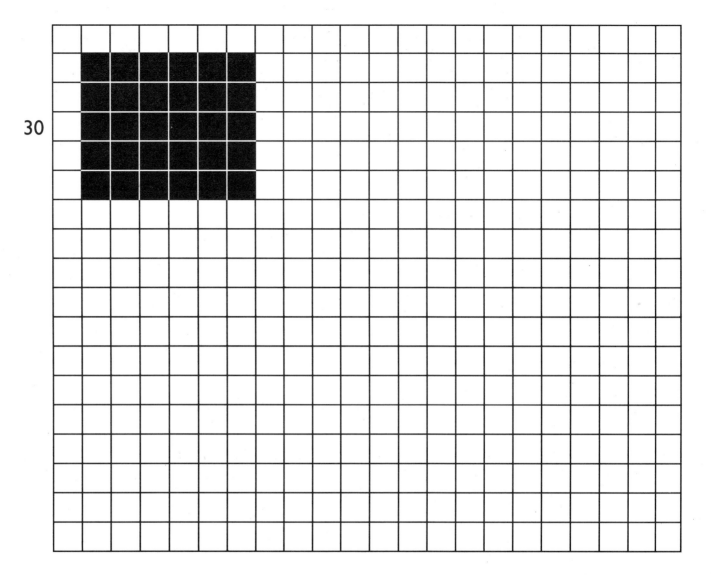

30

Use these
dominoes:

Make a path
like this one.
Each straight
line must have
18 dots. Draw
the dots.

Use all of the
same dominoes
to draw another
path. Each
straight line
must have
12 dots.

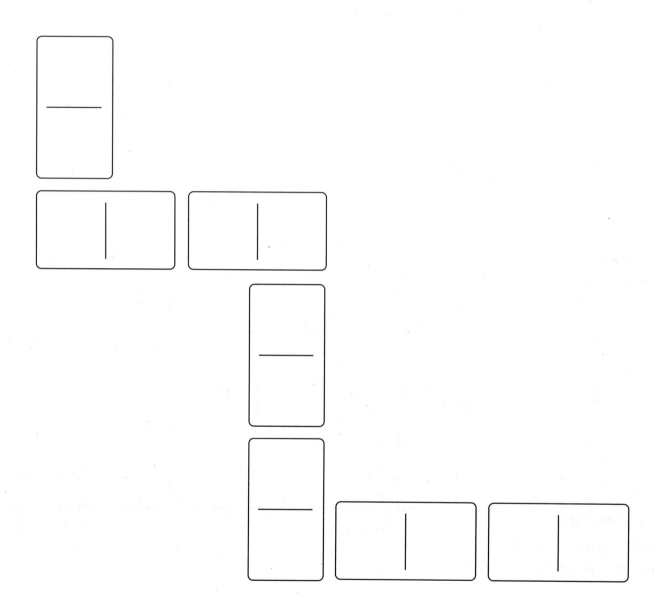

Color 4 rows of
9 squares red.
Color 9 rows of
4 squares green.
Color 6 rows of
6 squares blue.

In the space
beside each
group, write
the number of
squares colored.
What do you
notice about
those numbers?

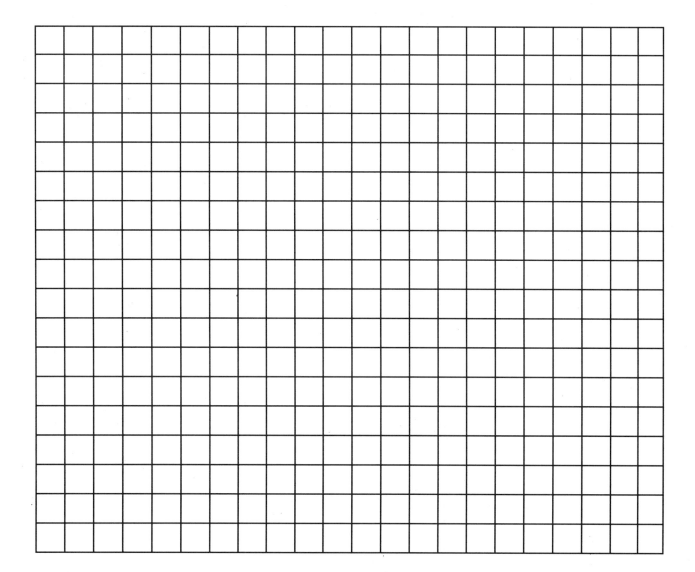

Use these
dominoes:

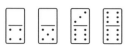

Cover the
square. Each
side must have
13 dots. Draw
the dots.

Write an
equation for
each side.

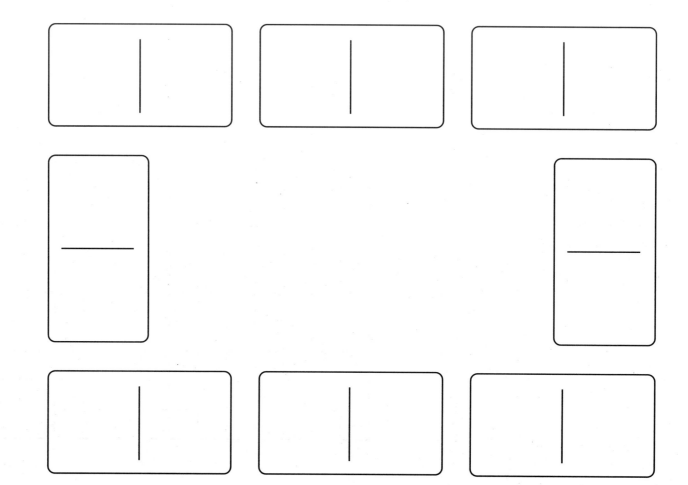

Using 1 color, find different ways to make 12 by adding the same numbers. Record each equation next to its grid.

$4 + 4 + 4 = 12$

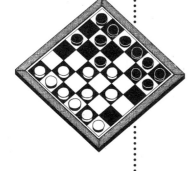

Use these
dominoes:

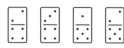

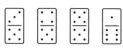

Make a path
like this one.
Each straight
line must have
19 dots. Draw
the dots.

Remove [:|::].
Use the rest of
the dominoes
to draw another
path. Each
straight line
must have
11 dots.

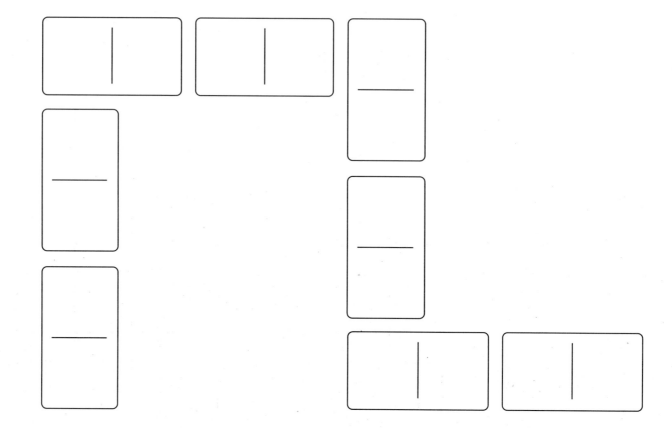

Using 2 colors, find different ways to make the sum equal 15. Record the equation next to its grid.

How many ways can you find?

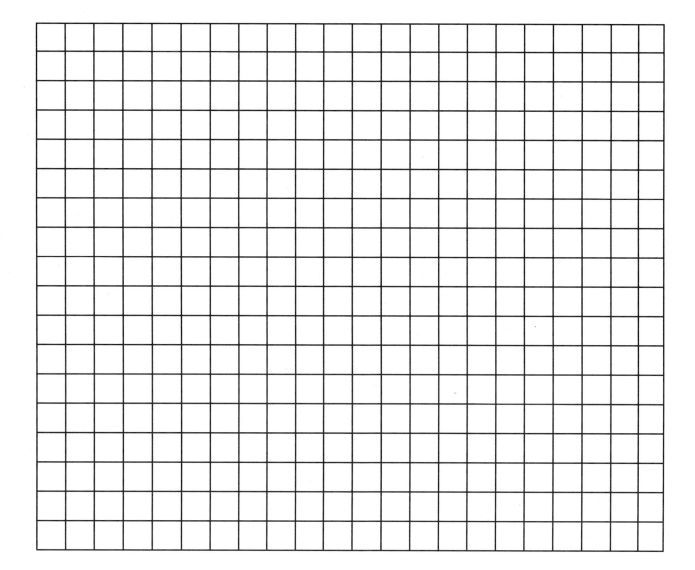

Use these
dominoes:

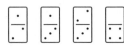
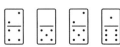

Cover the
square. Each
side must have
15 dots. Draw
the dots.

Write an
equation for
each side.

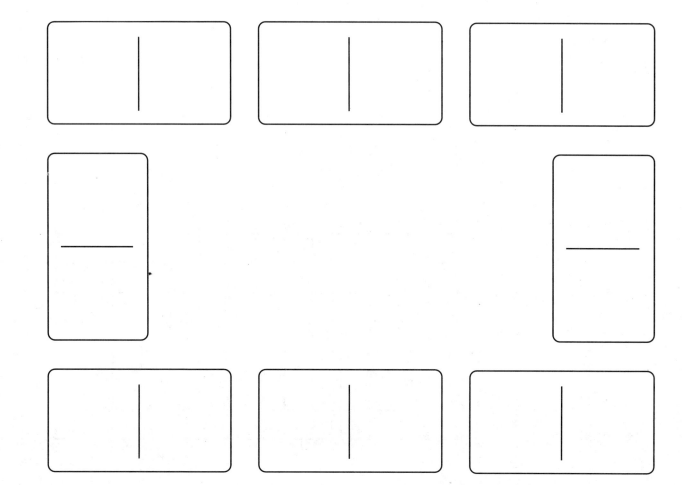

Using 1 color, find different ways to make 16 by adding the same numbers. Record each equation next to its grid.

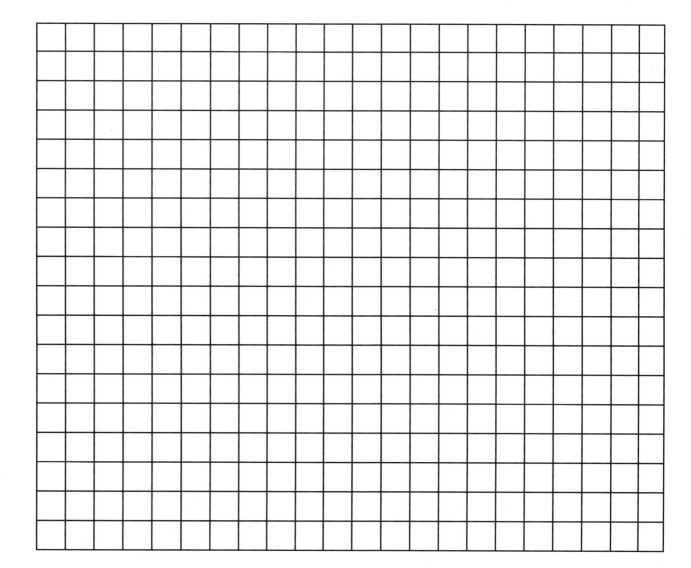

Use the blank domino and the 6 dominoes containing zero number of dots on one side. Make a path like this one. Each straight line must have 6 dots. Draw the dots.

Use all of the same dominoes to draw another path. Each straight line must have 7 dots.

Using one color, find different ways to make the product equal 24. Record the equation next to its grid.

How many ways can you find?

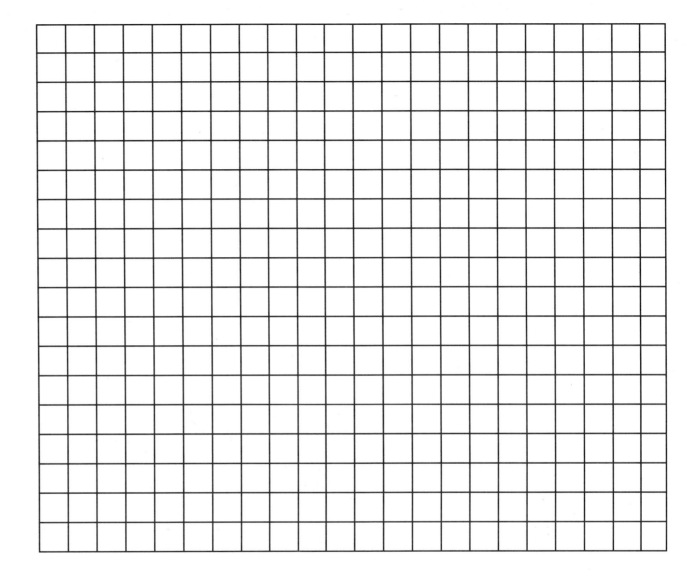

Use these
dominoes:

Cover the
square. Each
side must have
12 dots. Draw
the dots.

Write an
equation for
each side.

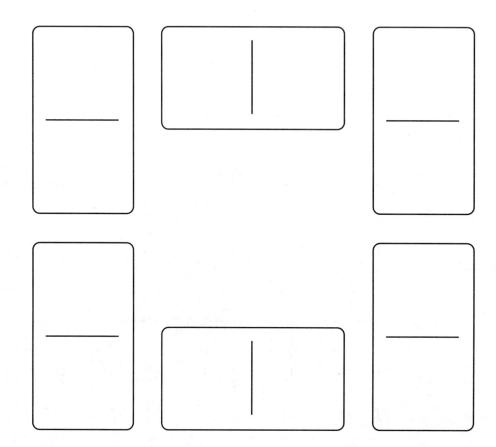

Using 1 color, find different ways to make the product equal 36. Record the equation next to its grid.

How many ways can you find?

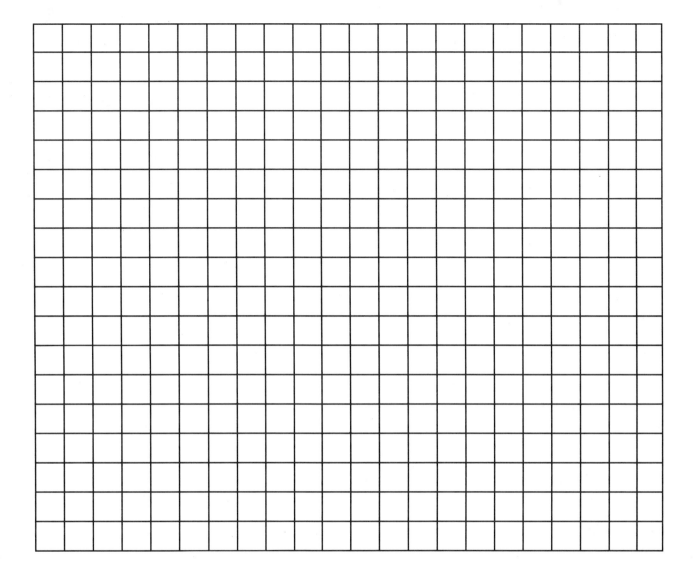

Use these
dominoes:

Make a path
like this one.
Each straight
line must have
11 dots. Draw
the dots.

Use all of the
same dominoes
to draw another
path. Each
straight line
must have 12
dots. Your
path can go
in different
directions.

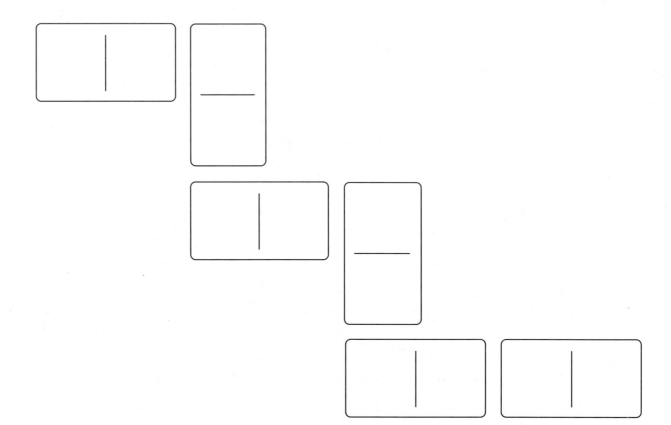

Using one color, find different ways to make the product equal 48. Record the equation next to its grid.

How many ways can you find?

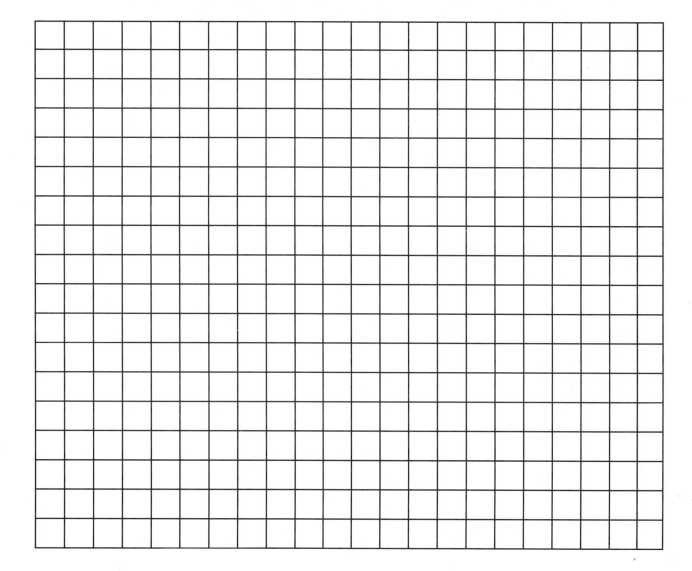

Use these dominoes:

Cover the square. Each side must have 16 dots. Draw the dots.

Write an equation for each side.

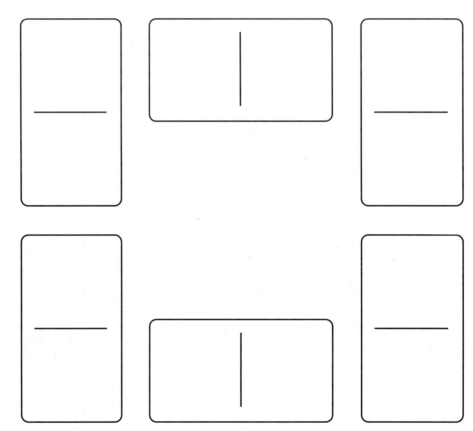

Color 6 rows of 8 squares blue. Color 8 rows of 6 squares green. Color 4 rows of 12 squares red. Color 12 rows of 4 squares yellow.

Write the number of squares you colored in that grid.

What do you notice about those numbers?

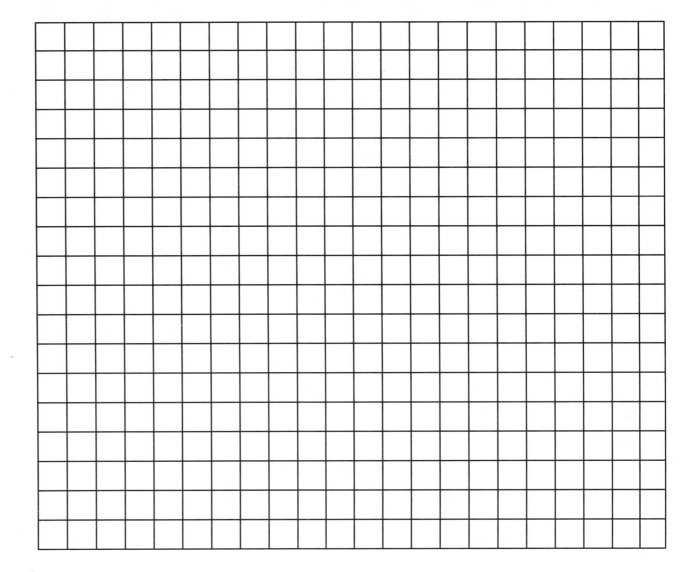

Use these
dominoes:

Make a path
like this one.
Each straight
line must have
13 dots. Draw
the dots.

Use all of the
same dominoes
to draw another
path. Each
straight line
must have
16 dots.

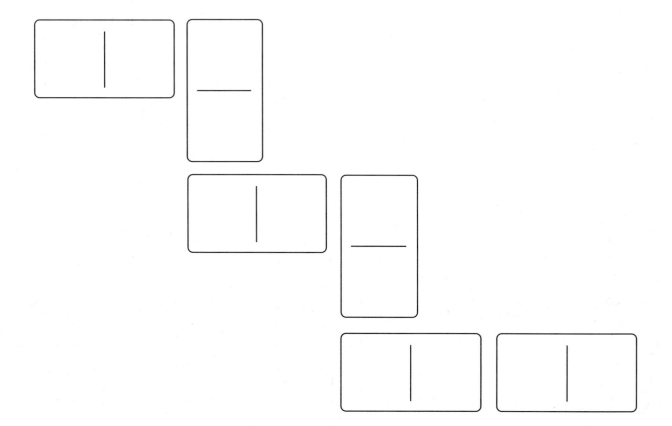

Using 2 colors, find different ways to make the sum equal 18. Record the equation next to its grid.

How many ways can you find?

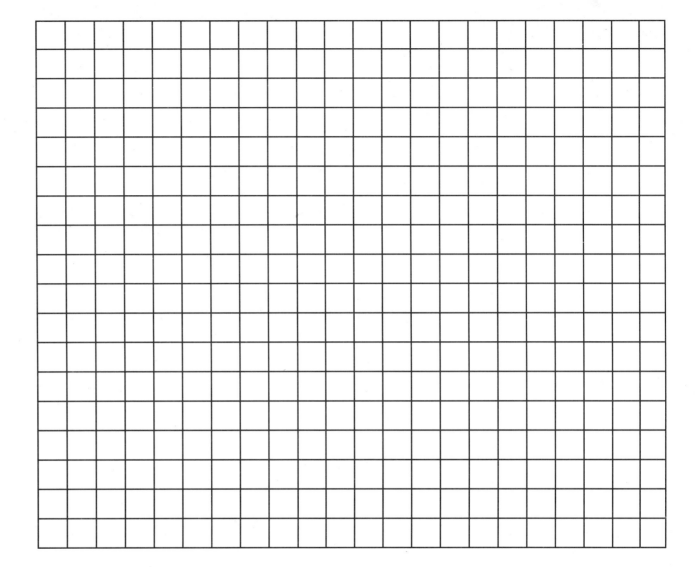

Use these
dominoes:

Cover the
square. Each
side must have
14 dots. Draw
the dots.

Write an
equation for
each side.

EXAMPLE
$2 + 2 + 4 + 6 = 14$

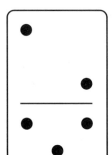

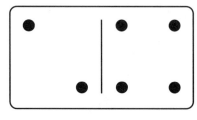

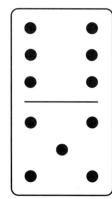

Using 1 color, find different ways to make the product equal 40. Record the equation next to its grid.

How many ways can you find?

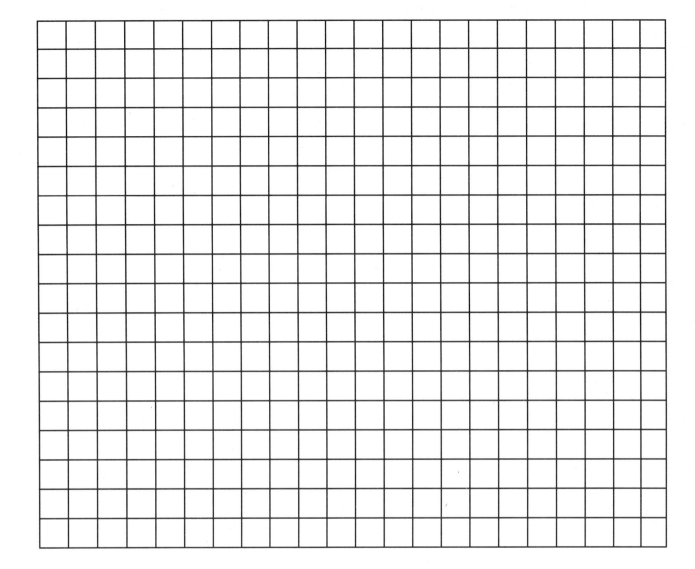

Use these
dominoes:

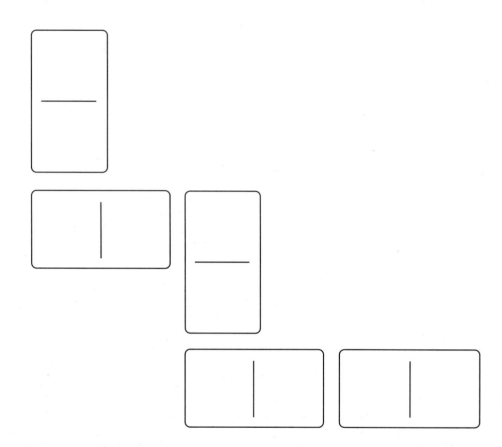

Make a path
like this one.
Each straight
line must have
3 dots. Draw
the dots.

Use all of the
same dominoes
to draw another
path. Each
straight line
must have
5 dots.

The Outlined Bible

An Outline and Analysis of Every Book in the Bible

GIVEN BY

ROBERT LEE

at the Mildmay Conference Hall Bible School, London

LONDON
PICKERING & INGLIS LTD.

PICKERING & INGLIS LTD.
29 LUDGATE HILL, LONDON, E.C.4
26 BOTHWELL STREET, GLASGOW, C.2
Fleming H. Revell Company, Westwood, New Jersey

SBN 7208 0025 0

TWENTY-FIFTH IMPRESSION

PREFACE

THE following Bible Studies, which have been designed and arranged to show at a glance the contents of each separate book of the Bible, formed part of a five years' course at the Mildmay Bible School, which I had the honour to conduct. The majority of them were planned and prepared with no idea whatever of publication, and that they have been published only at the urgent solicitations of many Missionaries and Christian workers who listened to them, and of friends in many parts who have been helped by them.

As a preparation for a more exhaustive study of the Word, this system is indispensable. In order to read the 66 books of the Bible with some degree of intelligence, it is necessary to understand something of their human authors, the various purposes they had in mind when writing them, their distinctive styles, and other peculiarities. It is also good sometimes to note the opinions of others concerning them, and thus be awakened into a more prayerful study of any book in the Divine Library that hitherto may have seemed dry and uninteresting.

Commenting on such studies as these, the late Dr. PIERSON wrote these timely words: "**In beginning the study of a book it is well to take a forward glance over its entire contents, as we look over the map of a country or district we are about to explore, to get the lay of the land, or from a mountain-top to get a survey of the entire horizon.**"

I need hardly say that these studies are SUGGESTIVE, and by no means exhaustive. The limited space at my disposal only permitted the barest of comments, and the rather large and unwieldy appearance is essential in order that each book may be seen at a glance. I ought also to say that, to be of the fullest service, these studies must be used as originally intended. When given, each one present at the School received a cyclostyled copy of the Analysis; during the Lecture they had it before them with the opened Bible; after the Lecture they took it home with them, and went carefully over the Bible book with its aid.

ROBERT LEE

ANALYSES of the BOOKS of the OLD TESTAMENT

Book.	Key Words or Phrase.	Message.
GENESIS,	BEGINNING,	The Failure of Man Met by the Salvation of God.
EXODUS,	REDEEM,	Redemption by Blood.
LEVITICUS,	HOLINESS, ATONEMENT,	Access to God Through Blood. Holiness of Redeemed Imperative.
NUMBERS,	SERVICE, SOJOURNING, WORK, WAR,	The Redeemed Saved to Serve. Beware of Unbelief.
DEUTERONOMY,	OBEDIENCE,	The Motive for and Necessity of Obedience.
JOSHUA,	POSSESS,	The Faithfulness of God.
JUDGES,	"RIGHT IN HIS OWN EYES,"	Spiritual Declension and God's Grace in Restoration.
RUTH,	REST, REDEEM,	Rest Through Redemption and Union.
I. SAMUEL,	PRAYED,	The Place and Power of Prayer in Life.
II. SAMUEL,	BEFORE THE LORD,	Be Sure your Sin will Find You Out.
I. KINGS,	AS DAVID HIS FATHER,	Jehovah, the Sovereign Ruler of Israel.
II. KINGS,	ACCORDING TO THE WORD OF THE LORD,	The Fulfilment of the Word of the Lord.
I. CHRONICLES,	THOU REIGNEST OVER ALL,	Jehovah as Sovereign Lord.
II. CHRONICLES,	PREPARETH HIS HEART,	Seeking and Serving the Lord.
EZRA,	THE WORD OF THE LORD,	The Word of God in the Life of His People.
NEHEMIAH,	PRAYER, WORK,	The Conditions of Successful Work for God.
ESTHER,	"FOR SUCH A TIME AS THIS,"	The Reality of the Divine Providence.
JOB,	TRIAL,	Trials and Suffering for our Education.
PSALMS,	WORSHIP,	Worship the Lord in the Beauty of Holiness.
PROVERBS,	WORDS TO RULE LIFE,	Godliness is Intensely Practical.
ECCLESIASTES,	UNDER THE SUN,	Life Without God is a Disappointment.
CANTICLES,	LOVE,	The Communion of Christ with His People.
ISAIAH,	SALVATION,	National Salvation through Judgment and Grace.
JEREMIAH,	BACKSLIDING, RETURN, AMEND, LOVED,	God's Certain Judgment. God's Eternal Love.
LAMENTATIONS,	"IS IT NOTHING TO YOU,"	The Misery of Sin. The Compassion of Jehovah.
EZEKIEL,	THE GLORY OF THE LORD,	The Goodness and Severity of God.
DANIEL,	"THE MOST HIGH RULETH,"	The Universal Sovereignty of God.
HOSEA,	RETURN,	God's Method in Restoring Backsliders.
JOEL,	THE DAY OF THE LORD,	The Value and Importance of Repentance.
AMOS,	PUNISHMENT,	National Sin means National Judgment.
OBADIAH,	RETRIBUTION,	The Perils of Pride and Anti-Semitism.
JONAH,	"FOR I KNEW,"	God, the God of the Gentiles.
MICAH,	"WHO IS A GOD LIKE UNTO THEE,"	God's Hatred of Injustice and Ritualism.
NAHUM,	UTTER END,	The Awful Doom of the Apostate.
HABAKKUK,	WHY?	God's Consistency in View of Permitted Evil.
ZEPHANIAH,	JEALOUSY,	God—a Jealous God.
HAGGAI,	THE WORD OF THE LORD,	God First in Life and Service.
ZECHARIAH,	"I AM JEALOUS,"	God's Care for His People.
MALACHI,	YE SAY,	Remember, Repent, Return, Rehearse.

ANALYSIS No. 1   **THE BOOK OF GENESIS**   MESSAGE   The Failure of Man under every condition met by the Salvation of God.

KEY WORD, "Beginning."   Key Verse, I. 1.

HATRED OF ENEMY

(1) There are two books in the Bible the great Enemy of mankind especially hates, and has bent all his energies to discredit, and they are Genesis and **Revelation.**

(2) He has attempted to overthrow Genesis by attacks of scientists and other critics, and Revelation by persuading men it is too mysterious.

(3) Why this dislike, think you? Because they both prophesy his downfall—Genesis tells us Who would bring this about, and Revelation gives details of its execution.

ITS GREAT VALUE

(1) In many respects it is the *most important book in the Bible.* Every great leading fact, truth and revelation is found here in germ—as the oak in the acorn. Melancthon stated: *"The whole book of Genesis excels in sweetness all other books and histories,"* and *"There is no more beautiful and lovable little book."*

(2) Dr. Bullinger says: *"Genesis is the seed-plot of the whole Bible, and it is essential to the true understanding of its every part. It is the foundation on which the Divine Revelation rests, and on which it is built up. It is not only the foundation of all Truth, but it enters into and forms part of all subsequent inspiration; and is at once the warp and woof of Holy Writ."* Genesis is the book of beginnings.

ITS AUTHOR AND ORIGIN

(1) The book was written by Moses. But how did he get his materials? Is it a mere compilation from ancient documents? Examine the old relics with this, and you will see the improbability of accepting that theory.

(2) Is it a written record of traditional lore? Many think so, and it is not as impossible as some imagine. Milton, in his "Paradise Lost", depicts Gabriel relating to Adam the wonders of Creation. This is pure fiction; but the Lord, no doubt, would communicate coveted knowledge to Adam, who told Methuselah, who told Noah, who told Shem, who told Abraham, who told Isaac, who told Jacob, who told Joseph, from whose writings Moses would learn it.

(3) But Acts VII. 37, 38 leaves us in no doubt as to its origin—it was received by Moses from God—it was born on Mount Sinai.

(4) Dr. Adam Clark writes: "The narrative is so simple, so much like truth, so consistent everywhere with itself, so correct in its dates, so impartial in its biography, so accurate in its philosophical details, so pure in its morality, and so benevolent in its design, as amply to demonstrate that it never could have had an earthly origin."

STYLE

It is written in prose, not poetry. This is important. Poetry forms handy clothing for myth and legend, as other ancient books. Thus Genesis is written, not in a mythical, but an historical style—for it is history and fact, not fable.

ANALYSIS

(1) It could be divided into eleven sections; the expression "the generation of" being the beginning of each section, except the first—as for instance, Section I., Chapter I. to II. 3. Section II., Chapter II. 4 to IV. 26. Section III., Chapter V. 1 to VI. 8, etc.

(2) But for easy analysis, taking "Beginning" as the key-word, we have nine sections:

DIVISION (A) PRIMEVAL HISTORY, COVERING A PERIOD OF OVER 2,000 YEARS								(B) Patriarchal History Over 300 Years.
(1) The Beginning of the Material Universe.	(2) Beginning of the Human Race.	(3) Beginning of Human Sin.	(4) Beginning of Revelations of Redemption.	(5) Beginnings of Human Family Life.	(6) Beginning of Godless Civilization.	(7) Beginning of Nations of the World	(8) Beginning of Confusion of Language	(9) Beginning of the Hebrew Race.
I. 1 to 25.	I. 26 to II.	III. 1 to 7.	III. 8 to 24.	IV. 1 to 15.	IV. 16 to IX.	X.	XI.	XII. to L.
1. Verse 1 gives us the original creation. 2. Isaiah XLV. 18 tells us that God did not create as we find it in verse 2. 3. Note 2 Peter III. 5, 6. 4. The six days were days of reconstruction.	1. Man created, not evolved. 2. Placed in charge of a reclaimed wilderness, for "Eden" is Accadian for ' wilderness."	NOTE— 1. Tampering with Word of God. The Woman subtracted from and added to the Word of the Lord. 2. She "Saw," "Took," "Gave."	1. First promise of a Redeemer, the beginning of all subsequent revelations. 2. The next time we meet the Cherubim we find no sword because of blood (Ex. XXV. 20).	1. First Family. 2. First family quarrel, and that over religion. 3. Note R. V. of Verse 7, where sin is likened to the crouching of a wild beast.	1. First city built, and city life originated by a murderer. 2. Note R.V. of IV. 23 and 26.	1. A very important section. 2. Here we have the title deeds of the nations.	1. A first attempt at unity apart from God. 2. This attempt at Babel to unify mankind will be repeated by Anti-Christ, see Rev. XVII.	1. This section is largely a biographical one. 2. We have history of Abraham, Isaac, and Jacob.

ITS MESSAGE

(1) Its distinctive message is: The failure of man under every condition met by the Salvation of God.

(2) It was necessary for man to know by failure his own weakness and insufficiency, before he would voluntarily choose God.

(3) In this book man is seen to fail: (1) Amidst ideal environment (Eden). (2) Under the rule of conscience (from Fall to Deluge), (3) Under Patriarchal rule (from Noah to Joseph). Note, the book begins with God, and ends with a coffin.

(4) But human failure is met by the Divine grace and activity. Where sin abounded grace did much more abound.

LIVINGSTONE AND EXODUS

During the Livingstone Centenary meetings, rightful stress was laid upon his love for, and devotional study of, the Bible. He made Holy Writ his constant study. Once, when in great peril, he read the Bible through four times. It appears that in later life the books of Genesis and Exodus were constantly in his mind, Moses being his favourite Bible hero. Thus were fed in that mighty man of God the fires of holy enthusiasm and courage.

EXODUS THE SEQUEL TO GENESIS

Between the close of Genesis and the opening of Exodus 3½ centuries intervene. Between the going down of Jacob to Egypt and the commencement of the persecution, 115 years must have passed. One has said that this " silence of 3½ centuries is almost awful in its grandeur, like the loneliness of Sinai in the mount of the Lord." Exodus is the sequel to Genesis. Genesis speaks of man's failure under every test, and in every condition ; but Exodus shows us God hastening to man's rescue, to man's redemption, coming forth to emancipate and enrich. Its key verses are as above—III. 8 gives God's declaration, and XII. 23 shows how it was accomplished. Exodus is the book of redemption. Note how the book opens and closes. It begins in darkness and gloom, yet ends in glory ; it commences by telling how *God came down in grace* to deliver an enslaved people, and ends by declaring how *God came down in glory* to dwell in the midst of a redeemed people.

THE PATTERN OF OUR REDEMPTION

In the construction of an engine or a ship, a design has to be drawn, and a pattern made. Our salvation was the design of God before the foundation of the world—the pattern we find in the Book of Exodus. " Exodus is the historical picture of the outworking of Divine Grace in the redemption and recovery of man by God to Himself by Jesus Christ, who is at once our great Apostle (Moses) and High Priest (Aaron)." " The story of Exodus is repeated in every soul that seeks deliverance from the enmeshing and enervating influence of the World. From this point of view, the book is human, from the first verse to the last. The things that happened were by way of figure, and they were written for our admonition." We study Exodus in order to see God's way of delivering sinful man, and His gracious and glorious purposes in thus rescuing him.

DIVISION

The book is in two main divisions, and five sections, as below :

(A) NARRATIVE I. to XIX			(B) LEGISLATIVE. XIX. to end	
(1) Bondage	(2) Redemption	(3) Education	(4) Consecration	(5) Worship
I. AND II.	III. TO XV. 21.	XV. 22 TO XIX.	XIX. TO XXIII.	XXIV. TO XL.
1. Here we have the sad condition of the people, whom God eventually redeemed. 2. Events : (a) Birth of Moses. (b) Adoption of Moses. (c) Renunciation of Moses. (d) Flight of Moses. (e) Marriage of Moses. 3. *Israel's awful suffering:* (a) Disturbed them. (b) Purified them (c) Unified them. (d) Disenchanted them.	1. Here we behold God coming down in grace to deliver Israel, and we see how redemption was accomplished, viz. : by blood. 2. Events : (a) Call of Moses. (b) Moses' return to Egypt. (c) Conflicts with Pharaoh. (d) Israel emancipated. 3. *Life of Moses summarised* : (a) 40 years thought he was somebody. (b) 40 years learning he was a nobody. (c) 40 years discovering what God can do with a nobody.	1. Here is begun the spiritual education of Israel ; all these events were designed to teach them absolute dependence upon God. 2. Events : (a) Marah and Elim. (b) Wilderness of Sin. (c) Rephidim. (d) Amalek and Jethro. 3. Note.—Elims generally follow the Marahs ; and Divine Love will sweeten the Marahs it does not remove.	1. Here we are taught that the re-deemed must do the Will of their Redeemer, and must consecrate themselves to His service. For His redeemed ones a Divine rule for faith and conduct is provided. 2. Event : The giving of the Moral Law. 3. Now He writes His Law upon the fleshy tables of redeemed hearts, and gives His Holy Spirit to cause them to walk in His ways.	1. Redeemed ones must be worship-ping ones ; and must only worship in God's own appointed way. 2. Event : The giving of the Ceremonial Law. 3. This is a very rich section. God designed *everything* about the Tabernacle, and consequently not one sacred article should escape our prayerful study.

ANALYSIS No. 3

KEY WORDS : "Holiness" and "Atonement."

THE BOOK OF LEVITICUS

MESSAGE 1. Access of Redeemed to God only through Blood.
2. Holiness of Redeemed imperative.

TITLE

Leviticus—the name commonly given to the third book of Moses—was the title given to it by the "Seventy" when they translated it from the original Hebrew into the Greek. Its Hebrew title is "Va-yich-rah," *i.e.*, "And He called." The former is a man-given name, inferring that it contains ordinances pertaining to the Levites (yet the Levites are only once incidentally mentioned (XXV. 32, 33); the latter is the Divine name, and is more in keeping with the contents, viz., God's call to the Redeemed to access, communion, and worship in His presence, and to holiness of body and soul.

TIME

The whole of the instructions given, and the events recorded in this book, come between April 1st, when they set up the Tabernacle (Exodus XL. 2, 17; also see Lev. I. 1), and May 20th, when they departed from Mount Sinai (Numbers X. 11). "Considered as embracing the history of one month only," wrote Dr. Parker, "this may claim to be the most remarkable book in the Old Testament."

FOR WHOM?

This is a book for redeemed people, showing how God is to be approached and worshipped. In Genesis we see man ruined, in Exodus man redeemed, in Leviticus man worshipping. All its types relate to worship, as those of Exodus relate to redemption. Leviticus is the book of Worship.

PECULIARITIES

(1) *Note how majestically the book opens.* It is the first of only three that have a like beginning, the other two being Numbers and Joshua. Such an introductory sentence ("and the Lord called") always indicates the communication that follows to be of first rate importance.

(2) A great Bible scholar has pointed out that in Leviticus "*The Holy Spirit is not once named*, though referred to in all the other books of the Pentateuch, because all here relates to Christ, and it is the Spirit's work to glorify Christ."

(3) *No other book in the Bible contains so many direct messages from Jehovah as this.* "The Lord spake," "said," or "commanded," are met with 56 times; "I am Jehovah," 21 times; "I am Jehovah, your God," 21 times; "I am," 3; and "I, Jehovah, do," twice.

MESSAGE

(1) *The* key-word of the book is "Holy." It is met with at least 87 times. Its next basal key-word is "Atonement," occurring at least 45 times.

(2) *The problem is, How can a sinful man approach a holy God?* How is he to gain access to God? Who is to decide this question? God alone must determine how. *This book declares that even His redeemed ones can only gain access to Him, with its consequent privilege of communion and worship, on the basis of sacrifice through shedding of blood.*

(3) It has also another message. One of the surprises of the book is its insistence on the holiness of the body, as well as that of the soul. *This book teaches that the redeemed must be holy, because their Redeemer is holy, XIX. 2.*

ANALYSIS

THE HOLINESS OF GOD

| Its Basal Message | | Teaching Definitely |

(1)	(2)
That because of that holiness, the	and also because of that holiness, the
# ACCESS	# HOLINESS
of the redeemed to Jehovah can only be secured on the basis of sacrifice through blood shedding. Key Verse XVII. 11.	of both body and soul of the redeemed is both imperative and compulsory. Key Verse XIX. 2.
I. TO X.	XI. to end.
1. THE FIVE OFFERINGS, each of which represents a distinctive aspect of the one offering of our Lord Jesus, I. to VI. 7	1. LAWS OF PURITY. - - - - - - XI. to XVI. Holy people must have (*a*) Pure food, XI. (*b*) Pure bodies, XII. to XIV. 32, (*c*) Pure homes, XIV. 33 to 57, (*d*) Pure habits, XV., (*e*) constant resort to the blood, XVI. This XVI. chapter is the great atonement chapter.
2. THE LAW OF THE OFFERINGS, giving particulars as to order, arrangement, etc., V. 8 to VI.	2. SUNDRY LAWS, in recapitulation. - - - - - XVII. to XXVI. Holy people must have (*a*) Pure worship, XVII. 1 to 9, (*b*) Sacred regard for blood, 10 to 16, (*c*) Pure morals, XVIII., (*d*) Pure customs, clothing, etc., XIX. to XXVI. (Note the feasts in Lev. XXIII.)
3. THE PRIESTHOOD : - - - - - - - VIII. to X. (*a*) Call, VIII. 1 to 5, (*b*) Cleansing. 6, (*c*) Clothing, 7 to 13, (*d*) Atonement, 14 to 29, (*e*) Anointing, 30, (*f*) Food, 31 to 36, (*g*) Ministry, IX., (*h*) Failure, X.	3. LAWS CONCERNING VOWS. - - - - - - XXVII.

THE BOOK OF NUMBERS

MESSAGE

The Redeemed
1. Are Saved to Serve.
2. Must Beware of Unbelief

NAME

Numbers is the name by which the fourth book of Moses is generally known, and is so called because it records two numberings of Israel—that at Sinai (chap. I.) and the one in Moab (chap. XXVI.); but its name in the Hebrew Bible is B'midbar, which means, " In the wilderness," and this seems the better title, as it covers all the events of the book, viz., all the wanderings and experiences of Israel in the wilderness. It is the book of the wilderness.

CHARACTER

The book is partly historical and partly legislative. It is the book of pilgrimage, of warfare, service, and, alas, of failure.

MESSAGE

This book has a three-fold message : (1) *One of its principal thoughts is that of service.* This is the message we meet with right on its threshold. The Lord's people are saved to serve. Note how significant is the order of the messages of these first four Bible books : In Genesis we see man ruined, in Exodus man redeemed, in Leviticus man worshipping, and now in Numbers, man in service. This is the Divine order. Only a saved and worshipping soul is qualified for service. (2) *Its second message is the indispensableness of order in service and walk.* Order is heaven's first law. Here we note how well organised the Camp and the service of the Tabernacle were, and how orderly the Lord desired the daily walk of the Israelites to be. (3) It has a third message : The failure of Israel looms large as we read its pages ; and that failure was due to unbelief, therefore *this book cries to every redeemed one : "Beware of unbelief"*! Thank God it was not all failure! In the last section we see Israel victorious owing to their restoration to God's favour.

ANALYSIS

(A) At Sinai. Time, 20 days. See I. 1, and X. 11.	(B) From Sinai to Kadesh. Time, 37 years, 11 months.	(C) In Moab. Time, 9 months, 10 days.
(1) Orderly **SERVICE** In the Wilderness	(2) Sad **FAILURE** In the Wilderness.	(3) Glorious **VICTORY** In the Wilderness.
I. TO X.	XI. TO XX., with XXI, 5 to 9, and XXV.	XXI. 1 to 4, and 10, TO XXXVI.
THE LORD'S SERVICE : 1. In battle - - - I. 2. In a well ordered camp - II. 3. In the Tabernacle - - III., IV. Note.—" Work " and " Service " rendered in R. V. Margin as " Warfare," IV. 3, 23. 4. In a pure camp - - - V. 5. In a Nazarite life - - VI. 6. In unsolicited gifts - - VII. 7. In Aaronic and Levitical service VIII. **Other Matters.** 1. Passover Legislation - IX. 1 to 14. 2. Guiding cloud - - IX. 15 to 23. 3. Trumpet legislation - - X.	This is a very sad section. There are eight murmurings altogether, as follows : 1. Against the WAY God led them, XI. 1 to 3. 2. The FOOD He fed them with, XI. 4 to 35. 3. Against the LEADER He set over them, XII. 4. Against the LAND He promised them, XIII.. XIV. 5. They murmured against God's righteous VERDICT pronounced on them, XIV. 39 to 45. 6. And against His APPOINTMENTS, XVI., XVII. 7. They murmured against THIRST, XX. 2 to 13. 8. And because of God's PROVISION, XXI. 4 to 9. During these 37 years Israel almost ceases to have a history ; it is almost a blank. The significance of the murmurings of XX. 2 to 13 lies in this : It was the first trial, and failure, of the new generation, showing they were no better than their fathers. Note the legislation of XV., XVIII., XIX.	The predominant note of this section is victory, though there are some failures. The old generation had passed away as punishment for their sin at Kadesh, and God now takes up Israel again. 1. *Victory over King Arad*, XXI. 1 to 3. 2. *Victory over King Sihon and King Og*, XXI. 21 to 35. 3. Balaam and Balak, XXII. to XXV. 4. Second census, XXVI. Showing a decrease of 1,820 since the numbering of Chapter I. 5. The law of inheritance, XXVII. 6. Joshua to succeed Moses, XXVII. 7. Ordering of the offerings and vows, XXVIII. to XXX. 8. *Victory over Midian*, XXXI. 9. Preparations to enter the land, XXXII to end.

THE BOOK.

Deuteronomy is the fifth and last book of Moses. *Its name means, " The Second Law." Not that it contains new laws,* but that the laws given at Sinai 39 years before are here reviewed and commented upon. And there was urgent need of such rehearsal. With two exceptions (Caleb and Joshua) the adults who had left Egypt and received the Law at Sinai had died, and *it was therefore necessary that the new generation should have the Law rehearsed and emphasized to them.* This Moses did in a series of eight discourses in the plains of Moab at the end of the 40 years' wanderings, and just one month before the nation crossed over the Jordan to take possession of the promised land. The addresses were first delivered orally, and then written (see I. 3, XXXI. 24 to 26).

JESUS' USE OF IT

One would judge that *this book was a special favourite of our adorable Lord* in the days of His childhood, youth, and manhood, for it was the only book from which He quoted in His conflict with the Tempter (see Matt. IV. 1 to 11, Luke IV. 1 to 13, with Deut. VIII. 3, VI. 16, VI. 13, and X. 20). Judging from the many quotations from it in their writings, it must also have been the favourite book of the prophets.

SATAN'S DREAD OF IT

This book has been most fiercely attacked by the Higher Critical School. The date of the book of Deuteronomy is a crucial question in the Higher Criticism of the Old Testament. The critics declare that the book was not written by Moses, but by some unknown author at least 600 years after, that the Pentateuch was " in great part composed to glorify the priesthood at Jerusalem, and that the book of Deut. in particular was produced to establish Jerusalem as the central and only acceptable shrine for the worship of Israel." *How comes it then that the name Jerusalem is not only entirely absent from Deut.* but also is not once mentioned in any other of the books of Moses? Remembering our Lord's use of Deuteronomy need we wonder at Satan's hatred of it, and attempts to discredit it?

SOME NOTABLE CONTENTS

This book contains (1) the first reference to the "children of Belial," (XIII. 13); (2) the first time we meet with the death by hanging on a tree, (XXI. 22. 23); (3) the only reference in the Old Testament to that great vision recorded in Exodus III. which led to Moses' call and Israel's deliverance, (XXXIII. 16, " Him that dwelt in the bush "); and the great prediction about a coming Prophet-Christ, (XVIII. 15 to 19).

MORE THAN A REVIEW

But this book is much more then merely a book of recapitulation and review of the law given at Sinai. It has forcefully been said that " it reviews the past with an eye to the future." *The whole book is a Divine treatise on obedience.* Moses already had tangible evidence, (see Numbers XX. 1 to 6), that the new generation were no better than their fathers, and he knew that everything depended upon their obedience—life itself, possession of Canaan, victory over foes, prosperity, happiness. So with all the force of his own ardent nature the Leader pleads with the new generation. He pointed out that God longed for their obedience (V. 29), because they were His own (I. 3, XIV. 1), because He loved them (IV. 37, VII. 7, 8), and desired to preserve and prosper them (IV. 1, 40, V. 29, VI. 2, 3, 24, etc.); and that out of gratitude to God for His amazing grace, mercy and privilege, they should render such obedience, (IV. 7, 8, V. 6, IV. 33, etc.) The full force and beauty of this book can only be discovered by reading it at one sitting. Oh, it is a heart stirring, heart moving appeal !

ANALYSIS

There are eight separate and distinct discourses, with a final chapter on the death of Moses.

(1) First Discourse. **Retrospect**	(2) Second Discourse. **Review**	(3) Third Discourse. **Warning**	(4) Fourth Discourse. **Covenant**	(5) Fifth Discourse. **Counsels**	(6) Sixth Discourse. **Instruction**	(7) Seventh Discourse. **SONG**	(8) Eighth Discourse. **Blessing**	(9) Death of **Moses**
I. to IV. 43.	IV. 44 to XXVI.	XXVII. & XXVIII.	XXIX. and XXX.	XXXI. 1 to 23.	XXXI. 24 to 29.	XXXI. 30 & XXXII.	XXXIII.	XXXIV.
1. Failure at Kadesh-Barnea, I. 2. Their wanderings, II. and III. 3. Application of this retrospect, IV. 1-40. 4. Cities of Refuge, IV. 41 to 43.	1. This is the longest of the discourses. 2. Here Moses reviews the moral, civil, and ceremonial law 3. Note V. 22, "and He added no more:" the completeness and finality of Ten Commandments.	1. Instruction as to a solemn ceremony to be performed on entrance into Canaan. 2. Note, the altar was built on mount of cursing, XXVII. 5. This is gospel.	1. This covenant gives the conditions under which Israel entered the promised land. 2. Observe the emphasis on circumcision of the heart, XXX. 6.	Last counsels of Moses to 1. All Israel, 1-6. 2. Joshua, 7 and 8. 3. Priests, 9 to 15. 4. Jehovah's warning, 14 to 21. Note the sadness of Jehovah's disclosure in these verses.	1. This is an address to the Levites, concerning the preservation of Deuteronomy. 2. Note R. V. of verse 26. Literally, " At" or "near the side of the Ark."	A sublime Psalm. Note by verse 44 it was sung as a duet by Moses and Joshua, Israel joining in the refrain.	This is really a remarkable prophetic utterance. Note the three S's in 29, 16, and 23: Saved. Separated. Satisfied.	1. It was a lonely death, as indeed every death is. 2. It was death with a vision. 3. And death in the Divine embrace. "Died by the kiss of God" is another rendering.

THE BOOK OF JOSHUA

WRITER

There is no reason to doubt that Joshua wrote this book. The Talmud asserts that Joshua wrote the whole of it except the last five verses, which were probably added by Phinehas, (see XXIV. 33). It certainly was written before the time of David (note XV. 63; David expelled the Jebusites), yea, *whilst Rahab was still alive* (see VI. 25).

CHARACTER

The book is the *story of a military campaign led by Joshua*, Moses' successor, by which Israel gained possession of Canaan. It is an aggressive book, thus bearing the same relation to the five books of Moses that the Acts does to the four Gospels.

MESSAGE

But it is much more than a mere history of a war, interesting though the story is. It has a four-fold message.

(1) *Its primary message is the faithfulness of God.* Study the key verses indicated above. He is faithful that promised. Of course He is: how could He be otherwise? This book declares and demonstrates the faithfulness of our God. It also

(2) Shows *the value of the twofoot rule* (I, 3), that to enjoy God's good gifts we must definitely appropriate them.

(3) Its third message is *God's horror and hatred of sin.* This war was punitive. The Canaanites were so sunken in sin, and so given up to sin and vices of the most awful nature, that God's flaming sword of justice had to be unsheathed.

(4) It has a fourth message. This military campaign typifies the warfare of the spirit. The Canaanites represent our lusts, besetting sins and spiritual enemies, and in the record we discover the *secret of an all conquering life.*

NOTABLE

One very notable fact concerning this book is *its introduction to a new method of teaching.* Up to this time God had spoken in dream, vision, or by angelic ministry; now there is the book of the Law written by Moses, and they are exhorted to hearken to God's voice in and through that book, (see I. 8). This arrangement continues up to date, only the book we have now is much larger than the one Joshua possessed, though just as authoritative. Do we value it enough?

ANALYSIS

(1) ENTRANCE Into the Promised Land.	(2) CONQUEST of the Promised Land.	(3) DIVISION of the Promised Land.	(4) FAREWELL of Joshua, their Leader.
I. TO V.	VI. TO XII.	XIII. TO XXII.	XXIII. AND XXIV.

1. Lord's summons to Joshua - I. 1 to 9.
2. Jehovah's appeal to Israel - I. 10 to 15.
3. People's hearty response - I. 16 to 18.
4. Rahab and the Spies - - II.
5. Passage of the Jordan - - III.
6. The two Memorials - - IV.
7. Effect of this on enemy - V. 1.
8. Reproach of Egypt rolled away, V. 2 to 10.
9. New Food - - V. 11, 12.
10. Their Captain - - V. 13 to 15.
 	
NOTE.
 	
1. Law, (as represented by Moses,) can give sinner no possession - - I. 2.
2. Value of Courage - - I. 6.
3. No water was seen by Israel when crossing Jordan. Look at R.V. of III. 16.
	1. Conquest of Jericho in an unusual way, VI. Note, during the six days, the only sound made was near Ark, (8), thus drawing attention to the Lord only.
	2. Sin of Achan - - VII.
	3. Conquest of Ai - VIII. 1 to 29.
	4. The Ceremony on Mount Ebal „ 30-35. Note, the Altar was built on Mount of Cursing.
	5. League made with the Gibeonites IX.
	6. Victory (a) at Gibeon - X. 1 to 27.
	    (b) at Makkedah X. 28 to 43.
	    (c) at Merom - - XI.
	7. List of Conquered Kings - XII.
	
	NOTE.
	
	1. Israel's sin of self confidence - VII. 3.
	2. In VII. 21, sin is traced in its four stages :
	    (a) "I saw," lust of the eyes.
	    (b) "I coveted," lust of the mind.
	    (c) "I took," act of the will.
	    (a) "I hid," act of the hand.
		1. Lord's message to Joshua - XIII.
		2. Division of the land - XIV. to XXI.
		3. The mistake of the two and a half tribes - - - - XXII.
		
		NOTE.
		
		1. Hebron, (fellowship,) became Caleb's because he was out and out for God, XIV. 14.
		2. Caleb's daughter could look well after her own interests - XV. 16 to 19.
		3. Joshua's noble and dignified reply XVII. 14 to 18.
		4. Joshua was the last to receive his inheritance. Like Caleb he was permitted to choose apart from lot, and he selected a barren place in a barren land no one else would have. XIX. 50.
			1. Joshua's last address,
			    (a) to the heads of the people, XXIII.
			    (b) and to all the people, XXIV. 1-28.
			2. Death of Joshua - - 29 to 31.
			3. Death of Eleazar - - - 33.
			
			NOTE.
			
			1. Genesis begins with God and ends with death; the book of Joshua both begins and ends with death.
			2. XXIV. 33. Priests had no possessions, yet this verse shows Phinehas had. Probably this was given to him as a special favour for special service.

THE BOOK OF JUDGES

MESSAGE
1. Our proneness to wander from God.
2. Results of such spiritual declension.
3. God's grace in pursuing & restoring backsliders

WRITER

The writer of this book is unknown. From the phrase found four times in the closing chapters, "In those days there was no king in Israel," (XVII. 6, XVIII. 1, XIX. 1, XXI. 25), we judge it *was written some time after the establishment of the monarchy.* Probably it was written by Samuel the prophet, the last judge in Israel, during his partial retirement from the leadership of the people on Saul becoming king. If so, then with what gusto he would record Gideon's great renunciation, (see VIII. 22, 23).

A SAD BOOK

(1) The book of Judges—*which takes its name from being the history of the 14 Judges* who ruled and delivered Israel—covers the period between the conquest of the land and the death of Joshua to the judgeship of Samuel and the introduction of the monarchy in Israel.

(2) It *is the Divine record of Israel's repeated departures from God,* and of sad national decay, one of the darkest periods of their history.

(3) The book of Numbers is a sad book, telling of 40 years wandering through sin; but the book of Judges is a far more sad and solemn book, for it tells of Israel's failure, not 40 but nearly ten times 40.

NOT ALL GLOOM

From the prominence given to Israel's repeated failures one gets the impression that the bulk of the 450 years under the Judges were spent in sin. Such, however, is really not the case, for of the 450 years there were no less than 350 years during which the people were loyal to God. This was an astonishing discovery to me. Of the state of things which existed during this happy period we have a charming picture in the book of Ruth. The erroneous impression is due to the emphasis and detail given of Israel's sin. Even 100 out of 450 years were far too many to spend unfaithful to God. How seriously God viewed these departures.

NOTABLE

The book is notable for several things. (1) *It has two commencements,* (I. 1, II. 6). (2) It contains the *oldest known parable in the world.* (IX. 8 to 15). (3) It contains the *greatest and grandest battle-song in the world,* (V). (4) It contains the *first record in history of the emergence of a woman into prominence and leadership of a nation,* (IV). Probably she was a widow.

MESSAGE

Being primarily the record of Israel's tragic relapses, this book is (1) *a revelation of the perpetual proneness of the human heart to wander away from God.* "Prone to wander, Lord, I feel it; prone to leave the God I love," is the bitter confession of many of God's people concerning the waywardness of their hearts. This book shows the awful possibility of spiritual declension after great spiritual blessing. (2) But, thank God, it is not only a book of Relapses, it is also a book of Deliverance. If there are 7 apostasies and 7 servitudes, there are 7 cries to God and 7 deliverances. *God is seen here pursuing and restoring His backslidden people.*

ANALYSIS

At first sight this book seems most disorderly. It certainly is not in chronological order. It ought to begin by II. 6 to 9, then chapter I followed by II. 10 to 13, and XVII. to XXI., and finally by II. 14, to end of XVI. But order is Heaven's first law, and there is a Divine reason for not writing it in chronological sequence. The outline shows this. In the first section we see Israel in dependence upon the Lord; in the second Israel forsaking the Lord, and the bitter results; and in the last we see the abysmal depths to which they sank.

(A) Introductory	(B) History of relapses, results of same, and recovery					(C) Appendix
(1) **DEPENDENCE** upon the Lord.	(2) **FORSAKING** the Lord, and some results.					(3) **ANARCHY** the final result.
I. to II. 5, Key I. 1.	Chapter II. 6 to XVI. Key verse to this section is II. 12.					XVII. to XXI. Key XVII. 6.
Israel began well but did not continue.	Soon Israel went astray, and II. 6 to 23 is a comprehensive summary of their subsequent history.					Confusion and anarchy
1. Lord consulted and result, I. 1 to 10.	Order of the seven apostasies.	Scripture.	Conqueror.	Length.	Deliverer and Judge.	1. In Church, or the religious life of the nation, XVII. and XVIII.
2. Judah began at home - I. 3, 4.	Apostasy: First.	III. 1 to 11.	Chushanrishathaim King of Mesopotamia.	8 years.	Othniel.	2. In home life, or the morals of the nation, XIX.
3. Capture of Adoni-bezek I. 5 to 7.	„ Second.	„ 12 to 31.	King of Moab and Philistines.	18 „	Ehud and Shamgar.	3. In the state, or the political life of the nation, XX. and XXI.
4. Imperfect victories I. 8 to 36.	„ Third.	IV. and V.	Jabin King of Canaan.	20 „	Deborah and Barak.	Note R.V. of XVIII. 30: the first idolatrous priest was Moses' grandson.
5. The Lord's rebuke II. 1 to 5. (For "an" R.V. reads "the" *viz* the Lord Himself.)	„ Fourth.	VI.-VIII. 32.	Midian.	7 „	Gideon.	
	„ Fifth.	VIII. 33-X. 5	Civil War, etc.		Abimelech, Tola and Jair.	
	„ Sixth.	X. 6 to XII.	Ammonites.	18 „	Jephtha, Ibzan, Elon, Abdon.	
	„ Seventh.	XIII. to XVI.	Philistines.	40 „	Samson.	

LITERARY VALUE

This book, which *derives its name from Ruth, the Moabitess, who figures as the chief person in the narrative,* is a literary and spiritual gem. The great literary authority of the 18th century, Dr. Samuel Johnson, introduced and read it to his friends in a London Club, a pastoral which he said he had lately met with, and which they imagined had only just been composed; and when they were loud in their praises of its simple and pathetic beauty, he informed them that it was only the story of Ruth which he had read them from a book they all despised—the Bible. There is nothing in human literature more beautiful than Ruth's address to her mother-in-law (I. 16, 17)—it is sublime.

THE BOOK, ETC

(1) *Writer.* Its writer is unknown. *It must have been written when the rule of the Judges had ended* on the introduction of the monarchy (I. 1), and *after the birth of David* (IV. 22), therefore we conclude that Samuel wrote it. It covers a period of 10 years (I. 4).

(2) *Appendix.* It is a kind of appendix to the book of Judges. But what a contrast it is to that book! It is like an oasis in a desert.

(3) *Notable.* It is notable because it is *the only instance in the Bible in which a whole book is devoted to the history of a woman.* "There are two books which bear the name of women: Ruth, a Gentile, who married a Hebrew husband; Esther, a Jewess, who married a Gentile husband."

ITS PURPOSE

(1) *One chief purpose of the book is the tracing of the genealogy of David,* and of David's Lord. The blood of Ruth ran in the veins of the Lord Jesus.

(2) It certainly is a love story, and is *designed to set forth the power of a pure love* to overcome all difficulties. Strange to say, it is not the story of a romantic love between a young man and a young woman, but the story of a young widow's passionate and devoted love for her mother-in-law.

(3) It most assuredly *gives a high ideal of wedlock.* Married life is treated in IV. 11 to 17 as a sacred and lofty companionship.

ITS TYPICAL VALUE

Typically it is of the utmost value. A greater than Boaz is here. *Boaz the kinsman redeemer is a type of Christ, Ruth being a type of us Gentiles. This story is a pre-intimation of the calling of the Gentiles.* The Moabite, shut out by Law (Deut. XXIII. 3), is admitted by Grace. (1) Ruth is a type of Gentile sinners: (*a*) stranger and afar off, (*b*) poor and needy, (*c*) related to Boaz by marriage, so are we related to Christ by the marriage of our human nature to His divine; (*d*) one nearer Kinsman, our fellow-creature, but he cannot help. (2) Boaz a type of Christ: (*a*) Lord of the harvest, (*b*) "Mighty Man of Valour" (II. 1, R.V. marg.). (3) Takes notice of us and treats us kindly (II. 5, etc.). (4) "And when in penitence we come and lie at His pierced feet, and beseech Him to spread over us the crimson mantle of His love, how immediate is His response" (see III). He speaks comforting words and loads us with blessing. (5) Redeeming us, and uniting Himself to us, loneliness ceases, we become fruitful and a blessing to others.

MESSAGE AND ANALYSIS

The primary message of the book is that of rest. Though the word is only found twice in it, yet the thought of rest permeates the whole. In the East the position of unmarried women is dangerous and trying—only in the house of a husband can she be sure of respect and protection. Elimelech forsook rest when he left the Promised Land. To leave Moab for Bethlehem seemed an impossible path to rest, as Naomi gravely and tactfully hinted (I. 11 to 13), but God's ways are not man's. *Ruth found rest through Redemption and union with her Redeemer.* For us there is no rest in the world but in union with our Divine Redeemer.

(A) Emigration to Moab and result. I. 1 to 5.	(B) Return to land of Judah and incidents. I. 6 to 22.	(C) Boaz and Ruth. II. and III.	(D) Boaz and Ruth. IV.
(1) **Rest Forsaken** I. 1 to 5.	(2) **REST DESIRED** I. 6 to 22.	(3) **REST SOUGHT** II. and III.	(4) **Rest Secured** IV.
1. Was this the famine referred to in Judges VI. 3 and 4?	1. After ten (4) disastrous years, Naomi decides to return to the land of Israel's rest.	1. Boaz, a man who had distinguished himself in war, (see R.V. marg. of II. 1), was probably absent on military service when Naomi returned, hence his ignorance (II. 5).	1. Boaz moves in the matter (1 to 8).
2. Out of will of God there could not be real blessing and prosperity.	2. Her two daughters-in-law intended to return with her, and actually started (7, 10), but warned, Orpah returned to her people and gods (15).	2. Ruth's act (in III.), in creeping softly to his resting place, and nestling under the corner of his long robe, was simply making a legal claim in the approved manner of the time.	2. Boaz and Ruth married (9 to 13).
3. Naomi permitted her sons to marry heathen wives.	3. Reaching Bethlehem, the whole city was moved, yet not one offered hospitality.		3. Naomi comforted and happy (14-19).
4. The wives treated their husbands kindly (8).	4. Note, "with her" (22),—only a backslider when restored can be made a blessing to others.		4. One of the many fine points of the story is that its concluding sentences are almost wholly devoted, not to the young and happy wife and mother, but to aged Naomi.

ANALYSIS No. 9

Key WORD, " Prayed," I. 10-27, VII. 5, VIII. 6. XII. 19-23.

FIRST BOOK OF SAMUEL

MESSAGE The place for, and the power of prayer in all experiences of life.

THE BOOK

(1) Of the six historical books of Israel this is the best known. From infancy the story of little Samuel (III.) and David and Goliath (XVII.), have drawn us ever with a lasting interest to it. Though history, it is presented to us in the most attractive garb of biography.

(2) It is thus named because Samuel is the prominent figure in it. Undoubtedly he wrote the bulk of it, Nathan and Gad completing it, (1 Chron. XXIX, 29).

(3) It gives a history of Israel from the time of Eli to the accession of David to the throne of Israel.

NOTABLE CONTENTS

The contributions of this book to religious vocabulary, theology, and experience, are remarkable.

(1) This book has the honour of *first giving and using the majestic title "Lord of Hosts,"* (I. 3). This is the first of the 281 occurrences of that name and title which denotes the God of Israel as the Lord of all the hosts of heaven and earth.

(2) The *name of Messiah is first found here,* a woman having the honour of first using it, (II. 10): " His Anointed," literally " His Messiah," Septuagint " His Christ."

(3) This book gives *the first of the five precious things in the Old Testament :* (1) Word of God, III. 1. (2) Redemption, Psalm XLIX. 8. (3) The death of His saints Psalm LXXII. 14, and CXVI. 15. (4) Lips of Knowledge, Proverbs XX. 15. (5) The thoughts of God, Psalm CXXXIX 17.

(4) It is here we *first find the word "Ichabod,"* (IV. 21,) *and " Ebenezer,"* (VII. 12,) *also " God save the King,"* (X. 24.)

(5) Here we are told that the *original name by which the Prophets were known,* long before they were called prophets, was " seer," (IX. 9.) This is a suggestive name, indicating their possession of gifts of perception and discernment, as well as a vision of God.

(6) It points out that *Samuel was the first of the noble line of the writing prophets,* (III. 20, with Acts III. 24, and XIII. 20) ; and indicates for the first time the existence of a school of prophets, probably an institution founded by Samuel, (X. 5, XIX. 20).

(7) *Its teaching on the Holy Spirit is important.* In its pages the Holy Spirit is seen as (1) author and channel of regeneration and a new heart, (X. 6, 9), as (2) the author of holy and righteous anger, (XI. 6,) (3) as the inspirer of courage and prudence of speech, (XVI. 13 with 18, " Prudent in matters " is in the R.V. " Prudent in *speech,*") (4) and our preservative from evil, (XVI. 14.)

MESSAGE

This book bears many messages. (1) It shows the suffering that polygamy brings, (I. 6). (2) The disasters that indulgent fatherhood brings, (II. 22 to 25). (3) The peril of mere ritualism and formalism, (IV. 3, " IT " not the Lord " may save us,") ; (4) of impatience, (XIII) and (5) only partial obedience, (XV). But the Key to THE message of the book is the meaning of Samuel's name and the oft occurrence of the words, " prayer " and " prayed." It is astonishing how full the book is of prayer. Indeed, it could be viewed as a treatise on prayer vividly illustrated from life. The very name of Samuel means " asked of God," and is a monument to a prayer presented and granted. Here we see prayer offered at all times. Therefore we take *the chief message of the book to be the place for, and the power of prayer in all experiences of life.* (1) Samuel given by God in answer to prayer, (I. 10 to 28). (2) Victory was given to Israel through Samuel's prayer, (VII. 5 to 10). (3) In sorrow at Israel's rejection of Jehovah as King evidenced by their request for an earthly King, (which rejection began in the days gone by, see Judges XXI. 25,) Samuel seeks the Lord in prayer, (VIII. 5, 6). (4) A praying man learns secrets from God, (IX. 15). (5) Not to pray for Israel Samuel considered to be a sin, (XII. 19 and 23). (6) Saul's final rejection seen in the Lord turning a deaf ear to his prayer, (XXVIII. 6).

ANALYSIS

Its contents may be grouped around the names of the three great personages of the book, Samuel, Saul and David.

Concerning (1) SAMUEL	Concerning (2) SAUL	Concerning (3) DAVID
Hannah's request for a son was answered by the gift of Samuel.	People's request for a King answered in the setting apart of Saul.	David anointed King as outcome of Samuel's mourning and prayers.
I. to VII.	VIII. to XV.	XVI. to XXXI.
BIRTH. 　1. Given in answer to prayer - - - - I. 　2. Hannah's prophetic prayer - - II. 1 to 11. CALL. 　1. Preserved in a place poisoned by Eli's two wicked sons　II. 12 to 26. 　2. Grave warning to Eli by unknown prophet　II. 27 to 36 　3. Lord revealing Himself to Samuel - - - III. MINISTRY. 　1. Capture of Ark and death of Eli - - IV. 　2. Ark seven months among Philistines- - - V. 　3. Return of the Ark - - - V. to VII. 　4. Victory through prayer - - - VII. 2 to 17.	CHOSEN. 　1. Samuel takes Israel's request for a King to the Lord in prayer - - - - - - VIII. 　2. Saul chosen to be King - - - - IX. 　3. Saul anointed King - - - - X. REIGNING. Saul's first great victory - - - - XI. Samuel's last public address to the nation - - XII. REJECTED. 　1. Saul's first downward step in the establishment of a standing army - - - XIII. 1 and 2. 　2. His second downward step - - - XIII. 3 to 14. 　3. A great victory - - XIII. 15 and XIV. 　4. Saul's terrible blunder - - - - XV.	ANOINTED. 　1. David selected and anointed - - XVI. 1 to 13. SERVICE. 　1. Saul's minstrel and armourbearer - XVI. 14 to 23. 　2. Slays Goliath - - - - - XVII. 　3. Love covenant between Jonathan & David, XVIII. 1-7 　4. Saul's jealousy and attempts to kill David, „ 8-20. EXILE. 　1. David's flight and wanderings - XXI. to XXX. 　2. Samuel's death - - - - XXV. 1. 　3. Death of Saul and Jonathan - - XXXI. WORDS- Note some of David's notable sayings, XXII. 23. XXX. 6 and 24.

ANALYSIS No. 10

Key Verse, V. 12.

Key Phrase:
"Before the
Lord."

MESSAGE: "Be sure your sin
will find you out."

SECOND BOOK OF SAMUEL

AUTHOR

Concerning the authorship of this book, 1 Chron XXIX. 29 has something to say, "The book of Nathan the prophet," and "the book of Gad the Seer," are supposed to be two of the several books referred to in the Bible that have perished. But the R.V. is very clear, giving "history" and "words" instead of book. *Second Samuel was undoubtedly written by Nathan and Gad, two of David's contemporaries.*

DESIGN

This book is almost entirely devoted to a history of David as King. It begins with his accession to the throne, and gives an account of the events during his reign of 40 years. *This book is therefore a history of the Kingship of David.*

CONTENTS

(1) The curious would like this to be noted, that in all the Bible *the word "Wench" is alone found here,* (XVII. 17.)
(2) *The first time a ruler is likened to a shepherd* is in V. 2. "Feed my people Israel," is literally "Shepherd my people Israel."
(3) It was David who *first described a king as "the Lord's Anointed,"* a phrase which gives a high and exalted conception of Kingship. (See 1 Samuel XXIV. 6, with 2 Samuel I. 14, 16, 21, II. 4, 7, III. 39 V. 3, 17, XIX. 10, XXII. 51).
(4) The incident related in VII. 1 to 17, teaches that *even our good purposes must be brought to God for His approval,* a lesson nowhere else taught so clearly in the Bible. How often we err in this respect, making the mistake that Nathan did (VII. 3).
(5) It contains *two notable parables :* the parable of the selfish one, (XII.), and the parable of the banished one (XIV. 1 to 20).
(6) It is in this book (XXIII. 2), that David claimed Divine inspiration for his Psalms, that *even his words* came from God.

MESSAGE

(1) *Its first message is the need of patience and dependence upon God for the fulfilment of His promises,* seen in II. 1, V. 1 to 3. Patience is a virtue for which special grace is given.
(2) *Its second and primary message is that on sin.* "Be sure your sin will find you out" is exemplified in several persons referred to in its narrative, (I. 14 to 16, II. 8, 9—Abner acted thus though he knew God's purpose, III. 9, 13, III. 27, IV. 11, 12) but more especially in David and his son Absalom. We have horrible details of one awful sin (XI. 4, XIII. 1 to 15). How swift was the Divine punishment! Yet, thank God, this book shows how ready God is to forgive (XII. 13). But fail not to notice, that *sometimes pardoned sin is punished* (XII. 14). The whole subsequent history of David is a record of punishment through his own, and on account of, his sin. This David recognised—see XVI. 10; there was little of brightness in David's life after his sin.

ANALYSIS

Though the two books of Samuel were originally one, yet they both have characteristics of their own. We have noted that the thought of prayer controls the 1st book of Samuel. Whilst we have the same prevailing thought here ("Enquired of the Lord," is one of its Key-phrases, II. 1, V. 19, 23, XXI. 1), THE Key-phrase is "Before the Lord." This means sometimes before the Ark of the Lord, but not always (as for instance, V. 3, though the Ark was in Gibeah, as VI. 3. XII. 16 means that he lay before the Lord in his own home). It was David's constant recognition of the presence of God with him always. *Note the various attitudes of soul* revealed by a study of this phrase, as shown in the following analysis :—

(A)	DAVID'S TRIUMPHS. Chapters I. to X.				(B) David's Troubles, XI.-XXIV.	
(1) David anointed King over Judah.	(2) David anointed King over all Israel.	(3) David consolidating the Kingdom.			(4) David's fall.	(5) Appendix.
David (a) **Enquired** of the Lord.	David's (b) **League** before the Lord.	David (c) **Danced** before the Lord.	David (d) **Sat** before the Lord.	David (e) **Preserved** by the Lord.	David (f) **Lay** in penitence before the Lord.	David (g) **Spake** unto the Lord.
Key II. 1.	Key V. 3.	Key VI. 16 and 21.	Key. VII. 18.	Key. VIII. 6 and 14.	Key. XII. 16,	Key. XXII. 1, XXIV. 17.
					XI. to XX.	
I. to IV.	V.	VI.	VII.	VIII. to X.		XXI. to XXIV.
1. News of Saul's death, I. 1 to 16. 2. David's elegy he called "The Song of Bow," (R.V. of 18), I. 17 to 27. 3. Anointed King of Judah II. 1 to 11. 4. Civil war. II. 12 to IV.	1. Crowned King over all Israel, V. 1 to 5. 2. Jerusalem made the capital, V. 6 to 16. 3. Victories, V. 17 to 25.	1. David copied from the Philistines, verse 4. 2. God cannot tolerate in His people what He overlooks in the worldling, verse 7.	1. David's desire to build the Lord's house, 1-3. 2. Forbidden, verses 4-13. 3. God covenants to build David a "house," 11.	1. Victories, VIII. 2. Mephibosheth, IX. 3. Great Victories, X.	1. Sin, XI. 2. Conviction; XII. 1-13. 3. Judgment : (a) Death of babe, XII. 14 to 23. (b) Ammon's Sin, XIII. 1 to 22. (c) Absalom's rebellion, XIII. 23 to XX.	1. Enquired of Lord, XXI. 2. Thanksgiving, XXII. 3. Last Words, XXIII. 4. Sin of numbering Israel, XXIV.

ANALYSIS No. 11. Key Phrase : "As David his father." XI. 4, etc.
Key Verses. XXII. 19 with IX. 4-9.

FIRST BOOK of KINGS

MESSAGE: Jehovah the Sovereign Ruler of Israel: blessing obedient, punishing disobedient, forgiving penitent.

THE BOOK

The author of this book is unknown. It certainly was *written whilst the first Temple was still standing* (VIII. 8). Consequently it is probable that Jeremiah, inspired by God, wrote it, incorporating records made by Nathan and Gad (1 Chron. XXIX. 29), and other writers. It is a history of the Kings of Israel and Judah, from David to Ahab and Jehoshaphat, covering a period of from 118 to 125 years.

NOTABLE CONTENTS

(1) In I. 50 and II. 23 we have the first recorded instances of using the horns of the altar as a refuge, *the first claims to the right of sanctuary.*

(2) It gives the *first instance of kneeling at devotions* (VIII. 54). Standing was the earliest practice (1 Samuel I. 26). In fact Solomon stood first before he knelt, (1 Kings VIII. 22). Baal worshippers bent their knees. This explains Judges VII. 5, 7 (why 9,700 of Gideon's troops who bent their knees—proving they had been, or were, worshippers of Baal—were rejected, and only the 300 who lapped were accepted,) and 1 Kings XIX. 18. However, kneeling at prayer has been sanctified for us by our Lord's use of that posture (Luke XXII. 41).

(3) It gives the *the first hint of a new chronology.* In 1 Kings VI. 1, the period between the Exodus and the beginning of the Temple building under Solomon, is given as 480 years, whereas it was 573 years. This has proved a stumbling block to many. But devout students of the Word have discovered that the difference of 93 years is exactly the length of time covered by the captivities in the book of Judges. This is the solution of the problem. This is God's spiritual chronology. "During those years Israel was not under Isra-El, not governed by God, but under the heel of the oppressor." God did not count the years of their captivity. The years lived out of His Will are not counted by Him. The sin and sins of these years are remembered until confessed, but the years are reckoned by Him as wasted and of no account.

(4) We have in V. 5 and VIII. 27 the first clear statement in the Old Testament *of a wonderfully spiritual conception of God.* Observe the Temple was not built as a House for the Lord, but for the "Name of the Lord." Pagan temples were intended by their builders for the actual residence of their gods. Solomon knew better. And the expression "Name of the Lord," is a very remarkable one.

(5) Notice V. 3, "his God," and V. 4, "my God." Solomon gloried in the fact that *his father's God had become his God.*

(6) Observe, (*a*) that it was *the old warrior* Joab who first noticed the sound of the trumpet (I. 41). (*b*) That in VIII. 3, we have the *only instance of the priests carrying the ark,* work the Levites always performed; and (*c*) that statement of *Jehovah dwelling* " *in the thick darkness,*" (VIII. 12,) which has been a comfort to thousands of tried souls. Art thou in spiritual darkness, my Christian brother or sister? Rejoice, for He is with you in that darkness! The darkness only shuts you *in with* (not from) your Lord. Note (*d*) the unexpected and *remarkable conception of Israel's mission in the world,* (VIII. 43, 60). Oh that Israel had ever remembered this!

ANALYSIS

THE (1) **Establishment** of the Kingdom : sad but necessary measures.	THE (2) **Glory** of the Kingdom : its unity and splendour.	THE (3) **Disruption** of the Kingdom : lamentable and fatal schism.	THE (4) **Decline** of the Kingdom : its deterioration and decay.
I. AND II.	III. TO X.	XI. TO XII. 24.	XII. 25 TO XXII.
1. Note "established." II. 12, 24. 45, 46.	1. Note III. 12, 13, IV. 30, VIII. 11	1. Note XI. 11, XII. 17.	1. Note XIV. 27, a symbolic act.
2. David prematurely aged (70), I. to 4.	2. Solomon's doubtful alliance, III. 1, 2.	2. Solomon's apostasy and death, XI.	2. Jeroboam's apostasy and death, XII. 25 to XIV. 20.
3. David's eldest living son's rebellion, I. 5 to 9.	3. First Divine appearance to Solomon, III. 5-15.	3. Ascension and folly of Rehoboam, XII. 1 to 15.	3. Rehoboam and Judah's awful apostasy, XIV. 21 to 31.
4. Nathan and Bathsheba's plot, I. 10 to 31.	4. The wisdom of Solomon, III. 16 to 28.	4. The disruption of the kingdom, Jeroboam becoming king of ten tribes, XII. 16 to 24.	4. Kings of Judah, XV. 1 to 24.
5. Solomon anointed king, I. 32 to 52.	5. The greatness of Solomon, IV.		5. Kings of Israel, XV. 25 to XVI.
6. David's last address and death, II. 1 to 12.	6. The Life's work of Solomon, V. to VIII.		6. Ahab and Elijah, XVII. to XXII.
7. Solomon's execution of various traitors, II. 13-46.	7. Second Divine appearing, IX. 1 to 9.		
	8. Fame of Solomon, IX. 10 to X. 13.		
	9. Wealth of Solomon, X. 14 to 29.		

MESSAGE

(1) This book is written to show the causes of the establishment and decline of the kingdom. It points out that, when loyal to God, Israel flourished, but when Israel departed from God their morals and their kingdom declined. The vision of XXII. 19, is very important. God sat as Sovereign on His throne dispensing mercy and grace to the penitent and obedient, but punishment and chastisement to the sinners.

(2) Note the new standard, "as David his father," (III. 3, 14, IX. 4, XI. 4, 33, 38. XIV. 8, XV. 3, 11). Man failed to reach even this human standard.

ORIGINALLY ONE BOOK

(1) In the original Hebrew, 1 and 2 Kings formed one book, as also did 1 and 2 Samuel, and 1 and 2 Chronicles. They were first divided by the Septuagint translators, when they translated the Old Testament into the Greek language. The explanation given is this: Greek requires at least one third more space than Hebrew, therefore the translators were compelled to divide them, either because the scrolls were of limited length, or to make the scrolls easy to handle.

(2) With this in mind, note the perfect order of the two books as one, as pointed out by Dr. Bullinger: "The book begins with King David and ends with the King of Babylon; opens with the Temple built and closes with the Temple burnt; begins with David's first successor on the throne of his kingdom, and ends with David's last successor released from the house of his captivity."

SCOPE OF THE BOOK

(1) This second book of Kings contains the history of Israel and Judah from Ahab to the captivity, a period of about 300 years.

(2) The *first half of the book is largely taken up with an account of Elisha's ministry of 66 years*. This book records 16 miracles by Elisha, whereas Elijah performed only eight. "The story of Elisha is almost entirely a record of his miracles, and the story of his miracles is almost entirely a record of deeds of beneficence." (See II. 14, 21, 24, III. 20, IV. 1 to 6, 16, 17, 35, 41, 43, V. 10, 27, VI. 6, 17, 18, 20, XIII. 21).

(3) The *second half of the book is taken up with events leading up to the fall of Samaria and captivity of Israel, and the fall of Jerusalem and captivity of Judah*.

(4) Israel had 19 Kings, not one being good, whilst Judah had 19 Kings and one Queen, eight of whom were good.

(5) Note (a) one of the best of Judah's Kings—Hezekiah, was the father of the worst of the Kings (XXI.); (b) the remarkable commendation of Josiah (XXIII. 25); (c) how nearly the only surviving descendant in the Davidic Royal line (XI. 1 to 3), and only existing copy of the Law (XXII. 8 to 20), perished.

KEY WORDS

This book abounds with Key-Words.

(1) *The phrase "Man of God," is found in it 36 times*, more than any other book in the Bible. God had His brave witnesses in those days.

(2) *The sad and tragic sentence, "Did that which was evil in the sight of the Lord" is met with 21 times* (III. 2, VIII. 18, XII. 2, 11; XIV. 24, XV. 9, 18, 24, 28, XVI. 2, XVII. 2, 17, XXI. 2, 6, 15, 16, 20, XXIII. 32, 37, XXIV. 9, 19). What they did no doubt was considered right according to earthly standards, but according to the Divine rule of faith and practice it was wrong.

(3) Thank God, we do meet with the reverse statement, "right in the sight of the Lord," but only eight times. (III. 18, XIII. 2, XIV. 3, XV. 3, 34. XVIII. 3, XX. 3, XXII. 2).

(4) *The phrase "the Word of the Lord," and its equivalent, are met with 24 times* (I. 17, IV. 44, VII. 1, 16, VIII. 19, IX. 26, 36, X. 10, XIV. 25, XV. 12, XIX. 21). —Observe man's "word" mentioned four, and six times, and met by the Lord's "Word," 21—XX. 4, 16, 19, XXII. 13, 16, 18, XXIII. 2, 3, 16, 24, XXIV. 2.

(5) *Note the prominence given to the Lord's anger* (XIII. 3, XVII. 18, XXIII. 26, XXIV. 20), *and wrath* (XXII. 13, 17, XXIII. 26).

MESSAGE

I have taken the trouble of jotting down these references because a study of them gives the message of the book. God's standard of worship and morals had been violated. To meet this Jehovah sent His "Men of God" to warn, and, if possible, lead back to the Lord. They came with a "Thus saith the Lord." Failing in this, His anger was roused, and He gave them over to the enemy. In all this He fulfilled His own Word.

ANALYSIS

The book gives graphic descriptions of the Lord's emotions at Israel's base treatment of Him—this is shown in the following Analysis.

(a) Closing Ministry of ELIJAH	(b) Long Ministry of ELISHA		(c) The Passing of ISRAEL		(d) The Passing of JUDAH
JEHOVAH (1) **IGNORED**	JEHOVAH (2) **DERIDED**	JEHOVAH'S (3) **ANGER**	JEHOVAH'S (4) **Compassion**	JEHOVAH'S (5) **Great Anger**	JEHOVAH'S (6) **Fierce Wrath**
I. 1 to II. 2.	II. 12 to 25.	III. 1 to XIII. 21.	XIII. 22 to XVI.	XVII.	XVIII. 1 to XXV.
(1) Key I. 3 and 16.	(1) Key, II. 23.	(1) Key, XIII. 3.	(1) Key, XIII. 23.	(1) Key, XVII. 11 and 18.	(1) Key, XXII. 13, 17, XXIII. 26, with XXIV. 20.
(2) The King's base conduct, I. 1 and 2.	(2) Elisha's inducement II. 12-15	(2) Elisha's long ministry, 66 y's.	(2) Kings of Judah:	(2) Last King of Israel: Hosea—bad.	(2) We owe a very great deal to Hezekiah, (see Analysis on Psalms.)
(3) Elijah's message and deliverance, I. 3 and 16.	(3) The "little children" of v. 23, in R. V. "young lads" i.e. young men.	(3) Kings of Judah:	(a) Amaziah - good.		
(4) Elijah's translation, II. 1-11.	(4) "Go up," was a blasphemous reference to Elijah's translation, and, in reality, was deriding the act of Jehovah.	(a) Jehoshaphat - good.	(b) Uzziah - good.	(3) In this chapter we have "a post mortem enquiry into the diseases that killed a nation."	(3) Kings of Judah:
(5) King of Israel: Ahaziah, bad.		(b) Jehoram - good.	(c) Jotham - good.	(4) Note the force of verse 23.	(a) Hezekiah, good. (b) Manasseh, bad. (c) Amon bad. (d) Josiah, good. (e) Jehoahaz, bad. (f) Jehoiakim, bad. (g) Jehoiachin, bad. (h) Zedekiah, bad.
		(c) Ahaziah - bad.	(d) Ahaz - bad.		
		(d) Joash - good.	(3) Kings of Israel:		
		(4) Kings of Israel:	(a) Jeroboam II. - bad.		
		(a) Jehoram - bad.	(b) Zechariah - "		
		(b) Jehoram - "	(c) Shallum - "		
		(c) Jehoahaz - "	(d) Menahem - "		
		(d) Jehoash - "	(e) Pekahiah - "		
			(f) Pekah - "		

FIRST BOOK OF CHRONICLES

A "KITTLE" BOOK

That brilliant Scotsman, Edward Irving, referred to this book as " The book of kittle (difficult or puzzling) Chronicles." And no doubt the majority of Bible readers and students agree with him as, on their own confession, they find little to attract and much to bewilder in these two difficult books. But it is well to remember that whenever a Bible book seems dry and uninteresting, it is so because the right Key to its study has not been found.

POINTS TO NOTE

(1) Students have noticed *a very clear resemblance in style and language between the two books of Chronicles and those of Ezra and Nehemiah.* Consequently the authorship of the former is generally ascribed to Ezra; and they must have been written during the Babylonian Captivity.
(2) Whilst Samuel and Kings concern both kingdoms of Judah and Israel, *Chronicles deals only with Judah.*
(3) The writer has more to say of the Temple and its ritual than of the wars of the Kings. It breathes an ecclesiastical atmosphere.
(4) *Prominence is given to the activities of the Lord on behalf of His people,* IV. 9, 10. V. 20 and 22. XI. 14. XII. 18, XIV. 2, 11. 15. XVIII. 13:
(5) *The justice of the Lord's judgments are declared* in V. 25, 26. VI. 15. IX. 1. X. 13, 14. XV. 2, 13. XXI. 19, (Note—the Lord spoken of as doing this Himself).

SUPPLEMENT ?

Greek translators gave the books the title—"Things Omitted." They noticed that much information is given in them not found in the other historical books, and by their title meant to signify that the books were supplementary to Samuel and Kings. Certainly much additional information is given, *e.g.,*—(1) The genealogy of Judah is enlivened by the episode of Jabez IV. 9, 10, who was a man of prayer, and because he asked much he obtained much. (2) A raid was made upon Philistia by part of Ephraim's family, whilst Ephraim was alive (perhaps Joseph still lived, see Gen. L. 23), which ended disastrously, VII. 21. Perhaps the feud between Israel and the Philistines began through this raid made whilst Israel was yet in Egypt. (3) The erection of a temporary home for the Ark by David (XV. 1, XVI. 1,) until the Temple was erected. This provision will be repeated before the erection of the Temple yet to be built, see Acts XV. 16, 17, with Ezekiel XL to XLVI. (4) Age at which the Levites began their ministry, originally 30 (Num. IV. 3,) changed to 25 by the Lord (Num. VIII. 24,) was further reduced by David to 20 (I Chron. XXIII. 27,) etc., etc. But these two books form much more than a mere supplement to the other historical books.

THE CLUE

As a matter of fact they form *"an independent work, in which the history of the chosen people is related afresh in a new manner, and from a new standpoint.* Whilst the same events are recorded, they are viewed from a different standpoint. In Samuel and Kings we have the facts of history; here we have the Divine words and thoughts about these facts. In the former books they are regarded from a man's standpoint; here they are viewed from a Divine standpoint." (Dr. Bullinger.)

ILLUSTRATIONS

Let us note a few facts in proof, and as illustrating this statement. (1) In 1 Samuel XXXI, we are simply told that the Philistines slew Saul; In 1 Chronicles X. 1 to 14, we are informed that the Lord slew him, and the reason is given; thus the Philistines were merely Jehovah's executioners. (2) In Samuel only one chapter (2 Samuel VI.) is devoted to an account of the removal of the ark to Jerusalem, but in Chronicles we have three (1 Chronicles XIII., XV., and XVI.), and in the Chronicles we are informed why the Lord slew Uzziah, and David's confession (XV. 2, 13), not referred to at all in the other books. (3) Two chapters in Samuel (2 Samuel XI. and XII.) are taken up in giving particulars concerning David's great sin, but in Chronicles we have not the slightest reference to it—this is in keeping with the character of God, for when He forgives He forgets—blessed be His name! There is a reference to David's second great sin (1 Chronicles XXI. 1), but only because it was necessary to do so in order to show what led up to the purchase of the Temple site. (4) In the account of this sin Chronicles (1 Chronicles XXI.) draws the curtain aside revealing the true mover of David, the other books being silent on this matter. (5) 2 Samuel II. 8, gives Ish-bosheth as name of Saul's son made king by Abner, but by Chronicles (1 Chronicles VIII. 33) we learn that he had another name, Esh-baal, *i.e.*, "Man of Baal." This son was probably born after his father's apostasy, and this idolatrous name hints that Saul had begun to worship Baal. This is only told in this book which gives the inner and deeper history. (6) In this book Jacob is always called after his spiritual name, Israel, I. 34, II. 1.

ANALYSIS

(1) GENEALOGIES.	(2) SAUL.	(3) DAVID.	(4) TEMPLE.
I to IX.	X.	XI. to XX.	XXI. to XXIX.
The book opens with an outline of primeval history from Adam to David. Note: Dwelling with the King must come before doing His work, IV. 23.	Saul's reign is passed over; Saul's overthrow and death are alone recorded.	1. David and his mighty men, XI., XII. 2. David and the Ark, XIII., XV., XVI. 3. David's prosperity, XIV. 4. David's desire to build Temple, XVII. 5. David's Victories, XVIII. to XX.	1. What led to acquisition of Temple site, XXI. 2. Material prepared for Temple, XXII. 3. Organization of Priests and Levites, XXIII. to XXVI, 23. 4. Organization of officers of state, XXVI. 28,-XXVII. 5. Closing scenes in David's life, XXVIII. and XXIX.

MESSAGE

"The Book of Chronicles is occupied from beginning to end with magnifying God, and giving Him His right place in Israel." Though often ignored and disobeyed, He is still the Sovereign Lord: "Thou reignest over all." Here we see the Lord active on behalf of those who trusted and served him; here is revealed the true mover to sin; here God's severities are justified, and God glorified in all His ways and works: In spite of the flood of iniquity He is seen sitting as King. By this book Israel's history is seen from the stand-point of Heaven. Remembering this, and also that it was written during the Babylonian captivity, students will easily see how timely and forceful its message would be.

ANALYSIS No. 14   "Prepareth his heart to seek   SECOND BOOK OF CHRONICLES   MESSAGE   Seeking and serving the Lord; the secret of a vital religion and a life of victory.

Key Verse, XX. 20   Key Phrase. God." XXX 19.

VALUE OF A RIGHT STANDPOINT

A party of tourists, after inspecting one of the famous objects of interest in Egypt, returned to their hotel, and compared notes on what they had seen. They were astonished to find that each had a different report to give, and there was every indication of a serious quarrel, until an old and experienced traveller restored the peace by declaring that they were all correct. The conflicting reports were accounted for by the fact that the party had viewed the object from different standpoints. In the study of Chronicles everything depends upon securing the right standpoint. It is important to note that in these two books the history of God's people is viewed from the *ecclesiastical, and not from the political standpoint; from the Divine, and not from the mere human point of view.* Let us illustrate this:

DIFFERENCES BETWEEN KINGS AND CHRONICLES

(1) In Kings VII. 8, we are simply told that Solomon built for Pharaoh's daughter a separate house, but Chronicles (2 Chron. VIII. 11), informs us that it was not built in Jerusalem, for Solomon felt that an idolatress, though his wife, should not reside in the holy city.

(2) Chronicles alone points out that in his apostasy, Jeroboam not only worshipped the golden calves, but also devils, (2 Chron. XI. 15).

(3) Not one redeeming act in Abijah's reign does Kings record, but in Chronicles (2 Chron. XIII.,) we have his devout address (5 to 12), and cry to God, (14, 18).

(4) It is only Chronicles that tells us that good king Asa neglected the Lord in his last illness, (2 Chron. XVI. 12); that good king Jehoshaphat in spite of XVII. 1 entered into a three-fold sinful alliance, (a) Matrimonial, 2 Chron. XXI. 6. (b) Military, XVIII. 3. (c) Commercial, XX. 35; that Athaliah had committed sacrilege (2 Chron. XXIV. 7); and why the Lord smote Uzziah with Leprosy (2 Chron. XXVI. 16 to 21).

(5) "Hezekiah's reign was divided into two great parts—his military exploits, and the reformation he made in the Temple, and in the worship of God. In 2 Kings (XVIII. 4 to 6), we have *three verses* about his reformation, but in 2 Chronicles *three chapters* (XXIX to XXXI); and with regard to military affairs it is just the reverse—three chapters in Kings are devoted to the secular history, whilst the religious reformation is dismissed in three verses."

(6) 2 Kings XXI. has much to say concerning Manasseh's wickedness, but it is only in Chronicles (2 Chron. XXXIII. 11 to 13) we are told of his captivity in Babylon, and his restoration to God and his throne. Because of this, he has been called "the Prodigal of the Old Testament."

(7) Note the remarkable phrase in 2 Chron. IX. 8: "The Lord . . . . set thee on His throne," It is on a par with 1 Chron. XXIX. 23.

KEY PHRASES AND MESSAGE

(1) In reading this book through one phrase is frequently met with, viz., "Seek the Lord." (VII. 14, XI. 16, XIV. 4, 7, XV. 2, 4, 12, 13, 15, XVII. 4, XIX. 3, XX. 3, 4, XXII. 9, XXVI. 5, XXX. 19, XXXI. 21, XXXIV. 3; also see XII. 14, XVI. 12). To seek the Lord meant blessing, success, victory.

(2) Prayer to, and reliance upon, Jehovah as the secret of success is further brought out in I. 1, XIII. 18, XIV. 6, 11, XV. 9, XX. 27, XXVI. 6, 7, XXVII. 6, XXXII. 8, 22. Also see XXIV. 24, XXVIII. 6, 19. Also note XX. 20.

(3) A prayerful study of these scriptures leads to the message of the book, viz., that seeking, believing, obeying, serving, and loving the Lord are absolutely requisite to the possession of vital religion and a spiritual and victorious life. And nothing less than this will satisfy the Lord or the deepest cravings of the soul.

ANALYSIS

(A) The Reign of Solomon. I. to IX		(B) The Kings of Judah. X. to XXXVI.	
(1) **LOYAL** to the Lord.	(2) **FORSAKING** the Lord.	(3) **SEEKING** the Lord.	(4) **SERVING** the Lord.

(1) Though it seems an impossibility to arrange the book in handy divisions, the above outline gives the contents in convenient form, and is in fact a summary of the history of the Lord's people narrated therein.

(2) During the reign of Solomon and three years of Solomon's son and successor (I. to XI.), the people were loyal to God, in spite of Solomon's fall, of which Chronicles gives no account. But eventually they "forsook the Law of the Lord," (XII. 1). Swift chastisement followed (2 to 4.), On Shemaiah the prophet delivering a message, the people humbled themselves, (6.) Abijah's reign also was not entirely bad, (XIII.)

(3) The first of the four great religious festivals took place under Asa (XV). It was continued by Jehoshaphat (XVII. to XX.), who sent travelling preachers with the Word of God throughout the land, (see XVII. 7 to 9, and XIX. 4). On the death of Jehoshaphat, under the reign of his son (XXI.), and grandson (XXII.), led by a wicked wife (XXI. 6), and mother (XXII. 3), Israel plunged into sin.

(4) The second great religious revival took place under Joash, inspired by Jehoiada the priest (XXIII. to XXIV. 16), but on the death of this good priest, led by the princes of Judah, Joash went astray (17 and 19), even slaying the son of his benefactor who sought to lead him back to the Lord (20 to 22). The dying man's words were twice used by the Lord Jesus, (Luke XI. 50, 51, and Matthew XXIII. 35, 36).

(5) The third of these great religious revivals took place under Hezekiah (XXIX. and XXX.), and the fourth under Josiah (XXXIV).

(6) Note the strange reward for faithfulness as given in R.V. of XXXII. 1. Testing often comes after faithfulness.

THE BOOK OF EZRA

KEY

(1) The key to the study of this book is *the life and master-passion of its writer*, Ezra, who wrote it about the year 457 B.C.

(2) Ezra was a descendant of Hilkiah, High Priest in the reign of Josiah, who found a copy of the Law. (read 2 Chron. XXXIV. 14).

(3) Though by birth a priest, he was not able to exercise his priestly duties as he was a captive in Babylon. Instead, he gave himself to the study of the Word of God (Ezra VII. 10), *becoming its great exponent*. How little the Law and other Divine Writings were known to the community at large is seen by a study of 2 Chron., Ezra, and Nehemiah. This book records how, mainly through Ezra's ministry, the Word of God gained for the first time in the history of Israel and Judah, its rightful position.

(4) The Word of the Lord, as read and expounded by Ezra, *came with the force of a new revelation*, and wrought wonders in the life of the nation.

(5) It has been suggested that the memory of Ezra has scarcely had fair play amongst Bible lovers. Certainly, we owe a very great deal to him. In addition to his powerful ministry of the Word, he wrote 1 and 2 Chron., Psalm CXIX. (which is a striking poem on the Word of God), instituted the wonderful system of Synagogue worship (the parent of our own), and, assisted by the great synagogue, settled the sacred Canon of Scripture. The revival under Ezra was a revival of Bible study and obedience to the revealed will of God. *The fruits of that movement are with us to-day*, though nearly 2,500 years have passed since then.

SECTIONS

(1) Until the third century, Ezra and Nehemiah were treated as a single book, and that may be one explanation of the abrupt close of Ezra.

(2) Ezra views the return *from the ecclesiastical standpoint*, Nehemiah *from the civil*; Ezra is the book of the Temple building, Nehemiah is the book of the Wall building.

(3) It is in two sections, Chapters I. to VI. dealing with the return under Zerubbabel, then, after a break of 57 years, Chapters VII. to X., the return under Ezra.

KEY-PHRASE

Its *Key-phrase is the Word of the Lord* referred to as "Word of the Lord" (I. 1), Law (III. 2), Commandments of the God of Israel (VI. 14), Book of Moses (VI. 18), Law of the Lord (VII. 10), Law of Moses (VII. 6), Law of Thy God (VII. 14), Words of the God of Israel (IX. 4), Commandments of God (X. 3, 5).

ITS MESSAGE

It gives a clear message on the place and power of the Word of God in the religious, social and civil life of His people.

ANALYSIS

(A) THE RETURN UNDER ZERUBBABEL (About 50,000). Chap. I. to VI.				(B) RETURN UNDER EZRA (About 2,000). VII. to end		
(1) RETURN OF ISRAEL In Fulfilment of The Word of the Lord.	(2) RE-ERECTION OF ALTAR In Obedience to The Word of the Lord.	(3) REBUILDING OF TEMPLE In Obedience to The Word of the Lord.	(4) RESTORATION OF TEMPLE RITUAL According to The Word of the Lord.	(5) THE STUDENT OF THE WORD OF GOD Commissioned.	(6) A GREAT TREMBLING at The Word of the Lord.	(7) REPENTANCE AND REFORM through The Word of the Lord.
I. and II.	III. 1 to 7.	III. 8 to VI. 14.	VI. 15 to 22.	VII. and VIII.	IX.	X.
1. Note I. 1. 2. As Daniel prophesied in the reign of Darius, probably he had something to do with this proclamation. 3. The very heathen assisted by their gifts, I. 6. 4. Whilst only 74 Levites returned, 4000 priests did so.	1. Note III. 2. 2. Before they thought of homes for themselves, their first thought was the House of God. 3. And they did not begin with the walls or Temple, but the Altar. 4. The atoning work must come first, and be at the heart of every real live movement.	1. Note VI. 14. 2. Hindrances to all real work for God are to be expected. 3. The Church must not have the help of the world, IV. 1 to 3. 4. This opposition disheartened them, hence the need of Haggai's message. (VI. 14.) (Read Haggai here.)	1. Note VI. 18. 2. About 23 years passed between the return of the exiles and the completion of the Temple. 3. Verse 17 is a proof that representatives of *All* the tribes returned (see VIII. 35).	1. Note VII. 10. 2. How Ezra loved the Word! 3. By verse 12 of chapter VII. we note how impressed the King was with Ezra's love and estimate of God's Word. O! so to live that representatives might learn to respect God's Book! 4. Note Ezra's loyalty to God and jealousy for God's glory, VIII. 21, 22.	1. Note IX. 4. 2. On his arrival he found things even worse than he expected. 3. Have *I* learned yet to tremble at the Word of God? (verse 4.) 4. Study, on your knees, Ezra's touching prayer and confession, (5 to 15.)	1. Note X. 5. 2. Here we see the Word of God at work, producing genuine repentance, and leading to separation. 3. In this book we have separation. (a) From Babylon I. (b) From worldly help, IV. (c) From leaning on the arm of flesh, VIII. 21 to 23. (d) From sinful alliance X. 10, 11.

ANALYSIS No. 16
Key Verses, I. 4, vi. 3.
Key Words, "Prayer" and "Work."
THE BOOK of NEHEMIAH
MESSAGE
Prayer, Pains, and Perseverance, the Conditions of Successful Work for God.

INTRODUCTION

(1) The Book of Nehemiah is largely *autobiographical*, and is the *last historical book* of the Old Testament.

(2) The book is a striking *revelation of the character of Nehemiah* He was born (probably of the Royal House of Judah) in exile, and became cup-bearer to the mighty king, Artaxerxes. Though comfortably situated in Shushan, and his circumstances all that could be desired, *his heart was in the ruined city of his fathers*.

(3) This life of ease, luxury, and certain substantial advancement he renounced at the call of God, for a life of toil, danger, and the heart-breaking work of a reformer. Have you ever given him the credit and honour he deserves for *his "great acceptance?"*

(4) *This book reveals him* as "a man of patriotism and courage—fearless, enthusiastic, and enterprising, a man of prayer and hard work, and one who feared God, and sought His blessing." "His character is without blot."

(5) *Between Ezra and Nehemiah* there is an interval of about twelve years. Nehemiah's administration covered a period of 36 years, and was marvellously successful, in spite of incessant and bitter opposition. *The book begins and ends with prayer.*

ANALYSIS

(1) The events which led to Nehemiah's appointment as Governor of Judah.	(2) The Building of the wall in spite of many difficulties.	(3) Nehemiah's wise organization and preparation, in view of his return to Babylon.	(4) Certain reforms accomplished after his return from Babylon.
I. TO II. 11.	XI. 12 TO VI.	VII. TO XII.	XIII.
1. Scene laid in the Royal palace.	1. After resting three days he privately inspected the ruins at night (II. 12 to 16).	1. Before the stirring dedication of the finished wall (XII. 27 to 43).	1. After a twelve years' absence at the Court of Persia, Nehemiah returns to find the need of another reformation.
2. In the month of December, from one of his own brothers, he learns of the sad state of Jerusalem (1 to 3).	2. Then inspires the people to work (II. 17-20).	2. Came arrangements for guarding the wall and city (VII. 1 to 4);	2. Note, the High Priest's sad fall, through a worldly alliance (XIII. 4).
3. This news led him to prayer (4 to 11). Note "God of Heaven."	3. The names and account of work done (III).	3. Census (VII. 5 to 73, XI., XII.);	3. Nehemiah deals very drastically with the offenders (8, 28).
4. This expression: " and to the prayer of Thy *servants* " (11) proves he was the moving spirit in a little circle of praying friends.	4. Nehemiah had six forms of opposition from the enemy . (*a*) Grief, II. 10, (*b*) Laughter, II. 19, (*c*) Wrath, IV. 1, (*d*) Mocking, IV. 1, (*e*) Conflict, IV. 8, (*f*) Subtlety, VI. 2, 3.	4. And the calling of a great and remarkable convention for the reading and exposition of the Word (VIII. to X).	4. Sabbath rest established, and wrong marriage ties dissolved.
5. After four months prayer, comes the enquiry and the commission of the King (II. 1 to 10).	5. More dangerous still, opposition from friends within: (*a*) Discouragement, IV. 10 to 23, (*b*) Selfishness, V.	5. Only reference to "pulpit" in the Bible is VIII. 4.	
	6. Wall finished in 52 days.		
	7. No account of his own work—of what he himself did.		

MESSAGE

(1) Its key words and key verses are as above: Prayer and Work, I. 4, and VI. 3.

(2) It has a peculiar and opportune message for Christian workers. It points out that the conditions of success in work for God are prayer, pains, and perseverance.

(3) **Nehemiah, the Model Worker for God.**

(*a*) A man with a heart at leisure from himself to sorrow over the sad state of Zion. (I. 4.)

(*b*) A man of prayer at all times, and under all circumstances, thus living in fellowship with God. (I. 5 to 11, II. 4, IV. 4, 9, V. 19, VI. 9, 14, XIII. 14, 22, 29, 31.)

(*c*) A man determined to become personally acquainted with the true state of affairs (II. 12).

(*d*) A man full of self-denying labours for the cause of God (II. 5).

(*e*) A man able to inspire others to work (II. 17, 18), as well as work himself (IV. 23).

(*f*) A man with a glorious conception of the sacredness and nobility of work for God. (Note VI. 3 to leave the work he was engaged in, even to meet the great ones of the district, he considered to be a " coming down").

(*g*) A man undismayed and undisturbed by opposition from without and within.

(*h*) A man ever ready to give God all the credit for any wisdom he displayed (VII. 5, with II. 12).

THE BOOK OF ESTHER.

PROBLEM.

(1) It is said that Luther declared himself so hostile to the book of Esther that he wished it did not exist. Many to-day have the same view. Certainly the book is a problem, and bristles with difficulties. At first sight the tone of the book does seem to be " of a wholly secular character, and to deprive it of any claim to be regarded as a book of spiritual teaching, and still less to be entitled to a place in the volume of Holy Scripture."

(2) Note (*a*) God's name is never mentioned, though the heathen king's name occurs 187 times. (*b*) It is never quoted in the New Testament. (*c*) It makes no reference to prayer, or any of the sacred observances of the Jewish Law. (*d*) The superstitious habit of observing lucky days by a heathen is its only approach to the supernatural.

FACT.

(1) Before hastily condemning it we should enquire what the view of the Jewish people is concerning it, and whether we really understand it or no.

(2) It is a fact that not only was this book accepted as part of the Canon, but *it was regarded by many of the Jews as peculiarly sacred.* It held a place in their view second to the five Books of Moses.

SOLUTION

(1) The very absence of the name of God is *its chief beauty*, and should by no means be considered a blot on it.

(2) Matthew Henry says : " If *the name of God is not here His finger is.*" This Book is, as Dr. Pierson called it, " *The Romance of Providence.*" By Providence we mean that in all the affairs and events of human life, individual and national, God has a part and a share. But that control is a secret and hidden one. Hence in this wonderful story, which teaches the reality of the Divine Providence, the name of God does not appear, " only the eye of faith sees the Divine Factor in human history ; but to the attentive observer all history is a Burning Bush aflame with the mysterious Presence."

(3) The Talmud gives Deuteronomy XXXI. 18. as another reason why God's name is not mentioned. Because of their sin, God had hidden His face from Israel. Yet, though hiding His face, He was not forgetful or unconcerned about His people, though He did it all under a veil.

(4) It has also been suggested that this book is an extract from the official documents of the Persian Court (II, 23). This would account for the omission of the name of God, and for its minute details.

AUTHOR.

(1) Nothing dogmatically can be said concerning its authorship. Augustine ascribed the book to Ezra, the Talmud to the Great Synagogue.

(2) The possibility is that Mordecai himself wrote the book—see chapter IX. 20.

DIVISION.

Curiously, all the events of the book circle around three Feasts ; therefore naturally it falls into three divisions.

---

(1)

The Feast of Ahasuerus,

and its sequel, I. and II.

1. A feast which lasted six months   -   -   -   I. 1 to 4.
2. Followed by a seven days' feast   -   -   -   1. 5 to 8.
3. The Queen's noble refusal and deposition   -   I. 9 to 22.
4. Between Chapters I and II. the king made his historic attack on Greece with an army of five millions, suffering a terrible defeat.
5. Selection and enthronement of Esther   -   II. 1 to 20.
6. Mordecai saves the life of the King   -   -   II. 21 to 23.

   Note : "Esther" is a Persian name meaning "The Star of the East," but her Hebrew name was Hadassah, meaning "Myrtle."

---

(2)

Events leading up to

The Feast of Esther,

and its sequel, III. to VII.

1. Mordecai's refusal to worship a descendant of the Agag whom Samuel slew   -   -   -   -   III. 1 & 2.
2. The Court busy-bodies tell Haman   -   -   -   3, 4.
3. Haman's Conspiracy   -   -   -   -   5 to 15.
4. The Fasting of the Jews   -   -   -   IV. 1 to 4.
5. Mordecai's message to Esther   -   -   -   5 to 14.
6. Esther's fast   -   -   -   -   -   15 to 17.
7. Esther interviews the King   -   -   -   V. 1 to 8.
8. Haman plots to slay Mordecai   -   -   -   9 to 14.
9. King's sleepless night and result   -   -   -   VI.
10. Esther's feast and result   -   -   -   -   VII.

---

(3)

Institution of

The Feast of Purim,

and its sequel, VIII. to X.

1. Esther's intercession and stratagem to save life of Israel, VIII.
2. Day of self defence   -   -   -   -   IX. 1 to 19.
3. The Feast of Purim instituted, which has been observed ever since by the Jews   -   -   -   IX. 20 to 32.
4. The greatness of Mordecai   -   -   -   -   X.

   Note : "Sending portions" IX. 19. It is believed that our observance of Christmas has been largely moulded on the customary keeping of Purim by the Jews, with its habit of sending portions.

ANALYSIS No. 18

Key Word: Trial. Key Verses, I. 9, with James V. 11.

THE BOOK OF JOB

MESSAGE

Trials and suffering sometimes come for our education, not always as chastisment.

OPINIONS

In the opinion of many, the book of Job is the most remarkable book in Holy Writ. *Tennyson called it "the greatest poem, whether of ancient or modern literature.* Luther regarded it as "more magnificent and sublime than any other book of Scripture." *Carlyle wrote: "I call that (Job) one of the grandest things ever written with pen."*

DATE

It is the most ancient book known. It must have been written about the time of Jacob. Note (1) total silence of the disputants on the miracles attending the Exodus. (2) Length of Job's life places him in the patriarchal times. (3) Job acted as high priest in his family, which was not allowed after the Exodus. (4) Eliphaz was descendant of Esau's eldest son called Eliphaz, who had a son called Teman (Genesis XXXVI. 10, 11).

AUTHOR

Unknown. *Job XXXII. 16 (note the "I") seems to shew that Elihu wrote it.* Though written in poetical form (with the exception of first two chapters, and part of last, which are prose), Job and the others were *actual* beings, so it is fact not fiction.

MESSAGE

Incidentally it shows how remarkably full were the theological knowledge and intellectual culture of the patriarchal age. Almost every important doctrine is found therein, in addition to scientific truths only fully discovered in our own time. But *the message of the book is on the mystery of suffering.* All suffering was thought to be on account of personal sin. Yet the apparent failure of God to reward His servants and punish His enemies as they deserved was a problem which always tried the faith of the Old Testament saints. Becuuse Job suffered so heavily his friends were sure he must have sinned dreadfully. But whilst this book does not solve, *it gives additional and welcome light on the mystery of suffering and pain,* proving that, as in Job's case, it is sent, not as chastisement, but as a test and revealer of character, and to educate and instruct. The Ancients asked: "How can this man be godly if he suffers?" We Christians say: "How can this man be God-like if he knows nothing of suffering?"

(1) JOB before the trial.	(2) Satan and the mystery of pain.	(3) The end of Job's patience.	(4) The heated and fruitless philosophical discussion of the mystery of suffering by Job and his four friends.	(5) Jehovah and the mystery of suffering.	(6) Job and "the end of the Lord."
I. 1 to 5.	I. 6 to II. 10.	II. 11 to III.	IV. to XXXVII.	XXXVIII. to XLI.	XLII.
JOB'S 1. Place: Uz, spoken of in Lamentations IV. 21, as identical with Edom. 2. Purity, verse 1. 3. Prosperity, verses 2-4. 4. Popularity. (See Chapter XXIX). 5. Piety, verse 5. By verse 4 we note that sons must have had homes of their own. Note: Job sought access to God through the blood of sacrifice. Verse 5.	SATAN'S 1. Admission into the court of Heaven. 6. 2. Restlessness, verse 7. 3. Power: its extent and limit. 4. Theory: that Job was only good for what he could get. 5. Declaration: he declared that suffering would annihilate Job's piety. 6. Theory,—proved to be wrong. Note: "The Sons of God" of verse 6 are shown by XXXVIII. 7, to have been angels.	Here endeth Job's patience, and here beginneth Job's complaining. Though he cursed not God, he cursed the day of his birth, placing amongst his curses what Satan placed amongst his blessings: 1. 10 with III. 23. Note: The "Seven days and seven nights" of II. 13 is the period of very great mourning.	1. There is a sameness in the arguments of Job's three friends, viz., all suffering is result of personal sin, therefore Job's great suffering proved him to be a great sinner and a great hypocrite. 2. In the first discourses of the three friends this statement is first elaborated, and *each discourse ends with an appeal to Job to repent of his sin,* when prosperity would return to him. 3. In the second series of discourses each deals exclusively with the terrible sufferings and end of the wicked. 4. The third series of discourses resembles the first. 5. Note Eliphaz backs up his arguments by lessons he had received from a remarkable dream or vision, Bildad from old proverbs he had read or heard, (as VIII. 2 to 13), Zophar from experience and reason. 6. Though Job holds the same views, he yet protests his innocence, and in XXI. brings forward a new argument, viz., that the wicked often spend their lives in prosperity. 7. The fourth friend, Elihu. comes nearest the truth, for he shows (XXXIII.) that suffering must be sometimes considered as God's discipline to bring the soul back.	1. "We are struck, first of all, by what God does not say. Hitherto the book has been one long argument, but there is no argument here. It is as though we were to learn that the *mysteries of Divine Providence are not to be settled by logic.* Rest does not enter the heart by way of intellectual powers." 2. "Job's thoughts were turned from himself to God. If he were unable to explain ordinary and well known facts (of natural history and science) how could he be capable of explaining the mystery of God's ways." 3. "The fact that God did not explain the mystery of suffering teaches us that He wants our confidence."	1. And what was the Lord's purpose in permitting suffering to Job? FIRST: To reveal Job's character. SECOND: Object lesson to others. "God's Blackboard." THIRD: To bring out a hidden sin, of which Job was unconscious, namely – self-righteousness. 1. Verse 6 is always the language of the true penitent. 3. Note the force of verse 10.

A TESTIMONY

All devout readers and students of the Psalms can understand and appreciate the glowing testimony of C. H. Spurgeon, written upon the completion of his great commentary on the Psalms, which took twenty of the best years of his life: "A tinge of sadness is on my spirit as I quit 'The Treasury of David,' never to find on this earth a richer storehouse, though the whole palace of Revelation is open to me. Blessed have been the days spent in meditating, mourning, hoping, believing, and exulting with David. Can I hope to spend hours more joyous on this side of the golden gate? The book of Psalms instructs us in the use of wings as well as words: it sets us both mounting and singing."

WHAT IT IS

The book of Psalms is a collection of 150 spiritual songs or poems, many of which were set to music for the Tabernacle and Temple worship. "They set forth the attitude of the soul in the presence of God when contemplating past history, present experience, and prophetic hope." "Every Psalm is a direct expression of the soul's consciousness of God."

AUTHORS

These sacred and inspired poems were written by various persons: Moses wrote one (XC.); David composed seventy-three Psalms; Sons of Korah eleven; Asaph twelve; Heman one (Psalm LXXXVIII.); Ethan one (Psalm LXXXIX.); Hezekiah ten; the remainder being anonymous.

DIVISION

(1) From ancient times the book was always understood to be in five sections, each ending with a doxology, (see R.V.)
(2) But why the book should be thus divided has been for ages a puzzling problem.
(3) It has been thought that in book 1 we have a collection by David of the Psalms he composed; in book 2 additional Psalms for use in the Temple, compiled by Hezekiah; in book 3 a compilation by Josiah; and in books 4 and 5 a collection by Ezra and Nehemiah. But this explanation is not wholly satisfactory.
(4) It is quite certain that the Psalms are not arranged in chronological order, else the oldest (XC.) would be the first.
(5) The proper solution is found in a right understanding of a very ancient Jewish statement: "Moses gave to the Israelites the five books of the Law; and *corresponding with these* David gave them the five books of the Psalms."
(6) The whole book thus forms a poetical pentateuch. This is splendidly brought out in "The Companion Bible" as follows:

BOOK I. Psalms 1 to 41.	BOOK II. Psalms 42 to 72.	BOOK III. Psalms 73 to 89.	BOOK IV. Psalms 90 to 106.	BOOK V. Psalms 107 to 150.
Corresponding with Genesis. Key-words VIII. 4, X. 18.	Corresponding with Exodus.	Corresponding with Leviticus.	Corresponding with Numbers.	Corresponding with Deuteronomy.
Subject: **Man : his state of blessedness, fall and recovery.**	Subject: **Israel's Ruin,** (42 to 49.) **Redeemer,** (50 to 60.) **Redemption,** (61 to 72.)	Subject: **The Sanctuary**	Subject: **The Earth**	Subject: **The Word of God**
1. Man in a state of blessedness, (I.) 2. "He is seen, (II. to VIII.,) fallen from his high position of blessing, at enmity with God, 3. That enmity culminating in antichrist (IX. to XV.); 4. But finally blessed by the gracious work of the 'Man Christ Jesus.'" (XVI. to XLI).	"In the Genesis book man is the central thought; in this Exodus book, it is the nation of Israel. It opens with the 'cry' from the depth of the ruin and oppression as Exodus does; and it ends with the King reigning over the redeemed nation, (Psalm LXXII.) brought 'again the second time' from the four corners of the earth, as it was brought the first time out of Egypt."	"In this the counsels of God are seen in relation to the Sanctuary, which is mentioned or referred to in nearly every Psalm of this third book. The Sanctuary is seen from its ruin to its establishment in the fulness of blessing."	As Numbers is the "Book of the Wilderness" or earth, so in this fourth section the earth is its central thought. "Blessing for the earth is needed, (Psalms XC. to XCIV.,) anticipated, (XCV. to C.,) and enjoyed, (CI. to CVI.)" Its first Psalm (XC.), was written during the wanderings in the wilderness.	All the teaching of this fifth section is grouped around the Word of God. "The book opens with Psalm CVII., which gives the key. 'He sent His Word and healed them,' while Psalm CXXIX. is the great Psalm of the whole book."

ANALYSIS No. 20

PURPOSE: Words to rule life. Key Verse IX. 10.

THE BOOK OF PROVERBS

ANTIQUE METHOD OF TEACHING

Proverbial teaching is one of the most ancient forms of instruction. From the earliest historical times every nation has had its proverbs. This method of teaching was well adapted to the times when books were few and costly, as the clear crisp sentences were so easily memorised. But even to-day, in this age of learning, proverbs are household words, and exert a mighty influence.

THE HOME OF PROVERBS

Without doubt, the East is the original home of proverbs. Nearly all the proverbs of Europe can be traced to the East, so our wise men declare. The finest and grandest collection of proverbs in the world is the book bearing that name in the Bible. And the Bible is an Eastern book. But this book is more than a collection of human wisdom. It is Divine Wisdom intended to rule our daily life. And we neglect it at our peril. It is designed to teach us how intensely practical godliness is.

AUTHORS

This book, written by inspiration of God, had a variety of human authors. Only in chapters X. to XIX. and XXV. to XXVI. have we proverbs conceived and written by Solomon. In chapters I. 6 to IX. 18, XIX. 20 to XXIV. we have "The words of the wise," (see I. 6, XXII. 17, XXIV. R.V.), i.e. words taught Solomon by his teachers. And in chapters XXX. and XXXI. we have the words of Agur and Lemuel. Out of the 3,000 proverbs Solomon "spake," (1 Kings IV. 32,) he was led to select many and "set in order" Eccles. XII. 9). Many years afterward "the men of Hezekiah, King of Judah," (Proverbs XXV. 1,) made a further selection from that vast store, preserved no doubt in the royal library. The book of proverbs was then complete as we have it to-day.

ANALYSIS

Solomon "set in order" the collection of Proverbs he had made, What "order"? Is there any "order" to be discerned in it? At the first glance it appears to be but a jumble. *But there is no disorder in any Divine Book.* A second glance reveals three divisions, marked by the phrase ':' The Proverbs of Solomon," (I. 1, X. 1, XXV. 1). But on a more careful inspection of these three divisions, striking differences are observed, especially in the pronouns—in some portions the pronouns are in the second person, and in others the third person. This, and other facts, has led Dr. Thirtle and others to decisive conclusions, viz., that when you have the pronouns in the second person, you have proverbs FOR Solomon, taught him by his teachers, but when you have pronouns in the third person, you have proverbs BY Solomon, taught BY him.

Introduction	PART I. Proverbs FOR Solomon	PART II. Proverbs BY Solomon	PART III. Proverbs FOR Solomon	PART IV. Proverbs BY Solomon	PART V. Proverbs FOR Solomon	PART VI. Proverbs by Augur	PART VII. Proverbs by a Mother
I. 1 to 5.	I. 6 to IX. 18.	X. 1 to XIX. 19.	XIX. 20 to XXIV.	XXV. to XXVI.	XXVII. to XXIX.	XXX.	XXXI.
1. Object and result of a study of this book. 2. Who will take heed?	Fourteen addresses, all introduced by the phrase "My Son." I. 8, 10, 15. II. 1. III. 1, 11, 21. IV. 1. 10, 20. V. 1. VI. 1, 20. VII. 1.	Note the second person, (Thy, Thee,) but the third person (He, Him, His, They Them).	Six addresses beginning with the formula, "My Son," XIX. 27, XXIII. 15, 19, 26, XXIV. 13, and 21.	Copied by men of Hezekiah from the royal library.	Begins without any formal introduction. Note again "My Son," XXVII. 11.	Verse 4 is "God Almighty's great conundrum spoken out of Eternity into time."	Sundry wise advice, and also praise of a virtuous wife.

TOPICAL SYSTEM OF STUDY

The best method of studying this Book is the topical method. Trace all this Book has to say on Fools, Wise Man, Heart, Sluggard, Righteous, etc., etc., and you will discover a mass of teaching. Here is a pattern study on the Fool.

A FOOL DEFINED.	A FOOL'S BELIEF.	A FOOL'S ACTS.	How to Treat a Fool.	A FOOL'S END.	A FOOL'S SAVIOUR.
One who trusts in his own heart, XXVIII. 26.	1. His way is right, XII. 15. 2. Detests the thought of departing from evil, XIII. 19.	1. Hates anything that makes him feel small, I, 7. 2. No self-control - XII. 16. 3. His words are very foolish - XII. 23. 4. Makes a mock at sin - XIV. 9. 5. Thinks little of his mother - XV. 20. 6. No concentration of thought or purpose, XVII. 24. 7. Food, XV. 14. (8.) No delight, XVIII. 2. 9. Mouth gets him into trouble - XVIII. 6-7.	XIII. 20. XXIII. 9. XXVI. 4 and 5.	III. 35. XI. 29, with Luke XII. 20.	1. Learn the A.B.C. of Wisdom, i.e. "the fear of the Lord." 2. And let the Lord be "made unto you Wisdom."

THE BOOK OF ECCLESIASTES

VALUE OF A KEY

(1) Some books of the Bible cannot possibly be understood and read with profit unless the key to their study be found. Perhaps no portion of Holy Writ more needs a Key than Ecclesiastes.

(2) The fact that *it has always been a favourite book with Atheists* startles us. It is said that Volney and Voltaire appealed to it in support of their sceptical philosophy. No one can deny that it contains statements at variance with the remainder of Bible teaching, and gives its approval to things Christians denounce. Read I. 15, II. 24, III. 3, 4, 8, 11, 19, 20, VII. 16 and 17, VIII. 15.

INDISPENSABLE

Even if we decide that the Book is contradictory and impossible to understand we cannot dispense with it, for it is quoted largely in the New Testament ; VII. 2, in Matt. V. 3 and 4. V. 2, in Matt. VI. 7. VI. 2, in Luke XII. 20. XI. 5, in John III. 8. XII. 14, in 2 Cor. V. 10. V. 1, in 1 Timothy III. 15. V. 6, in 1 Cor. XI. 10.

SCIENTIFIC FACTS

Then it contains scientific statements astoundingly accurate, " There is a danger in pressing the words in the Bible into a positive announcement of scientific fact, so marvellous are some of these correspondencies. But it is certainly a curious fact that Solomon should use language entirely consistent with discoveries as evaporation and storm currents (I. 6 and 7). Some have boldly said that Redfield's theory of storms is here explicitly stated. Without taking such ground, we ask, who taught Solomon to use terms that readily accommodate facts that the movement of the winds which seem to be so lawless and uncertain, are ruled by laws as positive as those which rule the growth of the plant; and that by evaporation, the waters that fall on the earth are continually rising again, so that the sea never overflows! XII. 6 is a poetic description of death. How that the "silver cord" describes the spinal marrow, the "golden bowl" the basin which holds the brain, the "pitcher" the lungs, and the "wheel" the heart. Without claiming that Solomon was inspired to foretell the circulation of the blood, twenty-six centuries before Harvey announced it, is it not remarkable that the language he uses exactly suits the facts—a wheel pumping up through one pipe to discharge through another?" (Dr. Pierson.)

CHARACTER

(1) There is no doubt that Solomon was its author (I. 1), and that it is *the dramatic autobiography of his life and experience when he got away from God, and tried* various methods of securing happiness. This book had its origin in the sad backsliding of Solomon.

(2) Did Solomon get right again? Was he ever restored? The concluding verses of this book seem to declare decisively in the affirmative.

KEY WORD

(1) It abounds with key-words. "Under the Sun," occurs twenty-nine times ; "Vanity," thirty-seven ; "Under the Heaven," three ; "Upon the Earth," seven.

(2) Its true key-phrase is " Under the Sun." It has been well called "the book of the natural man." It is significant that the covenant title "Jehovah" is not used once in the book. This book refers only to man in relation to his Creator. The book gives an account of a long experiment which the writer made in search of satisfaction and happiness. There is no "Thus saith the Lord" in the book. It is simply a work of argument and an appeal to reason, giving particulars of an experiment to live without God.

(3) But the Christian man is not merely "Under the Sun," but is above the sun, "seated" with Christ in the Heavenly places. And what the man "under the Sun" states to be impossible, the man of God above the sun knows and expresses to be gloriously possible, (I. 15 being answered by God in Isaiah XL. 4 and XLII. 16, with Luke III. 5, and XIII. 13—note printed heading to this page in Bible—also Phil. II. 15 ; and I. 9, answered in 2 Cor. V. 17, Rev. XXI. 5).

MESSAGE

The message of the book is that, apart from God, life is full of weariness and disappointment. It is well that Ecclesiastes is followed by the Song of Solomon, for the one is the complement of the other. " In Ecclesiastes we learn that without Christ we cannot be satisfied, even if we possess the whole world—the heart is too large for the object. In the Song of Solomon we learn that if we turn from the world and set our affections on Christ, we cannot fathom the infinite preciousness of His love—the Object is too large for the heart," The Analysis is as follows :—

THE (1) Problem I. 1-3.	THE EXPERIMENT (2) I. 4 to XII. 12.	THE CONCLUSION (3) XII. 13 and 14.
How to be satisfied and happy without God ?	*He sought satisfaction in* 1. *Science* I. 4 to 11, but he noted a horrid sameness in nature; in 2. *Mere wisdom and philosophy* I. 12 to 18, but all to no pupose; in 3. *Pleasure* II. 1 to 11, in mirth 1, drinking 3, building 4, great possessions 5 to 7, wealth and music 8. but found all empty ; he tried 4. *Materialism* II. 12 to 26, by living merely for the present, even trying 5. *Fatalism* III. 1 to 15, and 6. *Deism* III. 16 to end of IV., but found all wanting. He tried 7. *Religion* (without God) V. 1 to 8, and 8. *Wealth* V. 9 to end of VI., but without satisfaction. Finally he tried 9. *Morality* VII. 1 to XII. 12. Here we are in a purer atmosphere. Here he gets on to a higher platform. But even morality did not satisfy.	1. " Solomon stands before us, by turns, as the man of science, and the man of pleasure, the fatalist and materialist, the sceptic, epicurean and stoic, with a few earnest and enlightened interludes, till in the conclusion of the whole matter, he sloughs the last of these lying vanities, and emerges to our view the noblest style of man, the penitent and the believer." 2. Note "duty" is in italics – it is "This is the whole of man," *i.e.* to do this means that you are a whole, not a half man, therefore holy. 3. God alone can satisfy.

The SONG of SOLOMON

MISUNDERSTOOD

This is one of the most misunderstood books of the Bible.   Many Christians even question its right to be in the Sacred Library.

OPINIONS

Before condemning it, let us note the opinion of others.   The Jews have ever held this song in the greatest esteem.   They reckoned it amongst the holiest of books.   They compared Proverbs to the outer court of the Temple, Ecclesiastes to the Holy Place, and the Song of Solomon to the Holiest of all.   Jonathan Edwards, of revered memory, writes : "*The whole book of Canticles used to be pleasant to me, and I used to be much in reading it . . . . . . and found, from time to time, an increased sweetness that would carry me away in my contemplation.*"   The fact is this, the most spiritually minded men the world has ever known have revelled in its pages.

WHY MISUNDERSTOOD   It is misunderstood because unkind critics do not remember that it is

(1) Poetry and not Prose.   We give poets a wide license.   They also forget that it is
(2) An *oriental* poem.   Orientals revel in figures of speech we abhor.   There is nothing here that would offend the most modest oriental.
(3) It is a *parable*, therefore the question is rightly not one of inspiration, but of interpretation.
(4) It is important to note that it was sung annually on the eighth day of the Passover feast.   Therefore only those who know the Lord Jesus as their Passover Lamb can possibly understand it.

WHAT IS IT. ?

(1) Probably the book had a basis in actual fact, that an actual story of earthly love lies behind it, the story of Solomon and a maid of Shulam.   One writes: "It is a record of the real history of a humble and virtuous woman engaged to be married to a young man of like humble circumstances, who was tempted to transfer her affections to one of the richest and most famous men that ever lived.   It celebrates the victory of chaste love in humble life over all the attractions of worldly advantage, and all the allurements of courtly grandeur.   It is a revelation of the chaste and virtuous love which no splendour can dazzle, and no flattery seduce."

(2) But that is only the background and framework.   Dr. Duff, in his fine introduction to Rutherford's letters, says : " We find here startlingly shadowed forth, in the impassioned strains of loftiest oriental mataphorical imagery, often far too glaring for colder occidental habitudes of thought and feeling, the loving relationship, transporting fellowship, and warmly affectioned intercourse between Emmanuel—the God-man—and individual human souls."   And Mrs. Penn Lewis writes : " In the ' Song of Songs ' we have unveiled to us the heart history of the redeemed who is led on to know the Lord, veiled in language to be understood only by the teaching of the Eternal Spirit, we see how the Heavenly Bridegroom woos the soul for whom He died, leads it on from one degree of union to another, draws it with the cords of love to forsake itself and its own life, and then causes it to know, in real experience, one life with Him."

ANALYSIS

It can be divided into five sections, and in every section but two, (3rd and 5th), you have recorded absences between Bride and Bridegroom, result of such absences, but terminating in the union and delight of the severed ones.

(1) I. to II. 7.	(2) II. 8 to III, 5.	(3) III. 6 to V, 1.	(4) V. 2 to VIII. 4.	(5) VIII. 5 to end.
Verse. 1 Introduction - best of all the Songs of Solomon. 2 Desire for kiss of communion. 3 Bridegroom absent, yet name fragrant, and his love valued above all earthly joys 4 to 6. Confession of weakness, and unworthiness, but remembers past mercies 7 Longs to find her Beloved, though He hides Himself. 8 He directs her how to find Him. 9 to II. 2. At last the King suddenly reveals Himself ; and then we have His glowing description of Bride and her description of Him. 3 to 7. Testimony of the Bride showing that now she is satisfied.	In this section we again have absence between Bride and Bridegroom (verses 8 and 9); Bride asleep (10); the cry of the Bridegroom for His Beloved (10 to 13); Bride sheltering in the atoning sacrifice (14); Bridegroom turns her eyes to Calvary, her search for Him (III. 1-3), help of Watchmen (3), and her reward in finding Him (verse 4).	This section differs from the previous two, in that the Bride and Bridegroom are never absent the one from the other. She does not speak once; He alone speaks. It is here, for the first time, the Bridegroom calls the soul His Bride, see verse 8 R.V. In Chapter I. she is only His friend (R.V. marg for "O my Love"); In Chapt. II. 14, He calls her "Dove," because of the presence of the Holy Dove, the Holy Spirit within her. In IV. 8, He calls her " Bride," (verse 8, R.V.)	Begins again with the absence of the two. The Bride sleeps, but is wakened by Him ; too lazy to get up at first, but upon doing so finds her Beloved gone, She tells her grief to friendly daughters of Jerusalem, who ask her what there is about her Beloved different from others. She replies. Asked where He had gone, she suddenly remembers Then He returns, and describes the glory of the Bride in language that would not shock the most refined Eastern taste.	Here we see the Bride and Bridegroom once more together coming up from the wilderness. There is now wilderness no longer, nothing but the land flowing with milk and honey. The King reminds her of her former lowly position, (verse 5,) and the Bride bursts forth in her marvellous outline and description of true love.

THREE STAGES OF LOVE

1. At first the ruling thought of the soul is " My Beloved is mine and I am His," (II- 16).   At this stage we think chiefly of Christ as ours, and in some way for our pleasure.   2. Then we come to " I am my Beloved's, and my Beloved is mine," (VI. 3).   His ownership takes first place in our thoughts.   3. At last we come to " I am my Beloved's and His desire is toward me." (VII. 10), where the word " mine " is altogether dropped in the perfect assurance that to be His includes all.

THE BOOK OF ISAIAH

FOR YOUNG CONVERTS

When the great Augustine asked Ambrose which of the sacred books was best to be studied after his conversion, the answer was "Isaiah." Certainly *nowhere else in the Old Testament have we so clear a view of the grace of God*. This book has been called, "The Gospel according to Isaiah," and its writer has been called "The Fifth Evangelist," and "the prophet of Redemption." Because of this, and its noble language and rich vocabulary and style, we venture to think that the advice of Ambrose was excellent and worth copying.

THE PROPHET

Isaiah was *a man of Royal blood*, his father, Amoz, being a younger son of Joash, King of Judah. He was, moreover, *a man of strong and commanding personality, became a statesman, and wielded a tremendous influence for good in the State*. He married one who shared the prophetical gift, had at least two sons (VII. 3, VIII. 3 and 18), laboured for sixty years, and died a martyr, in the reign of Manasseh, at (so tradition states) the age of 120.

STYLE

He is one of the *most beautiful and sublime of all the prophetical writers*. He has been called the greatest of the prophets. With the exception of four chapters (XXXVI. to XXXIX.) it is all poetry, and most magnificent poetry it is! It abounds in metaphors, *e.g.* (II. 19, XXIV. 20).

For the topical method of Bible study this book provides a rich store of material. As for example—

TOPICAL STUDY

(1) There are *seven everlasting things in Isaiah*. (a) Salvation (XLV. 17). (b) Light (LX. 19). (c) Joy (XXXV. 10). (d) Strength (XXVI. 4). (e) Kindness LIV, 8), (f) Covenant (LV. 3). (g) Judgment (XXXIII. 14).

(2) Construct *from its pages a life of our Lord*: (a) Birth VII. 14 and IX. 6). (b) Family (XI. 1). (c) Anointing (XI. 2). (d) Character (XI. 3 and 4.) (e) Plain Diet and Simplicity of Life (VII. 15), (f) Gentleness (XLII. 1 to 4). (g) Death (LIII.). (h) Resurrection (XXV. 8). (i) Glorious Reign (XI. 3 to 16, XXXIII., etc.)

(3) Note *Its teaching concerning the Holy Spirit* (X. 27, XI. 2, XXXII. 15, XL. 7 and 13, XLII. 1, XLIV. 3, LIX. 19 and 21, LXI. 1 LXIII. 10).

(4) Search for *its teaching concerning Comfort* (XL. 1, LI. 3, 12, LXVI. 13, LXI. 2, 3, 12, LXIII. 9, also XLIII. 1, 2, L. 10).

(5) Also note (a) Its hint concerning the Trinity ("Us" VI. 8). (b) The marginal rendering of XXVI. 4, and LIX. 15. (c) Its prophecy concerning the end of war (II. 4, XI. 9, XIV. 7). (d) Its three "Blesseds" XXX. 18, XXXII. 20, LVI. 2). (e) Lord as King of Israel (VI. 5, XLIV. 6, and XLIII. 15). (f) Remnant of Israel to be saved (I. 25 to 27, II. 2 and 3, VI. 13, XI. 11, XVIII. 7, XXVII. 12, 13), etc., etc.

KEY WORDS and MESSAGE

(1) "*The Holy One of Israel is a phrase peculiar to this book* It is only found in three Psalms (71, 78, 79), twice in Jeremiah (50 and 51), and in 2 Kings XIX. 22, where Isaiah is the speaker. This phrase and simply "Holy One" are met with quite thirty-three times. Evidently the vision he saw when he heard the Seraphim crying "Holy, Holy, Holy," had impressed him, and he could only think of the Lord as the Holy One.

(2) *Another word peculiar to this book is the word* "Salvation." In no other book of the Old Testament, except the Psalms, is this word so frequently found. Isaiah's own name means "Salvation is of Jehovah." This is its message, as at the head of this Analysis.

ANALYSIS

This book falls naturally into three parts. Part I. begins by the Lord giving the reason for impending Judgment and Captivity of Israel, but ends with the blessing and regathering of Israel. Part II. gives the Lord's intervention and deliverance of Israel. Part III. is in three sections, two of which end with the refrain: "There is no peace saith my God to the wicked," and the third with the death of the wicked. Part I. begins with a Vision (VI.); Part III. begins with a Voice (XL). Then notice Part III. begins and ends like the New Testament, *i.e.* with John the Baptist in the Wilderness, and a new Heaven. Notice also that interspersed with the threats and announcements of judgment are cheering promises of blessing and assurances of a glorious restoration.

(B) DENUNCIATORY	(B) HISTORICAL	(C) CONSOLATORY
The Holy One of Israel **Provoked, Rebuking, and Judging,**	The Holy One of Israel **DELIVERING,**	The Holy One of Israel **Comforting, Redeeming, Enriching.**
I. to XXXV. Key I, 4, V. 24, XXXI. 1.	XXXVI. to XXXIX. Key XXXVII. 23.	XL. to LXVI. Key XL. 1, XLIII. 3, 14, XLIX. 7, LIII. 3. LX. 17.
1. Concerning JUDAH and JERUSALEM, I. to XII. Degradation of people, call of Isaiah, and Immanuel the Divine Child, Israel's only hope.	HEZEKIAH'S 1. TROUBLE, XXXVI.	1. Section One. Dominant Note is "COMFORT," XL. to XLVIII.
2. Concerning SURROUNDING NATIONS, XIII. to XXIII. Babylon, Moab, Damascus, Egypt, Tyre.	2. PRAYER and DELIVERANCE, XXXVII.	2. Section Two. Dominant Note is "SUFFERING SERVANT," Chapter LIII. is the central one XLIX. to LVII.
3. Concerning the WORLD, XXIV. to XXXV. A remarkable section, very largely future.	3. SICKNESS, XXXVIII. 4. FOLLY, XXXIX.	3. Section Three. Dominant theme is "FUTURE GLORY." LVIII. to LXVI.

ANALYSIS No. 24   Key Verses: III. 12. 22.   XXXI 3.   THE BOOK OF JEREMIAH   MESSAGE   The certainty of God's judgment because of sin, yet the tenderness and eternity of the love of God.

Key Words: Backsliding, Return, Amend, Loved.

SOME GLOWING OPINIONS

"This book stands to this day second only to the Psalms as the most spiritual book in the Old Testament," is the testimony of that great Scotch divine, Principal Whyte. "So far as we have a data for judgment, Jeremiah was the healthiest, youngest, bravest, grandest man of Old Testament history," writes Dr. W. W. White. Isaac Williams says : 'There is nothing in all Scripture so eloquent of love and sorrow and consolation as the XXXI. and XXXIII. chapters of Jeremiah. No words can be found in any language of such touching beauty." Surely snch eulogium must come as a shock to those who have not seen any beauty in Jeremiah !

THE LIFE OF JEREMIAH

Unlike many of the prophets, Jeremiah has much to say concerning himself. He was a priest by birth (I. 1), and was called by the Lord to the prophetic ministry at an early age (I. 6). Pleading his youth (only twenty-one), inexperience, and deficiency of speech (I. 6), as reasons for not responding to the call, he was assured that Jehovah ordained him to this work before his birth (I. 5), and he then received the Divine enduement (I. 9) and commission (I. 10). He was commanded not to marry, (XVI.) The message he had to bear was a stern and solemn one, and eost this tender-hearted and truly patriotic man of God much sorrow. The delivery of this message of judgment wrung his heart. His ministry was not acceptable: his own family (XII. 6) and his own towns men (XI. 18 to 13) conspired against him. The people of Jerusalem also conspired against him (XVIII. 18), ard eventually beat him and put him in the stocks (XX. 1 to 3). Released, he was assaulted and nearly lost his life, (XXVI.) He suffered imprisonment several times, (XXXVII. 11 to 15, XXXVIII.) On the fall of Jerusalem he was released by Nebuchadnezzar. and assisted the new governor, but on the assassination of the latter by Gedaliah, he was compelled against his will to accompany the refugees io Egypt. Here he met his death by stoning after a ministry of forty years.

JEREMIAH'S CHARACTER

He was not " a man mighty as Elijah, eloquent as Isaiah, or seraphic as Ezekiel, but one who was timid and shrinking, conscious of his helplessness, yearning for a sympathy and love he was never to know—such was the chosen organ through which the Word of the Lord came to that corrupt and degenerate age." Why the selection of such a man for so stern a mission? Ah, it takes a tender-hearted individual to deliver with force and pathos a stern message of judgment. Tone is important. Jeremiah was the prophet of the broken-heart.

SOME UNIQUE CONTRIBUTIONS

This book alone of all the Bible books declares (1) that the Ark will have no place in restored Israel (III. 16). (2) " Rising up early and speaking " is a phrase only found in Jeremiah (eleven times VII. 13, &c.,) with the exception of 2 Chron. XXXVI. 15, which probably Ezra the Scribe borrowed from Jeremiah. (3) It contains that unique phrase "The generation of His wrath" (VII. 19), and (3) "neither could they blush," a charge that they had lost the power of blushing, so shameless was their sin (VIII. 12). Also note his prayers, (I. 6, IV. 10, XII. 1-4, XIV. 7, 8, 11, 21, XV., XVII., 13-18, XVIII. 13-18, XX. 7, XXXII. 16-25.)

ANALYSIS

The book is a combination of history, biography, prophecy. It is not written in chronological order.

(A) CALL	(B) MINISTRY					(C) RETROSPECT
(1) JEREMIAH'S **Call & Commission**	(2) IN JUDAH **Before Fall of Jerusalem**	(3) FALL OF **Jerusalem**	(4) To remnant in land **after Captivity**	(5) **In Egypt**		(6) **Captivity of Judah**
I.	II. to XXXVIII.	XXXIX.	XL. to XLII.	XLIII. to LI.		LII.
Introduction (1 to 3), Call (4 to 8). Enduement (9 and 10), and Encouragement (11 to 19).	Taking the usual formulæ of Prophetical utterance: "The Word of the Lord came," as a guide, there appears to be 51 distinct prophecies in this book.	Some particulars of the fall.	History and prophecy mingled.	1. To Jews, XLIII. to XLV. 2. To Gentile Nations, XLVI, to LI.		The Book begins by foretelling of Judgment, and ends with its fulfilment.

MESSAGE

In reading through this book certain words are frequently met with—" Forsake " and " Forsaken " twenty-four times. " Backslider " and " Backsliding," (with the exception of once in Proverbs, and three times in Hosea, only found in Jeremiah), thirteen times ; " Return " forty-seven times. Jeremiah is a book full of messages for backsliders. Judah had forsaken the Lord—Jeremiah uttered warnings of impending judgment, and besought the people to return to the Lord and amend their ways, as Jehovah still loved them tenderly.

TEXTS FOR PREACHERS

Forsaking a fountain tor a broken cistern, II. 13. Insufficiency of mere reformation, II. 22. False and unskilful personal dealing, VI. 14. Old paths the best, VI. 16. Lost opportunities, VIII. 20. What to glory in, IX. 24. Need of regeneration, XIII. 13. The Lord a stranger, XIV. 8. Premature decay, XV. 9. The Word of God, XV. 16, XXIII. 29. Condition of heart by nature, XVII. 9. Second chance here, XVIII. 4. Righteousness personified, XXIII. 6. See also other important truths in XXIV. 7, XXXI. 16 and 31 to 34, XXXIII. 3, XLIX. 11.

ANALYSIS No. 25

Key Texts : I. 12. II. 17. III. 22 & 33.

LAMENTATIONS of JEREMIAH

MESSAGE 1. The misery that sin brings. 2. The love and compassion of Jehovah for the subjects of His Wrath.

AUTHOR ETC

(1) This book was written by Jeremiah, after the third siege and fall of Jerusalem. In the Sept. version this book is prefaced with these words : " And it came to pass, after Israel was taken captive, and Jerusalem made desolate, that Jeremias sat weeping, and lamented with this lamentation over Jerusalem, and said." Note—*Instead of exultation over the fulfilment of his prophecies he mourned and wept: this fact is well worth our notice.*

(2) On the face of the Hill of Calvary, the green hill without the city wall where our dear Lord was crucified, is a dark recess known as "Jeremiah's Grotto." This is held to be the place where the prophet sat and gazed at the ruined city, and composed this wail of a broken heart. If this is so, *how suggestive it is to find that the mourning patriot's tears for the woes of the city should have been shed so near the spot where the rejected Saviour should suffer for the sins of that city,* and indeed of the whole world.

(3) Jewish patriots chant this book every Friday at the wailing place in Jerusalem, and it is read in every Jewish Synagogue on the fast of the ninth day of August, the day set apart to mourn over the five great calamities which have befallen the nation.

OPINIONS

Principal Whyte writes : " There is nothing like the Lamentations of Jeremiah in the whole world. There has been plenty of sorrow in every age, and in every land, but such another preacher and author, with such a heart for sorrow, has never again been born. Dante comes next to Jeremiah, and we know that Jeremiah was that great exile's favourite prophet." We could quote the opinions of others, but this is sufficient.

A Greater than Jeremiah here

There is no doubt that we have a greater than Jeremiah here. Dr. Schofield suggestively remarks : " The touching significance of this book lies in the fact that it is the disclosure of the love and sorrow of Jehovah for the very people whom He is chastening—a sorrow wrought by the Spirit in the heart of Jeremiah." This book foreshadowed the wailing of the Lord Jesus over the approaching desolation of the Holy City. Many passages are charged with Messianic meaning : I. 12, II. 15, III. 14. 15, 19, 30.

STYLE

Each lament is arranged in acrostic form, which is necessarily obscured in our translation. " The Hebrew alphabet contains twenty-two letters. Each chapter in Lamentations also contains twenty-two verses, and each verse begins with one of the twenty-two letters of the Hebrew alphabet in order, except Chapter III., which has sixty-six verses, three commencing with A, three with B, and so on ; the last chapter is a little irregular." It is thought that this acrostic method was adopted as an aid to memory.

ANALYSIS

There are five poems as indicated by the Chapters. In each poem, except the last, there are references to the sad ruined condition of the city, followed by a justification of God in dealing so sternly and drastically with His people, and a reference to passers by. Each poem ends with a prayer to the Lord, with the exception of the fourth, but this is made up by the last, which is all prayer. The gem of the whole book is III. 22, 23,

FIRST POEM	SECOND POEM	THIRD POEM	FOURTH POEM	FIFTH POEM
The City represented as a **Weeping Widow** mourning in solitude.	The City represented as a **Veiled Woman** now mourning amidst the ruins.	The City represented as, and by, the **Weeping Prophet** mourning before Jehovah the Judge.	The City represented as **GOLD** dimmed, changed, degraded.	The City represented as a **SUPPLIANT** pleading with the Lord.
I.	II.	III.	IV.	V.
Jerusalem is graphically represented as a widow bereft of her children, sitting alone in the night, weeping. Note the characteristic utterances, "None to comfort," 2, 9, 17, 21: and "No rest," 3. "No pasture," 6; "No comforter." 9.	Here is a vivid description of the siege of Jerusalem. In this second poem the prophet dwells principally on God as the author and inflicter of these sore punishments.	This is considered one of the most remarkable poems in the Old Testament. This poem differs from the others in that the prophet identifies himself with his people, making their miseries and sorrows his own.	1. City—by a series of contrasts the horrors of the siege are depicted, 1 to 10.	There was no closing prayer in the previous poem, but this is one long earnest appeal to Jehovah.
1. The City in her calamity, 1 to 7.	1. The City—siege and ruin, 1 to 14.	1. City—prophet a man of affliction, 1-20.	2. Judgments—God justified, 11 to 16.	1. City—Calamity, 1 to 6.
2. Judgments—God justified, 8 to 11 & 18.	2. Passers by—their scorn and cruel taunts, 15, 16.	,, ,, of hope, 21-36.	3. Edom's cruelty, 17 to 20.	2. Sin—confession, 7.
3. Passers by—appeal for sympathy, 12-19.	3. Judgments foretold, 17.	2. Judgments—God justified, 37 to 39.	4. Retribution on Edom, 21 & 22.	3. Suffering, 8 to 18.
4. Prayer—appeal to the Lord, 20 to 22.	4. Prayer—to the Lord, 18 to 22.	3. Appeal to nation, 40 to 54.		4. Appeal to the Lord, 19 to 22.
		4. Appeal to the Lord, 55 to 66.		

C*

ANALYSIS No. 26.

Key Phrase: "The Glory of the Lord." I. 28; X. 4, 18; XLIII. 2.

THE BOOK OF EZEKIEL.

MESSAGE:

The goodness and severity of God.

EZEKIEL.

Ezekiel was a priest belonging to the aristocracy of Jerusalem, (I. 1 to 3,) and, at the age of twenty-five, just eleven years before the destruction of the Temple, was carried captive to Babylon. He was contemporary of Jeremiah and Daniel. In Babylon he dwelt in his own house (VIII. 1). He was married, but his wife died in the year when the final siege of Jerusalem began (XXIV. 18). He began his ministry five years after reaching Babylon, at the age of thirty, when Jeremiah was approaching the end of his great and tragic career.

HIS MISSION.

By false prophets the captives were led to imagine that Jerusalem would not be destroyed, and they would soon be restored to their beloved city and land. Jeremiah heard of this, and from Jerusalem wrote and sent them a letter (Jeremiah XXIX). Ezekiel began his ministry the following year, endorsing all that Jeremiah had said, and endeavouring to convince them that *before they could ever hope to return to Jerusalem they must return to their Lord.* Though the task was a difficult one, and though at first he met with very great opposition, ultimately he was blessed with success, and his people's return to their Lord and their land was largely the fruit of his ministry.

PROPHET OF THE SPIRIT.

Each of the three great Prophets emphasized one Person in the Blessed Trinity. *Ezekiel is the Prophet of the Spirit, as Isaiah is the Prophet of the Son, and Jeremiah the Prophet of the Father.* The ministry of the Spirit is most noticeable in this book. There are at least twenty-five references to the Spirit. See II. 2, III. 12, 14, 24, etc. His name means "whom God strengthens," and the Agent in his strengthening was the Holy Spirit.

NOTABLE TRUTHS.

(1) Ezekiel speaks of Israel in Egypt more than any other Prophet. It is only in this book (XX. 1 to 9) that we learn of *Israel's Idolatry in Egypt, and of God's thought to destroy them there because of it.* How near they were to destruction ! But God can do for His own name's sake what He cannot possibly do for ours, and He spared them.

(2) It is *in this book alone that we learn of Satan's past history,* (XXVIII. 11 to 19.) Here we get a glimpse into the history of our great Adversary.

(3) It is here only that we have *very full details of the Temple yet to be built* (XL. to XLII.), *and of the new river* (XLVII).

ANALYSIS.

(1) This is a book many do not care to read. One reason is because such do not understand its key, structure, and message.

(2) *Its key phrase is "The Glory of the Lord,"* which occurs fourteen times in the first eleven chapters. In the Old Testament "the Glory of the Lord" means the visible light which shone between the cherubims in the Most Holy Place in Tabernacle and Temple proclaiming the presence of God. Before the destruction of the Temple, Ezekiel in vision saw the Glory of the Lord leave the Temple. There is in IX. 3 a brief statement of this fact, further particulars being given in chapter X. As he looked he saw above the ark and cherubims the likeness of God's throne, which had wheels, and was therefore a kind of royal chariot (X. 1). Then the Glory of the Lord removed to the threshold of the House (4), then from off the threshold and stood at the door of the east gate (18 and 19), then from the Temple and City to Olivet (XI. 22 and 23). *Thus slowly, reluctantly, majestically, the Glory of the Lord left the Sanctuary and the City.* But the Glory has yet to return (XLIII). Ezekiel's ministry began with a vision of God, and it closes with a vision of God among His people. Blessed consummation ! Its message is the severity of God to His backslidden and unrepentant people, and His goodness to the penitent.

(1) Preparation and call of the Prophet.	(2) Prophecies of destruction of Jerusalem.	(3) Prophecies against seven nations.	(4) Glorious Prophecies in relation to Israel's future
THE **APPEARANCE** of the Glory of the Lord.	THE **DEPARTURE** of the Glory of the Lord.	**GOD'S GLORY** and the surrounding nations.	THE **RETURN** of the Glory of the Lord.
I. to III.	IV. to XXIV.	XXV. to XXXII.	XXXIII. to XLVIII.

The appearance of the Glory and the result in the Prophet's life.
 	
1. Opened Heavens and a vision of God the Son as Man on the Throne, I.
2. The workers:
  (a) Commission, II.
  (b) Food, III. 1 to 3.
  (c) Task, 4 to 11.
  (d) Enduement, 12 to 14.
  (e) Duties, 15 to 21.
3. The appearance of the Glory of the Lord. III. 22 to 27.
	Reasons of departure of Glory of God. He begins his ministry to Israel :
	1. Siege of Jerusalem foretold - IV.
	2. Horrors of the siege - V.
	3. A remnant to be preserved - VI.
	4. Its awful desolation - VII.
	5. Idolatry in high circles of Society - VIII.
	6. Remnant marked for preservation IX.
	7. **Departure of the Glory** X. & XI.
	8. Punishment delayed but certain - XII.
	9. False Prophetesses - XIII.
	10. Various Old Testament parables, with other important teaching, all calculated to lead to the reformation and repentance of Israel. XIV. to XXIV.
		God of Glory acting in defence of His people.
		
		These seven prophecies were uttered in the interval between the knowledge of Nebuchadnezzar's siege (XXIV. 2), and the news that Jerusalem was taken (XXXIII. 21). Observe, God was against these heathen nations, not only because of sin of idolatry, but because of their ill-treatment of Israel.
		
		1. Ammon, Moab, Edom, Philistines, XXV.
		2. Tyre XXVI. to XXVIII.
		3. Egypt, XXIX. to XXXII.
			Preparation for return of the Glory of Lord. Preparations given after a 3 years' silence. Many consider this the richest portion of whole book.
			1. Promise of restoration to the penitents, XXXIII.
			2. The Good Shepherd, XXXIV.
			3. Gospel according to Ezekiel, XXXVI.
			4. Great National Revival depicted, XXXVII.
			5. Israel's future enemies vanquished, XXXVIII. and XXXIX.
			6. The New Sanctuary yet to be erected, XL. to XLII.
			7. **Return of the Glory of God**, XLIII.
			8. The mysterious Prince, XLIV.
			9. Division of Jerusalem, XLV. and XLVI.
			10. Life-giving Waters, XLVII.
			11. Division of the Land, XLVIII.

THE BOOK OF DANIEL

Key Verses: II. 22, IV. 25.

DANIEL

(1) Daniel, like Ezekiel, was among the captives carried to Babylon on the occasion of Nebuchadnezzar's hostile invasion of Palestine, (I. 1 to 3).

(2) It is believed that he belonged to a family of high rank, if not of the Royal House, and that he was taken to Babylon at the age of sixteen, eight years before Ezekiel. If that is so, then Daniel was among the number captured in the first invasion, in the third year of Jehoiakim, whilst Ezekiel was taken in the second invasion.

(3) His whole life from that time was spent in Babylon (see I. 21, a period of sixty-nine years), and in a vile court he lived a saintly life, so much so that in Ezekiel XIV. 14 to 20, and XXVIII. 3, he is referred to as a pattern or model of righteousness.

(4) Though belonging to a captive race, and never swerving in his devotion and loyalty to Jehovah, he rose to the highest position in the State, and exercised his own powerful political ministry in three Kingdoms, those of Babylon, Media, and Persia.

PROPHET

He was not only a public State servant, but he was also a prophet of God. His prophecies—which deal more fully with Gentile nations than with his own Jewish nation—are amongst the most remarkable in the whole of the Bible.

LORD'S IMPRIMATUR

In Matt. XXIV. 15 our Lord set His seal upon this book as inspired of God. Our Lord's own title, "Son of Man," is based on VII, 13.

MESSAGE

It has several messages. The Lord's loyal and obedient servants, (1) often are blessed with worldly success, (I. 9, 20, II. 48, 49,) and (2) are trusted with His secrets (II. 19, 22, 47); (3) in times of suffering and trial they have the comfort of His presence, (III. 25.) (4) It also sounds a loud warning against pride, (IV. 30 to 37,) (5) and not honouring and glorifying God, (V. 22 and 23). But its chief message is its proclamation of the universal sovereignty of God, (IV. 25).

ANALYSIS

It is in two main divisions—the first dealing chiefly with historic events, the second with visions and then with interpretations. Daniel's name means either "God my Judge," (suggestive of God's defence of him,) or, "Judge of God," i.e., one who delivers judgment in the name of the Lord, and suggests six minor divisions as follows:—

(A) HISTORICAL (Written by Daniel in the third person)					(B) PROPHETICAL (written in 1st person)
(1) HEATHEN **Customs** Judged.	(2) HEATHEN **Philosophy** Judged.	(3) HEATHEN **PRIDE** Judged.	(4) HEATHEN **Impiety** Judged.	(5) HEATHEN **Persecutors** Judged.	(6) THE **Nations** of the **World** Judged, and establishment of the Everlasting Kingdom.
I.	II.	III. and IV.	V.	VI.	VII. to end.
1 Though Daniel was dedicated to Baal, (his new name indicates that he was to be "favourite of Baal"), he remained true to Jehovah. 2 The Palace food—meat killed with blood, and offered to idols—he and his companions refused to take. 3. God blessed him and his companions for their loyalty, and gave them success.	1. Heathen philosophers failed to tell dream. 2. The interpretation of this dream gives the course and end of Gentile world dominion, from Daniel's day to end of this age. 3. Note the Stone (II. 34, 35), does not grow until it has broken into pieces the great image. It is *after* this total destruction of Gentile dominion that God's Kingdom is set up.	1. The erection of this great image was Nebuchadnezzar's attempt to unify the religions of his empire by self-deification. 2. This attempt will be repeated by the Beast, the last head of the Gentile World-dominion, (Rev. XIII. 11 to 15, XIX. 20). 3. Note the significance of the rise of the present day religion of Humanism.	1. By death of Belshazzar. 2. From inscriptions found and deciphered, we know now that Belshazzar and his father Nabonidus ruled jointly over Babylon and the Empire. 3. That whilst Belshazzar fell in the capture of the Imperial City, his father surrendered at Borsippa.	1. Daniel must have been about 80 years old when this trial befel him. 2. Daniel put "God rst," and the Lord defended him. 3. See how God was glorified by the loyalty of His Servant.	1. **Vision of Beasts,** Chapter VII. In Chapter II. the World Kingdoms are seen by the heathen King in their *outward* unity and glory, yet without life, a metal colossus. In this chap, they appear to the prophet of God in their real character, as instinct with life, *mere beast life,* terrible animal power. 2. **Vision of Ram and Goat,** Chapter VIII. Giving further particulars concerning the Medo-Persian and Macedonian Kingdoms, (verses 5 to 8 so impressed Alexander the Great that he preserved Israel). 3. **Vision of the Seventy weeks,** Chapter IX. This is a most remarkable chapter. The seventy weeks are seventy periods of seven years each. 4. **Vision of the Lord,** Chapter X. In verses 1 to 9 and 16 to end we have the vision of the Lord, but in verses 10 to 15 an angel appears. 5. **Further Prophecies concerning Daniel's time to end of time,** Chapters XI. to XII. 3. 6. **Closing Words,** Chapter XII. 4 to end.

THE PROPHET

(1) Hosea, contemporary with Amos, Isaiah, and Micah, laboured in Samaria, though in his later years, having long appealed to his doomed countrymen in vain, he retired to Judæa.   It is believed that the latter portions of this book were written in Judæa.

(2) He was spared many years to labour for his Lord.   *From I. 1, we judge that his ministry was exercised seventy-two years.*   It has been calculated that if he began his prophetic ministry at the age of twenty, he would die at the age of ninety-two to ninety-eight.

(3) *He had a very sad domestic trial*—the unfaithfulness of his wife—and God spoke to Israel through that lamentable trouble.   This is the pivot of the whole book.

HIS MISSION

Hosea's message was principally to Israel (i.e, the Ten Tribes).   The name Ephraim occurs in this book over thirty-five times, and the name Israel with equal frequency, whilst Judæa is not mentioned more than fourteen times, and Jerusalem is never mentioned.

CHARACTER

(1) Hosea's writings are more poetical than most of the prophets—they abound in striking metaphors.

(2) The attribute of God most in Hosea's thoughts is "Lord."   The aspect of the Divine character on which Hosea dwells most fondly is that of husband and wife.   (Israel is Jehovah's Bride, whilst the Church is the Lamb's Bride).

ANALYSIS

(1) Some consider Hosea to be the most difficult of all the prophetic books.   It certainly is not an easy one to study.

(2) At first sight there does not seem any order in it, but after much study one sees beautiful order.

(3) *It is in reality a clear treatise on repentance.*   It is a book for backsliders.   Here we have a delightful exhibition of God's methods in the restoration of a backslidden people.

(1) ISRAEL'S IGNOBLE CONDITION when selected by God	(2) ISRAEL'S AWFUL FALL	(3) ISRAEL'S RANSOM PRICE PAID	(4) The TERRIBLE RESULTS of ISRAEL'S FALL pointed out by the Lord	(5) ISRAEL'S PENITENT CRY	(6) The LORD PROBES Israel's Wounds before applying the healing balsam.	(7) The Prophet's FINAL APPEAL TO ISRAEL	(8) The Lord's gracious reply: ISRAEL'S FINAL RESTORATION
I.	II.	III.	IV. to V.	VI. 1 to 3.	VI. 4 to XIII.	XIV. 1 to 3.	XIV. 4 to 9.
1. Hosea's marriage with an abandoned woman. (2) (Calvin and others think it is only a parable. But there is no reason for not taking it to be a literal fact). 2. Birth of two sons and a daughter, significant names being given to each, (4 to 9.) 3. The marriage was to teach Israel, (and is it not true too, of every believer to-day!) that they were not selected by God because of any worthiness in themselves, for they were as unworthy of honourable marriage as Gomer. 4. In verse 2 Hosea shows that Israel's troubles began by departing from God. See how he ends this book (XIV. 1).	1. The unfaithfulness of Hosea's wife a picture of Israel's unfaithfulness to God, (1 to 5). 2. Chastisement, (6 to 13). 3. Verse 14 with VIII. 13 seems to suggest that Israel has to have another Egyptian and wilderness experience. 4. Finally to end in Israel being restored to the Lord for ever, (19). Note: By God's blessing our valleys of Achor (trouble) become doors of blessing and places for song, (15).	1. Though the prophet's wife has deserted him he is still to love her notwithstanding her conduct, (1.) 2. He enters into an agreement by which a certain provision is made for her (2) on certain conditions (3). 3. But it does not seem that they were to live together yet. 4. Fulfilled in Israel to-day. Not living as Jehovah's wife, but *living a separate life*, (4 and 5). 5. Evidently David has again to reign over Israel, (5).	1. No morality, (1 to 5.) 2. Wilful ignorance) 6 to 11), and idolatry, (12 to 19.) 3. But the crowning calamity of all was the hiding of the face of the Lord. See Chap, V. verse 15. (Compare IV. 7 with XIV. 8. There is a powerful Gospel lesson here. The first gives us a picture of a nation hugging its idols, and the second, the same nation throwing them away. "I have heard Him" is the secret.)	1 This will be the decision of the remnant in the last days. 2. Note the force of verse 3. To unrepentant Israel, He is as "a lion," (V. 14,) but to repentant ones as the gentle, fertilizing showers. 3. If our goodness proceeds from God, it will not be as the "morning cloud" or "early dew," verse 4.	1. To make sure that Israel is thoroughly repentant the Lord probes their wounds to test and deepen their penitence, 2. Note the metaphors used to describe the character and condition of Israel. VI. 4. VII. 4, 8, 11, 12. VIII. 7, 9. X. 1, 11, 12. XII. 1. 3. Note the pathos of XI. 8.	An appeal of the prophet to Israel, etc. 1. Confess that their sad state was entirely due to own sin. 2. A repudiation of all hope of help in man. 3. And with every sign of true, genuine repentance. Note. How comforting last clause of verse 3 is for fatherless.	1. Healing verse 4. 2. Loved by Lord 4. 3. Refreshed by Lord 5. 4. Growing 5. 5. Beauty 6. 6. Fragrance 6. 7. Fruitfulness 6 8. Companionship of Lord 7. 1. Note magnificent conclusion in verse 9. 2. Healing their backsliding means more than forgiving the backslider — it means that Jehovah will cure or remove the cause of the backsliding.

THE BOOK OF JOEL

JOEL

(1) Nothing is known of the prophet Joel beyond the short introduction he gives of himself in 1. 1.

(2) The first one to bear that name in Scripture was Samuel's elder son (1 Samuel VIII. 2), and it means "Jehovah is my God."

(3) Probably he was the very earliest of the prophetic WRITERS, exercising his ministry in Judah in the early reign of Joash, (2 Kings XI. and XII.) He would in his youth have known both Elijah and Elisha.

NOTABLE

(1) Competent literary authorities declare that, from standpoint of style, *this small book is a literary gem.* Its "style is pre-eminently pure, and is characterised by smoothness and fluency, strength and tenderness."

(2) But it is specially notable for three things. (*a*) It contains the grandest description in all literature of locust devastation. (*b*) It gives the first intimation of the outpouring of the Spirit upon ALL flesh (II. 28, 29); and (*c*) its prophecies are remarkable for their scope, extending from his own day to the end of time.

OCCASION

(1) There had been a very severe visitation of drought, and a plague of locusts, spreading ruin on every hand.

(2) Though Moses (Duet. XXVIII. 38 and 39), and Solomon (1 Kings VIII. 37) had mentioned locusts as one of the instruments of Divine chastisement, the people in this instance had not recognised them as such.

(3) Joel's mission was to point out the sad condition of the national spiritual life as the reason why the plague was sent, and to exhort to national repentance as the essential step in returning to God.

PROPHETIC

(1) But Joel also pointed out that the invasion of locusts was only a type of another more terrible invasion.

(2) No doubt this prophecy had a partial fulfilment in the swarms of heathen who invaded the land in those days.

(3) But there are details which have never yet had a fulfilment, and are yet future, for the last days.

KEY

(1) The Key to the understanding of the book is the phrase "The Day of the Lord," I. 15, II. 1. 11, 31, III. 14.

(2) "The day of the Lord" "will commence with the removal of the Church. It is the day when the Lord will judge and interfere once more directly in the course of this world's politics. It lasts for a thousand years."

(1) The National Calamity **Described and Interpreted**	(2) **The Day of the Lord Foreshadowed**	(3) The Day of the Lord **Foretold**	(4) **Intervention for Israel** BY **THE LORD**	(5) **This THE reason** WHY ISRAEL **Should Repent**	(6) The Lord's glorious response TO ISRAEL'S **Repentance**
I. 1 to 14, 16 to 20.	I. 15.	II. 1-10, III. 9-15.	II. 11, III. 16.	II. 12 to 17.	II. 18-29, III. 1-8 & 17-21.
1. The unparalleled Calamity (1 to 3). 2. Desolation described (4-13). 3 National Fast urged (14). 4. The mourning of the Prophet (16 to 20).	The prophet sees in this attack of locusts an emblem of a more terrible attack by swarms of heathen soldiers in his day, but more particularly in the last days yet to come.	1. Numbers of and injury done by enemies. II. 1-10 2. Lord's challenge to Israel's enemies. III. 9-15. 3. Promise of preservation of a remnant. II. 30-32.	1. The Lord's sudden and swift intervention to save Israel from annihilation. 2. III. 16, "Hope of His people" is in R.V. "a refuge unto," and in marg. of A.V. "a place of repair," or "harbour."	1. Note "Therefore." 2. The Lord's voluntary intervention THE reason given why Israel should repent and turn to the Lord. 3. A rent heart (13) is followed by a rent veil (Matt. 27-51) and rent Heaven (Isa. 64-1).	1. Blessing (18 and 19). 2. Emancipation (20). 3. Prosperity (21 to 27). 4. Outpouring of Spirit (28, 29). 5. Judgment of Gentile Nations. (III. 1 to 8) 6. Full Kingdom blessing. (III. 17 to 21).

MESSAGE

Joel has been called "the prophet of Religious revival." He saw that genuine repentance lay at the foundation of all real revival, and this he laboured to produce. This is a book of repentance. A rent heart is followed by a rent Veil, and Heaven, *i.e.* access to God and Pentecostal blessing follow true repentance.

THE BOOK OF AMOS

THE PROPHET

(1) Amos was a native of Tekoa, a place twelve miles from Jerusalem, and six from Bethlehem. He therefore belonged to Judah.

(2) He was not a courtier like Isaiah, or a priest like Jeremiah. but an ordinary working man. He was a herdsman, and a "dresser" (I. 1 R.V.) of sycamore trees. "Dresser" means "nipper" or "pincher"—the sycamore fruit, (the wild fig only eaten by the very poorest,) can only be ripened by puncturing it.

(3) He was contemporary with Hosea and Jonah. *Though a native of Judah he prophesied in and against Israel.*

THE TIME

(1) "Two years before the earthquake" (I. 1), he commenced his prophetic ministry at Bethel Amos foretold this earthquake, (V. 8, VI. 11, VIII. 8, IX. 5, R.V.)

(2) This earthquake must have been of exceptional severity, for Zechariah speaks of it nearly 300 years later as an event well remembered (Zechariah XIV. 5).

A MODEL WORKER

Incidentally this book provides us with a treatise on preaching, and portrays Amos as a model worker for God. Note :—

(1) *His humility.* He makes no attempt to hide the bare facts of his past life and employment ; he was not ashamed to make known his lowly birth and occupation. There was in him an entire absence of "side." His exaltation to prophetic rank did not spoil him.

(2) *His industry.* Owing to his trade he often lived a solitary life, yet he spent it in communion with God, and in close observation ot nature. The illustrations scattered through this book are all drawn from his every-day life, proving his keenness of sight and originality of mind.

(3) *His wisdom.* He did not preach over the heads of the people, but employed terms quite familiar to all of them.

(4) *His cuteness.* He caught the attention of the people right away by speaking first against their enemies.

(5) *His faithfulness.* He was not a tickler of the popular ear, but dealt faithfully with the people, making straight tracks for their consciences.

(6) *His steadfastness.* He refused to be turned off from the work God had given him, (VII. 10 to 17.) He kept his eye on his Divine Master.

(7) *His message.* He had a "Thus saith the Lord," a message direct from God. It was a timely one, too, suitable to that God-forsaking age.

(8) *His success.* He was blessed with wonderful success, (VII. 10.) He wielded an influence over the whole land.

MESSAGE

Amos' burden was one concerning punishment. He had a stern message for that luxurious and self-indulgent age. He was the prophet of woe. The book shows that national sin means national judgment, and whilst the sin of individuals will be judged at the Great White Throne, nations are judged in this world and in time. The history of the world proves this,

ANALYSIS

A great Bible teacher divides this book into fonr sections ; it also falls into five sections, both of which are shown as follows :

(a) DECLAMATION.	(b) PROCLAMATION.		(c) REVELATION.	(d) RESTORATION.
(1) **PUNISHMENT** of SURROUNDING NATIONS.	(2) **PUNISHMENT** of JUDAH and ISRAEL.	(3) THREE **DISCOURSES** AGAINST ISRAEL.	(4) **VISIONS** concerning ISRAEL.	(5) **RESTORATION** of all ISRAEL.
I. 2 to II. 3.	II. 4 to 16.	III. 1 to VI. 9.	VII. 1 to IX. 10.	IX. 11 to 15.
1. Here are prophecies against surrounding nations, who were occupying territory given to Israel by God. 2. Though sent expressly to Israel, he opens his ministry in announcing coming judgment on these six heathen nations, (a) To gain the attention of Israel. (b) To show Israel that God is no respecter of persons when sin is concerned.	1. The thunder-storm of God's wrath rolls over all the surrounding Kingdoms, touches Judah (as in verses 4 and 5), and at length falls with crashing effect upon Israel. 2. Note the charges God was compelled to lay at their door (II. 4, 6, 7, 8 etc.)	1. Each of these three discourses begins with "Hear"! 2. Address to Israel, and to "whole family," i.e. Judah as well. 3. In IV. 2, he rudely dispels the fond idea Israel hugged in its national pride, viz., that to the favoured nation of Jehovah no harm could happen. 4. In chapter V. we have a discourse on "seeking the Lord."	Vision ; 1. Of grasshoppers, VII. 1. 2. Of fire - " 4. 3. Of plumb-line " 7. 4. Summer fruit VIII. 1. 5. Of the Lord IX. 1. Note "standing on the altar." The only time "chapel" is mentioned in the Bible is in this book, VII. 13.	Here is foretold the Lord's return and the establishment of the Davidic Kingdom. 1. Restoration - - 11. 2. Possession - - 12. 3. Prosperity - - 13, 14. 4. Perpetuity - - 15.
NOTABLE VERSES. Quaint expression in I. 3 and other verses, "For three transgressions " etc,	NOTABLE VERSE. II. 13, God burdened with sins as a waggon with sheaves.	NOTABLE VERSES. 1. IV. 12. 2. III. 3. 3. VI. 1.	NOTABLE VERSES. 1. VII. 1, "After King's mowing"—let God have His part. 2. VIII. 11.	NOTABLE VERSE. IX. 15.

THE BOOK OF OBADIAH

OBADIAH

Absolutely *nothing is known of the writer* of this book. Several Obadiahs are mentioned in the Old Testament, but there is nothing to indicate that any of them wrote this book. His name means "The Servant," or "The Worshipper of Jehovah." It is difficult to locate the time when the book was written, but verses 10 to 14 *clearly prove that it must have been written after the fall of Jerusalem,* 2 Chronicles XXXVI. 17 to 21.

PURPOSE

This is the shortest book in the Old Testament. It is a brilliant prophetic cameo. It forms a sharp manifesto against the fierce Idumeans, who were the perpetual enemies of Israel. It gives the character, career, doom, and downfall of Edom.

HISTORY

The Edomites, or Idumeans, were the descendants of Esau. They were a proud, bitter, resentful people, ever seeking an opportunity to harm Jacob's descendants. Governed at first by Dukes, and afterward by Kings (Genesis XXXVI.), they were in their golden age when Israel were led out of Egyptian bondage. Israel and Edom were perpetually at war. *When Nebuchadnezzar captured Jerusalem, Edom rejoiced over Israel's downfall, and cruelly took part in the plundering and massacre,* (see Psalm CXXXVII. 7.) In days gone by God had commanded his people to treat Edom kindly, (Deuteronomy XXIII. 7), but now their atrocious conduct had filled up their cup of iniquity, and sentence of condemnation and annihilation was passed upon them. After Israel's restoration, Cyrus, king of Persia, overcame them, slaughtering thousands of them. They received another crushing defeat by the Jews, under the Maccabees, and slowly disappeared as a nation until their very name perished.

ANALYSIS

EDOM'S (1) HUMILIATION	EDOM'S (2) CRIME	EDOM'S (3) DOOM
Verses 1 to 9.	Verses 10 to 14.	Verses 15 to 21.
Note the steps in Edom's humiliation.	Note the telling description of Edom's sin.	At first sight this section seems to deal exclusively with Judah's glorious restoration, but on closer scrutiny it is seen to be introduced only to show how and when Edom's destruction was to be brought about.
1. The Lord at work influencing the nations (R.V. for heathen) against Edom, (verse 1.)	1. "Violence against thy brother Jacob," (verse 10,)	1. Verdict announced, (verses 10 and 15.)
2. In consequence, the small nation of Edom was "despised," (verse 2.)	2. Refused help, ("stoodest on the other side,"j and acted as the conquerors, (verse 11.)	2. Israel would be delivered, sanctified, and enriched, (17,) and after this would be an instrument in Edom's destruction, (18,) and possess the land of Edom, etc., (verses 19, 20.)
3. They would be dragged out of their apparently impregnable refuges, (verses 3 and 4,)	3. They rejoiced at Jacob's discomfiture and jeered at them, (verse 12.)	3. This came to pass in the time of the Maccabees – though verses 19 to 21 have yet a more glorious fulfilment.
4. They would be despoiled, but not as by thieves. (verses 5, 6,)	4. They also took a share in looting. (verse 13.)	4. What a glorious finish: "The Kingdom shall be the Lord's.
5. Neighbouring nations with whom they had entered into covenant, would break their agreements and rend them, (7,)	5. And, worse than all, hunted the fugitives and handed them over to the enemy, (verse 14.)	
6. Even the noted wisdom of their counsellors, (verse 8,) and the strength and courage of their soldiers, would be taken away, and would fail them.		

MESSAGE

This wee book has a two-fold message—a warning against sinful pride and godless defiance (verse 3), and against hating and harming the Jews, whose cause God Himself will undertake, and whose enemies He will destroy.

GOSPEL

What a gospel gem is here in 17 and 18! This gives the preliminaries to victory—delivered, sanctified, and enriched, I shall be able to live the all-victorious life.

THE BOOK OF JONAH

LITERARY VALUE

That eminent literary authority and author, Charles Reade, declared that the book of Jonah *is the most beautiful story ever written in so small a compass.* It is a perfect gem, and is simply full of teaching.

HISTORY

This book forms one of the battle-grounds of modern destructive criticism. By many it is considered to be only an allegory, with no historical background whatever. But 2 Kings XIV. 25, proves Jonah to be a historical personage. Then the historical character of this man is vouched for by our Lord (Matt. XII. 39 to 41). Therefore we have no hesitation in affirming that here we have fact not fiction; history, not fable.

THE PROPHET

(1) Jonah was of Gath—hepher, near Nazareth, therefore a Galilean, proving that the Pharisees lied when they said "out of Galilee ariseth no prophet." (John VII. 52). Nahum and Malachi also were of Galilee.

(2) *He began his prophetic career as Elisha closed his.* Some ancient Jewish authorities were of the opinion that Jonah was the widow's son of Zerephath, whom Elijah raised from the dead.

(3) A prophecy of his is preserved for us in 2 Kings XIV. 25 to 27. He was therefore a fully accredited prophet.

KEY Chapter IV. verse 2 is the Key, giving the clue to the whole book. Why did Jonah disobey the Lord? (1) Not because of cowardice—there are abundant evidences of his courage in this book. (2) Nor was it because he was "out of sympathy with foreign missions." (3) Nor was it out of regard for his own personal honour as a prophet. (4) *The motive that moved him to disobey God was a false patriotism.* Assyria was Israel's great enemy. He wished to leave them to perish in their sins, and thus Israel would be rid of their ancient foe. To go and preach to them might lead to their salvation, and their consequent preservation. And this he wanted to avoid.

ANALYSIS

(1) The Prophet's Commission	(2) The Prophet's Disobedience	(3) The Prophet's Prayer	(4) The Prophet Re-commissioned	(5) The Prophet's Success	(6) The Prophet Reproved
I. 1 and 2.	I. 3 to 17.	II.	III. 1 to 3.	III. 4 to 10.	IV.
1. He must have been an experienced prophet when the call came. 2. This book begins abruptly, "Now" seems to indicate that this was a continuation not a beginning of his ministry. 3. Nineveh was indeed a "great city." It was about sixty miles in circumference, covering 216 square miles, with a population of 600,000.	1. The prophet deliberately disobeyed the Lord 2. "He paid the fare thereof." We always have to "pay" when we disobey Him. 3. Note the four "prepared" things in this book. I. 17; IV. 6 to 8. 4. How like the sleep of the sinner is I. 6. 5. Salvation through substitution is taught by I. 15.	1. This was the prayer of one in great trouble, and 2. In a strange place. Note: 1. Its disjointed condition. 2. Its graphic description	1. Oh, the joy of not being cast off for faithlessness and disobedience! 2. He had to carry the Lord's message! "the preaching that I bid thee." 3. The prophet readily obeyed.	1. Jonah was successful because he was a living witness of the truths he proclaimed. Looking upon him they would get a gleam of hope. 2. Note — Nineveh "believed God" and repented.	1. Jonah had a lingering hope that destruction would come to the Assyrians. 2. God gave him an object lesson. 3. Note the abruptness of its finish. "God's tender accents are the last that reach the ear—the abruptness of the close makes them the more impressive."

LESSONS

(1) It shows how futile are man's efforts to frustrate the Divine purposes of grace.

(2) Its chief message is the statement found in Roman III, 29. It was designed to teach God's people that He was the God of the Gentiles as well as of the Jews, that He had purposes of grace and love toward them as well as toward Israel. This lesson Israel never learned in spite of the eloquent teaching of this book.

TYPE

(1) In Matt. XII. 38 to 42, Jesus declared that Jonah was a type of His own entombment and resurrection, and the people of Nineveh an example of true genuine repentance.

(2) Jonah is typical, not only of the Lord, but of Israel. Dr. Bullinger has very suggestively pointed this out. "Jonah is God's ambassador sent to preach repentance to the Gentiles. So was Israel. He objects to Gentiles being thus blessed, and flees from the unpleasant task. He is visited by a divinely sent storm, and is thrown into the sea. So Israel is now cast into the sea of the nations; but, like Jonah, is not lost, for presently Israel will be cast up on the earth, and become the ambassadors of Jehovah, and the conveyors of blessing to the Gentiles."

ANALYSIS No. 33
KEY TEXTS, vi. 8, vii. 18.

THE BOOK OF MICAH

MESSAGE

God's
1. Hatred of Injustice.
2. Hatred of Ritualism.
3. Delight in Pardoning.

WRITER

(1) Nothing is known of Micah beyond that stated in I. 1, viz. that he belonged to Judah, was contemporary of Isaiah, and that Isaiah must have been prophesying seventeen or eighteen years before he began his ministry. Though a countryman, his ministry was principally to the cities.

(2) His name means " Who is like Jehovah," and is an index to his character. To him God was everything. He had an exalted conception of the Holiness, Righteousness. and Compassion of God. He closes his book by exclaiming " Who is a God like unto Thee?" and he meant what he said. Judging by his writings, he was a man of wonderful power, calm, sane judgment. tenderhearted yet faithful, and for all this he gave God the credit. (III. 8.)

NOTABLE

It is notable for several reasons: (a) It is written in an entrancing style. It is full of poetic beauty, and in consequence is a favourite with students of the minor prophets. (b) It contains a remarkable prophecy concerning Jerusalem, III. 12, (c) and the future glory of Jerusalem, IV. (d) It locates the birthplace of the Saviour, V. 2; (e) and, as Dean Stanley says, it contains " one of the most sublime and impassioned declarations of spiritual religion that the Old Testament contains," VI. 6 to 8. (f) And, to crown all, in VII. 18, 19, we have, as Dr. Pierson says: "a little poem of twelve lines in the Hebrew . . . . . one of the most exquisite things to be found in the entire Old Testament, and would alone be sufficient to prove that this Bible is the Word of God, for there is nothing like it in all the literature of men."

QUOTED

An author is proud of the day when he is quoted either in print or on the public platform. There are three notable occasions when Micah was quoted: (a) By the elders of the land, saving by so doing the life of Jeremiah, Jer. XXVI. 18, and Micah III. 12. (b) Quoted on the Magi arriving at Jerusalem, Matt. II. 5, 6, Micah V. 2; and (c) by our Lord when sending out His twelve disciples, Matt. X. 35, 36, Micah VII. 6.

ANALYSIS

Some hold the view that it contains three addresses, each beginning with the word " Hear." But, unfortunately for this view, this word is found five times, not three, I. 2. III. 1, 9, VI. 1, 2, Like Isaiah, it falls into two clear divisions: Denunciatory, I. to III., then Consolatory, IV. to VII. It bears a striking resemblance to Isaiah. It has been regarded by some as a summary of the predictions of Isaiah, in fact " Isaiah in shorthand"; but, of course, it is a book separate and distinct. It falls into four sub-sections.

(A) Denunciatory I. to III.	(B) Consolatory IV, to end.		
"WHO IS A GOD LIKE UNTO THEE?" IN			
(1) WITNESSING (Key for this section is I, 2).	(2) CONSOLING (Key IV. 4).	(3) PLEADING (Key VI. 2, 3).	(4) PARDONING (Key VII. 18).
I. to III.	IV. and V.	VI.	VII.
1. The prophet and his hearers, I. 1, 2. 2. Practical description of the Lord coming forth in Judgment to witness against Israel, I. 3, 5. 3. Cause of the Judgment, I. 5. 4. Destruction of Samaria foretold, I. 6, 7. 5. An invasion of Judah, I, 8, 9. 6. And the consequent panic, I. 10 to 16. 7. Apostasy from God and injustice to man condemned, II. 8. The ruling classes denounced, III. 1 to 11. 9. Destruction of Jerusalem graphically foretold. III. 12.	1. Observe the great change in tone. The Lord, who witnessed against Israel, is seen here consoling her by declarations of coming glories, IV. 1 to 5. 2. Israel, though scattered, is to be gathered, IV. 6 to 8. 3. And, though the Babylonian captivity was certain, they should be delivered, IV. 9 to 13. 4. All this will come about through Jesus, V. 1 to 3, the Everlasting One. 5. Israel's future glory, V. 5 to 15.	1. This is a most touching Chapter. How appealingly the Lord pleads, 1 to 5. 2. He requires a spiritual worship and service, 6 to 8. 3. Sin and evil denounced and judged, 9 to 16. Note. the prophet speaks in verse 8 of God's requirements but he has nothing to say about God's gift. We cannot meet God's requirement without first receiving God's great gifts of righteousness and life.	1. The prophet mourns, 1 to 4. 2. Even the home had been invaded by deceit and hatred, 5 to 6. 3. The prophet turns to God (7), rebukes the enemy (8), makes humble confession of Israel's sin (9), confidently counts upon God for the future (10 to 17), and closes by declaring the fulness, freeness and faithfulness of the Lord's pardon.

NAHUM

Nahum, the writer of this book, was a native of Elkosh, (I. 1.) There is an Elkosh in Assyria, situated a few miles north of the ruins of Nineveh, and where a tomb has long been pointed out as that of the prophet's; but authorities, for several reasons, reject this place for that of *Elkosh in Galilee.* This latter place, though in ruins, was pointed out to Jerome as Nahum's by a native guide.

HISTORICAL SETTING

To get the right historical setting is important to the right understanding of this book. It is clear that Nahum was a native of Galilee, and was contemporary of Hezekiah and Isaiah. Upon the Assyrian invasion and deportation of the ten tribes, he escaped into the territory of Judah, and probably took up his residence in Jerusalem, where he witnessed, seven years afterwards, the siege of that city by Sennacherib, and the destruction of the Assyrian host, when 185,000 perished in one night, as recorded in 2 Kings XVIII. and XIX. Undoubtedly there are references to this in Nahum I. 11, etc. Shortly after this event Nahum wrote this book.

SUBJECT

This book has but one theme, the destruction of Nineveh. It was written about 150 years after the mission of Jonah. The revival, or rather the repentance, at the preaching of Jonah, sincere though it was, was not durable, and had been replaced by a complete and deliberate apostasy from God. They were not merely backsliders—they were far, far worse, they were apostates, deliberately rejecting and challenging the God they had accepted and worshipped (see 2 Kings XVIII. 25, 30, 35, XIX. 10 to 13). The Lord accepted the haughty Assyrian challenge (XIX. 22 to 23), and Nahum was chosen to record the prediction of the final and complete overthrow of Nineveh and her empire—an empire which had been built up by violence and cruel oppression, and which was doomed to perish in a violent and extraordinary way. All this prophecy came to pass eighty-six years afterwards. Nahum's book is one great " at last."

STYLE

Nahum forms a beautiful, vivid, pictorial poem on the grandeur, power, and justice of God, and on the conflict between Jehovah and this cruel and defiant world empire of Nineveh. A great student of the prophets writes : " None of the minor prophets seem to equal Nahum in boldness, ardour, and sublimity. His prophecy forms a regular and perfect poem ; the exordium is not merely magnificent, it is truly majestic ; the preparation for the destruction of Nineveh, and the description of its downfall and desolation, are expressed in the most vivid colours, and are bold and luminous in the highest degree."

ANALYSIS

The book falls into two sections, introducing us first to the Judge, then to the judgment.

(A) THE JUDGE I. 1 to 7.	(B) THE JUDGMENT I. 8 to end.			
	(1) THE VERDICT. I. 8 to 14.	(2) THE APPLICATION. I. 15.	(3) THE VISION. II.	(4) THE CERTAINTY. III.
1. The book opens with a declaration of *who* and *what* God is, giving "a sublime and powerful statement of those attributes of God which constitute the basis of all His actions towards the children of men." 2. Under the figure of a storm is set forth the overwhelming majesty of God.	1. Condemned to extinction (8 and 9). 2. Nineveh was captured whilst defenders were drunk (10). 3. Without doubt verse 11 refers to Rabshakeh (see 2 Kings XVIII. 17 to 37. 4. Name to be blotted out (14).	1. The first chapter closes with a warning to Judah. 2. This is an appeal to Judah which, coming after what had been said of Nineveh, is most impressive—God would deal with them severely if they turned not from the error of their ways.	The picture given of the siege and fall of Nineveh, and the desolation which followed is of the most vivid and graphic character. The prophet sees, and makes his hearers see, all the horrid sights of the tragic scene.	1. The Victor and the vanquished (1 to 3). 2. The cause of the overthrow (4). 3. The certainty of this judgment (8 to 10). 4. Various other particulars are here given of the siege.

MESSAGE

Its message is two-fold : (1) It is a message of comfort (Nahum's name means "Comfort") to a harassed and fearful people in peril through the cruel and awful military power of Assyria. Note how comforting I. 7, 12, 13 would be. (2) It is a message of warning, showing that all that God can do with an apostate people and nation is to destroy it.

The Book of HABAKKUK.

LITERARY EXCELLENCE.

(1) Viewed simply as literature (though it is infinitely more than that !) this book stands *pre-eminent for its literary beauty*. It is said that Benjamin Franklin read Habakkuk to a literary circle in Paris, winning their unanimous tribute of admiration for an author of whom not one of them had ever heard before.

(2) Habakkuk's description of the majesty and self-revelation of God in Chapter III. *stands supreme ;* and the whole of the book is written in a *strongly lyrical character*, approaching nearer to the Psalms in structure than any other of the prophetical writings.

WHO WAS HABAKKUK?

(1) What he writes concerning himself, explains the resemblance of his writings to the Psalms. He was not only a prophet (I. 1), but also one of the Levitical choristers in the Temple (III. 19). Beyond this, nothing further is known of the prophet.

(2) Judging from I. 5, 6, which speaks of the Chaldean invasion as still future, though imminent, he must have lived and laboured in the latter part of the reign of Joash (see 2 Kings XXII. 18 to 20). The invasion took place five years after.

GRANDFATHER OF REFORMATION.

(1) This prophet is actually the *Grandfather of the Reformation*. The great doctrine of justification by faith Paul learned from Habakkuk, and Luther learned it from Paul.

(2) One would conclude that this book must have been a favourite with Paul, for he quotes I. 5 in his warning to the unbelieving Jews at Antioch, (Acts XIII. 41), and that famous statement of II. 4 he quotes three times, (Rom. I. 17, Gal. III. 11, Heb. X. 38).

CONVERSATIONAL.

(1) This book is unique in that *quite two-thirds of it is a conversation between the prophet and his Lord.*

(2) Habakkuk has not only been called " The Prophet of Faith," but also " The Free-thinker among the Prophets." " He could not square his belief in a good and righteous God with the facts of life as he sees them." He was troubled with the " Why ?"

(3) Yet in all this mystery and perplexity, true to his name, (his name means " to embrace," " to cling.") he clung to God, and, pouring out his difficulties to Him in prayer, waited patiently (II. 1) for the Divine explanation.

(A) The First Conversation.		(B) The Second Conversation.		(C) Prophet's Hymn and Doxology.
(1)	(2)	(3)	(4)	(5)
He was perplexed with the silence and forbearance of God in permitting evil to continue, and pours out his soul to God.	God answers by stating His silence did not mean ignorance or indifference, but that He was about to bring punishment upon that sinful nation.	The Lord's reply, though it solved one difficulty, raised another, viz.: how a pure God could chastise Israel by a nation far far worse than themselves.	To this the Lord replies that He was not unmindful of the wickedness of the instrument, and would presently punish them very very sorely.	Finding all his difficulties solved, and God's "hush!" taking possession of his soul, he pours out his whole being in a thrilling hymn of prayer, praise, and confidence in God.
I. 1 to 4.	I. 5 to 11.	I. 12 to II. 1.	II. 2 to 20.	III.
Prophet's perplexity at 1. Lord's neglect of his prayers (2), 2. And apparent indifference to sin and suffering (3 and 4).	God replied that He 1. Was about to do something incredible (5). 2. That He would use the Chaldeans to chastise Israel for their sin (6). 3. And gives a graphic character sketch of the Chaldeans (7 to 11).	Prophet declared his difficulty to believe that 1. The Eternal and Holy God (12 and 13) 2. Could chasten a sinful people by a people more sinful (12 and 13). 3. And permit them to catch men as fishes (14 and 15) 4. When they glorified themselves (16 and 17). 5. The prophets patience, II, 1.	1. God bade the prophet to write very plainly what He was about to say (2). 2. What God was about to do would come to pass (3). 3. Those counted righteous through their faith would be preserved from those terrible sorrows (4). 4. And then God gives five woes against Chaldeans.	1. Prophet prays that God would revive His delivering grace (2); 2. And that, in the execution of judgment, He would remember mercy (2). 3. Then he gives a description of the majesty of the Lord at Sinai, and in going before Israel to possess Canaan (3 to 15). 4. Remembrance of all this brings rest to his soul (16). 5. And confidence in God (17 to 19).

THE BOOK OF ZEPHANIAH

WRITER

Very little is known of Zephaniah, the writer of this book. By I. 1 we learn that he was *probably a prince of the Royal house of Judah*, being a descendant of Hezekiah. He is supposed to have been a youth. His name means "Hidden of Jehovah." Perhaps he had his name in mind when he wrote II. 3.

WORK

He began his prophetic ministry in the early days of the reign of Josiah (B.C. 641-610). He foretold the doom of Nineveh (II. 13), which came to pass in B.C. 625; and in I, 4, he denounces various forms of idolatry, which were swept away by Josiah. Without doubt *he was mainly responsible for the revival under Josiah.* Tradition states that he had Jeremiah as colleague.

KEY WORDS

There are three. 1. "The Day of the Lord" is mentioned seven times and forms one key to the study of this book. 2. "In the Midst" is another striking key phrase. 3. But *the* key word is "Jealousy." There is a jealousy which must never be associated with God, a jealousy which is always suspicious of faithlessness, and constantly on the lookout for evidences of same. Milton speaks of such jealousy as "a lover's hell." What a hell on earth is that home wherein such jealousy exists! But there is another kind of jealousy which is the natural outcome of love, and that is the nature of God's jealousy. *He so loves His people that He cannot bear a rival, and must have their whole-hearted devotion;* and He will do everything He can to secure this, even going to the length of awful judgments, as here.

CONTENTS

On taking up the book to read, one is simply appalled at its contents—stern denunciation, dire threatenings, there is nothing but mutterings and threatenings of wrath—but remembering Cowper's fine phrase that chastisement is "the graver countenance of love," we see in all this the proof of God's love. But if the book begins with woe, it ends with singing, and though the first two sections are full of gloom and sadness, *the last section contains the sweetest love song in the Old Testament.*

Division A The Lord "in the midst" for JUDGMENT (Key III. 5, with I. 7,) Chapters I. 1 to III. 8.		Division B The Lord "in the midst" for SALVATION (Key III. 15 & 17) Chap. III. 9 to end.
(1) The devouring fire of the Lord's jealousy kindled in "the whole land" of Israel. —(Note I. 18).	**(2)** The devouring fire of the Lord's jealousy kindled over "all the earth" amongst Gentiles —(Note III. 8.)	**(3)** The devouring fire of the Lord's jealousy *quenched,* and the Lord at "rest in His love." —(Note III. 17.)
I. 1 to II. 3, and III. 1 to 7.	II. 4 to 15, and III. 8.	III. 9 to end.
1. Threat of Judgment, I. 2 to 7.	1. Judgment on Israel's local enemies, literally fulfilled in those days, II. 4 to 15.	1. Israel's repentance (9), followed by Israel's restoration (10), humility (11, 12), Sanctification (13), rejoicing (14), and deliverance (15).
2. Those on whom the Judgment will fall, I. 8 to 13.	2. Judgment on Israel's world-wide enemies yet to be fulfilled, III. 8, with II. 10, 11.	2. Note the singing of the Lord, III, 17.
3. Nearness of the day of the Lord, I. 14 to 18. (Partially fulfilled in the invasion of Nebuchadnezzar, but its full and complete fulfilment is yet future.)		3. The Lord told Job (XXXVIII. 7) that when He laid the foundations of the earth " the morning stars sang together and all the sons of God shouted for joy"; but He was silent.
4. Call to repentance, II. 1 to 3.		4. The first time we read of His singing, is in connection with redemption (Psalm CV. 43, margin).
5. The sad moral state of Jerusalem in the prophet's time, III. 1 to 7.	Truly wonderful and amazing are the above.	5. Was Matt. XXVI. 30 the last time He sang? The last time He sang was no later than the last conversion.
		6. And when Israel is restored He will sing.

TIME

"The second year of Darius" in which Haggai prophesied was B.C. 520.   Confucius, the celebrated Chinese philosopher, flourished in China at this time.

WRITER

We know nothing about Haggai beyond the fact that he was a prophet working in conjunction with Zechariah.   He was probably born at Babylon during the captivity.   His name means "My Feast," and may have been given to him in joyous anticipation of the return from captivity. He began to prophesy two months before Zechariah; but whilst Zechariah prophesied for three years, Haggai only prophesied three months and twenty-four days.

OCCASION

Sixteen years had passed since the return from captivity.   Ezra III. states that the first thought and care of the people was the rebuilding of the altar and the Temple; but difficulties cropped up.   Eventually, political intrigues stopped the work, and the zeal and enthusiasm of the people died away in the face of these prolonged difficulties; and although the storm spent itself and passed by, the workers did not return to their work.   Then came a season of distress—the harvest failed, there was drought, and trouble and sorrow (I. 6, 9 to 11).   Haggai was sent to interpret the calamity, and urge them to have done with their sinful sloth and despondency.   The result was good.   In twenty-four days the people began to re-build.   Then other comforting and cheering messages were given.

STYLE

Each book in the Bible has a style of its own.   The style of Haggai is plain, simple, curt, business-like.   He was fond of interrogation (e.g. I. 4, II. 3, 12, 13), which compels thought and attention.   Certain phrases he often repeats, as "Saith the Lord," and "Lord of Hosts," twelve times each; "Consider," quite four times.   "The word of the Lord" occurs five times, and marks the division of the book.   There were five messages, delivered on separate and distinct occasions.

(1) First Message (Sept 1st)	(2) Second Message (Sept. 24th.)	(3) Third Message (Oct. 21st.)	(4) Fourth Message (Dec. 24th)	(5) Fifth Message (Dec. 24th.)
A STERN MESSAGE of **REBUKE**	A COMFORTING MESSAGE of **COMMENDATION**	A CHEERING MESSAGE of **ENCOURAGEMENT**	AN ASSURING MESSAGE Concerning Cleansing and **BLESSING**	A STEADYING MESSAGE Concerning **SAFETY**
I. 1 to 11	I. 12 to 15.	II. 1 to 9.	II. 10 to 19.	II. 20 to end.
1. Disheartened, and disinclined for work, they tried to excuse themselves by a mistake in the reckoning of years, verse 2. 2. Calamity stated and interpreted, verses 6 to 11. 3. People urged to work, verse 8.	1. Rebuke has desired effect, verse 12. 2. At once, Haggai had given to him from the Lord, one very short but most comforting message, verse 13. 3. And that message had a stirring effect, verse 14.	1. As they laboured, they were disheartened by the fact that, owing to their poverty, the Temple would be inferior to Solomon's. 2 Haggai cheered them by declaring that its glory would be greater than the former one. Jesus stood in it.	1. By question and answer, Haggai dwelt on the impurity of the people. 2. But that impurity had been removed. 3. Now there was blessing for them.	1. Evidently II. 6, 7, had troubled them. 2. By the figure of the "signet." they were taught how the Lord esteemed, valued, and cared for them; 3. And also, how safe they were in troublous times.

MESSAGE

1.   "God first" in life and service, is the message of the Book.   It is an Old Testament commentary and illustration of 1 Cor. xv. 58.
2.   Haggai stands before us a model worker for God, a pattern for us to copy.
   (a)   He effaced himself.   He spends no time in giving details about his life and service.   He exalts his Lord.
   (b)   He ever had a "thus saith the Lord."   He was the Lord's messenger.
   (c)   He not only rebuked, but cheered; not only criticised, but commended and stimulated by word and example.
   (d)   He not only preached, but practised.   He lent a hand, see Ezra V. 1, 2.

THE BOOK OF ZECHARIAH

AUTHOR

(1) Zechariah, the prophet of Restoration and Glory, was probably born in Babylon. The difference between Ezra V. 1, VI. 14, and Zech. I. 1 can be easily explained. Probably his father died in his infancy, and then his grandfather Iddo (Neh. XII. 4 and 16), reared him.

(2) He was thus *priest as well as prophet.* The three names are very suggestive when put together—Zechariah "Jehovah remembers," Berechiah "Jehovah blesses," Iddo "the appointed time." Thus these three names form a key to the meaning of the book. Note the keywords of the book, "Jealous," "Jealousy."

MISSION

(1) He was contemporary of Haggai, being the younger of the two (II. 4) and *his mission was to encourage the despondent.*

(2) He encouraged the disheartened *by prophesying, in glowing terms, of the glory to come to Israel in far off ages.*

(3) This is *the* Divine method of encouragement—taking our eyes off the sad present to the glories of the future. He exercised his ministry for three years.

STYLE

Zechariah was one of the greatest of ancient inspired seers, and his fourteen chapters are full of the most striking visions recorded in the Old Testament. *He was a great poet, and was thus a fitting companion to plain, practical Haggai.*

DIVISION

(1) It is in two principal divisions—the first division falls into three sections, the second into two. The book consists of five separate and distinct messages.

(2) "Instead of this book being all fulfilled prophecy, as some would have it, it is indeed mostly unfulfilled, and even some of the prophecies which, on the surface seem to have seen a fulfilment, were only in part realised."

(A) First Division—APOCALYPTIC. Chapters I. to VIII.			(B) Second Division—PROPHETIC. IX. to End.	
(1) **First Message**	(2) **Second Message**	(3) **Third Message**	(4) **Fourth Message**	(5) **Fifth Message**
I. 1 to 6.	I. 7 to VI.	VII. to VIII.	IX. to XI.	XII. to end.
An earnest call to repentance. He reminded them of their fathers' sin (2), and of the captivity which resulted thereby (6), and exhorted them to flee from those sins (4) In lamenting their departed greatness, they must not forget the cause. Note: "Take hold," in verse 6, is in margin of A.V and in R.V. "Overtake." Judgments as well as blessings follow and overtake us. ———	Eight visions, all given in one night, and all designed for encouragement. I.—**The Material Side of Future Prosperity** 1. *Myrtle Trees, I. 7 to 17.* Israel, lowly and downtrodden, watched and prayed for. 2. *Horns and Smiths, I. 18 to 21.* Foretelling the overthrow of Israel's enemies. 3. *Measuring Line, II.* Revealing the glorious prosperity of Jerusalem, as result of the overthrow of the enemies. II.—**The Spiritual Side of Future Prosperity** 4. *Joshua, the Priest, III.* Picture of national pollution, cleansing, and restoration of nation to priestly service. 5. *Candlestick, IV.* Result is that Israel is able to be God's lightbearer to the world 6. *Flying Roll, V. 1 to 4.* Israel becomes a moral force in the world through the Word of God. 7. *Ephah V. 5 to 11.* Application of the law of God. 8. *Four Chariots. VI. 1 to 8.* Agency at work for Israel. Conclusion, symbolic crowning	1. This third message was uttered nearly two years later. 2. It is a fourfold answer to an enquiry made by a deputation from Babylon concerning the necessity of observing certain feasts they (not God) themselves had instituted. 3. The fast of the fifth month observed the destruction of the Temple, and that of the seventh month was kept on the anniversary of the murder of Gedaliah, (Jer. XLI.) 4. Answer first, VII. 1 to 7. Answer second, VII. 8 to 14. Answer third, VIII. 1 to 17. Answer fourth, VIII. 18 to 23.	1. The prophecies of this fourth message have hnd a partial, but yet not a full and complete fulfilment (see IX. 8). 2. The prophecies of the fifth message are all wholly future. 3. The prophecies are not in chronological order. **Concerning the King.** 1. The Coming of the King, IX. 9, only partially fulfilled. 2. The Rejection of the King. (a) Price paid, XI. 12, 13. (b) Shepherd slain, XIII. 6, 7. (c) Scattering of people, XI. 7 to 11. 3. The Second Advent of the King. XIV. 3 to 8. 4. The Victories of the King, IX. 8, XII. 1 to 9, 10 to 14, XIII. 1 to 5. 5. The Programme of the King, IX. 10 to 17, X. XIV. 9 to 21.	

THE BOOK OF MALACHI

ANGEL'S NAME

(1) Malachi is *the unknown prophet with the angelic name.* Nothing is known of him. Some even think that his name is unknown, Malachi being only a title descriptive of his official position, meaning " My Angel " or " Messenger."

(2) He not only bore this name, but unlike a good many of us, *he was proud of his name,* loving to repeat it, *e.g.* speaking of Levi, as an example of the true priesthood, he says " he is the *Messenger* of the Lord of Hosts," II. 7; he described John the Baptist as God's "*Messenger,*" and speaks of our Lord as " the *Messenger* of the Covenant," III. 1.

DIALOGUE

(1) This book is notable for its dialogue style. One evidence of a backslidden state is the hyper-critical spirit. God's people were in a sad spiritual condition, and consequently were prepared to call into question anything and everything, even God's own statements. All their words of criticism had been noted by the Lord—" Ye say " is met with quite a dozen times, I. 2, 6, 7, 12, 13, II 14, 17, III. 7, 8, 13, 14 He keeps account also of the statements of others, I. 4.

(2) But God not only took note of their sayings—He combated them, as a mere casual study of the above texts will show.

A PORTRAIT

(1) Malachi was the last of the prophets. " His prophecies therefore have a grave and solemn importance, and on two accounts. First as showing the state of the remnant who, in the tender mercy of God, had been brought back from Babylon; and secondly, because of the correspondence of the position of this remnant with that of God's people at the present moment. As there was nothing between them, so there is nothing to intervene between ourselves and the expectation of the Lord's return."

(2) In Israel's state, as revealed by Malachi, we have a telling portrait of our own time and age.

ANALYSIS

The book falls into two sections and three subsections, as follows:

(A) EXPOSTULATION, Chap. I. and II.		(B) PREDICTION, Chap. III. and IV.
(1) **A Message of Love**	(2) **A Message of Rebuke**	(3) **A Message of Hope**
I. 1 to 5.	I. 6 to II. 17.	III. and IV.
1. God's declaration of His love for Israel (2).	To the Priests—	A Series of Prophecies Concerning:
2. Israel blindly questions that love for and to them. (2)	1. Did not give God reverence and honour due to Him (6).	1. John the Baptist's Advent and work (III. 1),
3. The Lord condescends to give one of the many proofs (3 to 5).	2. Offered to God what they would not dare offer the Governor (8);	2. The coming and work of the Lord, all yet in the future (III. 1 to 6).
NOTE: In the Old Testament we get the declaration of God's love for *Israel* (2); in the New Testament we have announced God's love for the *World.* (John III. 16).	3. Refused to work except for gain (10).	3. The sad state of His people prior to His coming (III. 7 to 15).
	4. God's determination that, in spite of Israel's failure, His name should be great (11).	4. Yet even then there will be a faithful remnant (III. 16 to 18).
	5. Their utter failure (II. 1 to 9).	5. The Day of the Lord (IV. 1).
	To the People—	6. His advent has no terrors for His faithful ones (IV. 2 to 4).
	1. Guilty of sins against one another (II. 10),	7. Elijah to come again before the Day of the Lord (IV. 5).
	2. Against God in the family (II. 11 to 17).	

MESSAGE—Remember His love; repent of your sins; return to Him; rehearse His love, grace, and promised advent to one another.

ANALYSES of the BOOKS of the NEW TESTAMENT

Book.	Key Words or Phrase.	Message.
MATTHEW,	"KINGDOM,"	Jesus as the Messiah King.
MARK,	STRAIGHTWAY,	Jesus as the Servant.
LUKE,	SON OF MAN,	Jesus as the Ideal Man.
JOHN,	BELIEVE,	Jesus as the Eternal Son of God.
ACTS,	"BEGAN,"	The Work Continued by the Spirit.
ROMANS,	RIGHTEOUSNESS,	Justification by Faith.
I. CORINTHIANS,	"OUR LORD,"	The Lordship of Christ.
II. CORINTHIANS,	COMFORT, MINISTRY,	The Nature of Comfort. The Performance of Ministry.
GALATIANS,	FAITH,	Christ the Deliverer.
EPHESIANS,	THE CHURCH,	The Church, the Body of Christ.
PHILIPPIANS,	ALL,	Christian Unity to be Maintained at all Cost.
COLOSSIANS,	"HE IS THE HEAD,"	The Glory and Dignity of Christ.
I. THESSALONIANS,	"WAIT FOR HIS SON,"	The Coming of the Lord *for* His People.
II. THESSALONIANS,	"DAY OF THE LORD,"	The Coming of the Lord *with* His People.
I. TIMOTHY,	"HOW THOU OUGHTEST TO BEHAVE."	Designed to Accomplish (1 Tim. 4. 12).
II. TIMOTHY,	ASHAMED,	Loyalty to the Lord and to Truth.
TITUS,	"THYSELF A PATTERN,"	God's Ideal for the Christian Church.
PHILEMON,	RECEIVE,	The Practice of Christian Forgiveness.
HEBREWS,	BETTER,	A Right Conception of the Glory of Christ.
JAMES,	FAITH, WORKS,	Faith Shown by its Works.
I. PETER,	SUFFERING,	How We May Suffer to the Glory of God.
II. PETER,	REMEMBRANCE,	Purity and Loyalty Amidst Corruption and Apathy.
I. JOHN,	KNOW, FELLOWSHIP,	The Life of Fellowship with God.
II. JOHN,	TRUTH,	Truth Must be Received and Obeyed.
III. JOHN,	"FELLOW-HELPERS",	Hospitality. Domineering Leadership.
JUDE,	KEEP, KEPT,	Keeping the Faith and Being Kept.
REVELATION,	REVELATION,	Jesus, the Gloriously Triumphant One.

The GOSPEL ACCORDING TO St. MATTHEW

VALUE

(1) Renan, the sceptic, described this Gospel as "*the most important book of Christendom—the most important book that has ever been written.*"

(2) We are quite agreed as to its importance, but, instead of saying "the most important," we would prefer to say "one of the most important."

WRITER

(1) It was written by Matthew the converted publican, (IX. 9.) He is called Levi in Mark II. 14. Evidently he was re-named Matthew by our Lord.

(2) It is only in his Gospel that the despised name of Publican is associated with his apostolic name of Matthew. (Matthew means "Gift of God.")

(3) He seems to have been a man of means. Modestly he makes no reference to the "great feast" he made on his call to the ministry, (Luke V. 29,) or his great sacrifice in following Christ. But for this authorship, Matthew would have been one of the least known of the Apostles.

PURPOSE

(1) The book was written originally in Hebrew, and was specially designed for the use of the Jews, consequently the Old Testament is often quoted.

(2) One characteristic word in this book is the word "Fulfilled." He makes no less than sixty references to the Old Testament writings as fulfilled in Christ.

(3) There is no discord between the four Gospels as some imagine. Each wrote with a specific purpose in view. Each gives a different portrait of the Lord Jesus. The portrait Matthew gives of Jesus is that of King. The word "Kingdom" is met with fifty-five times, "Kingdom of Heaven" thirty-two times, "Son of David" seven times.

(4) This book shows that the mission of Jesus was primarily to the Jews, (X. 5-6, XV. 24.) The "Gospel of the Kingdom" preached by Jesus and His disciples, (IV. 23, X. 7,) was not identical with the Gospel preached to-day; the former is the good news that God was about to set up on the earth a political and spiritual kingdom, ruled over by Jesus, as the Son of David, whereas the latter has to do with God's spiritual sway. The Gospel of the Kingdom was preached up to the rejection and crucifixion of Jesus, but will again be preached just before the great Tribulation (XXIV. 14) and second Advent of Jesus as King. The Gospel we preach to-day is good news concerning salvation through Christ, and the calling out of a people for Himself, viz. : the Gospel of the Grace of God.

ANALYSIS

(1) Birth of the King	(2) Fore-runner of the King	(3) Testing of the King	(4) Proclamation of the King	(5) Laws of the King	(6) Ministry of the King	(7) Rejection of the King	(8) Entry of the King	(9) DEATH AND Resurrection OF THE KING
I and II.	III.	IV. 1 to 11.	IV. 12 to 25.	V. to VII.	VIII. to XI. 19.	XI. 20 to XX.	XXI. to XXV.	XXVI. to XXVIII.
The genealogy and birth of the King with the worship of the Eastern Kings (wise men) and the persecution of Herod the usurper. The Lord Jesus is the last in Jewish history whose descent from the Royal line of David can be fully and clearly established.	1. All notable persons in the East have forerunners, so Jesus. 2. John the Baptist announced the imminence of the Kingdom, and baptized the KING.	1. Here the Lord Jesus met and vanquished the tempter, refusing to gain the Kingdom in any way but God's. 2. "The first Adam fell in Eden surrounded by creature comforts; the second Adam conquered in the wilderness, His body enfeebled by long abstinence."	1. Jesus did not come to found the Church but the Kingdom. Here He makes His Royal Proclamation. 2. The Kingdom of God is made up of all in Heaven and Earth who submit themselves to Him, and the entrance into that Kingdom is by the new Birth, (John (III.) The Kingdom of Heaven is the visible establishment of the Kingdom of God on the earth.	1. The Sermon on the Mount is only for disciples. It is the code of laws especially for Christ's earthly Kingdom which He will set up by and by, though it has a message for us. 2. The Sermon on the Mount has a moral application to the Christian.	1. The King actively at work healing and teaching amongst His people Israel. 2. Note R.V. of VIII. 6: "servant" is rendered "boy"— a most affectionate term, showing the servant had endeared himself to his master.	1. This is a section of very great importance. Israel had practically rejected its King. Now the establishment of the Kingdom is postponed, and Jesus, for the first time, gives hint of a new departure, the creation of a new Society —the Church. 2. Note XII. 14, followed by the "mystery" teaching of XIII.	1. The official entry of the King into His capital, and His final and public rejection. 2. Note XXV. 41. No earthly judge makes the criminal's doom a matter of personal relationship to himself— Christ does. To depart from Christ means to depart from all hope.	1. Jesus was slain because He declared He was King. Note specially XXVII. 11, 12, 29, 37, and 42. 2. The rending of the Veil (XXVII. 51), followed the rending of the heart of Christ.

D*

ANALYSIS No. 41
Key Word, "Straightway." Key Verse, X. 45.

The GOSPEL ACCORDING TO St. MARK

MESSAGE
Jesus as the Servant

WRITER

(1) The writer of this second Gospel was not an Apostle, but only an associate of the Apostles, just an ordinary worker.
(2) He was the son of one of the Marys of the New Testament, who evidently was a person in comfortable circumstances. (Acts XII. 12).
(3) He was nephew of Barnabas, and it was owing to him that Paul and Barnabas disagreed. (Acts XV, 36-41).
(4) It is thought that Mark was converted through Peter; at any rate he became the companion of Peter, and recorded his utterances.

ORIGIN

The early Fathers, notably Clement of Alexandria, describe the impression made by the graphic preaching of Peter, the anxiety of his hearers to possess in writing what had delighted them when heard, their coming to Mark, Peter's companion, with the entreaty that he would record for them his master's words, Mark's compliance with the request, and Peter's apostolic sanction to the work. Justin Martyr refers to it as the "Memoirs" or "*Gospel of St. Peter.*"

PURPOSE

(1) It was written, so it is believed, at Rome for the Romans. Consequently (1) there are very few references to the Old Testament Scriptures. (2) Jewish words are explained (III. 17, V. 41, VII. 11 and 34, XIV. 36); also Jewish customs (VII. 3, 4, XIV. 12, XV. 42). (3) Latin words are frequently used, *e.g.*, Legion, Centurion, etc.
(2) The whole tone of the book reflects Peter's energetic and impulsive nature, and thus was admirably fitted for the Roman citizen, who was a "hustler"— a man of action.
(3) The portrait it gives of the Lord Jesus is that of the Servant, or the Ideal Worker. As the average Roman cared little for doctrine or teaching, but a great deal for action, in this Gospel the deeds of our Lord are emphasised and not His words.

ANALYSIS

This book almost baffles any attempt at analysis. It is so crowded with incidents. Yet we see five clear divisions.

(1) The Arrival and Identity of the Servant	(2) The Fidelity of the Servant	(3) THE SERVANT AT WORK The Character and Nature of His Work.	(4) The Servant Obedient to Death	(5) The Risen AND Glorified One STILL a Servant
I. 1 to 11.	I. 12 and 13.	I. 14 to XIII.	XIV. and XV.	(XVI.)
1. There is no genealogy, and no mention of His birth and infancy. Important as these events are, they are out of place in a description of a servant. 2. He is a servant to All, not merely to the Jew. 3. The Servant is the Son of God, declared in verse 1 and announced in verse 2. 4. He is fitted for His ministry by the Spirit. **Lesson:** I, too, cannot serve God acceptably unless I am His child through faith in Christ Jesus, and have also the witness and enduement of the Spirit.	1. Only in this book is it recorded that in His temptation, He "was with the wild beasts." 2. David, before he entered upon his service for God and Israel, did battle with wild beasts. 1 Sam. XVII. 34 to 36.) 3. In this temptation the Divine Servant was loyal to God. **Lesson:** I must be loyal to God, and, by His grace, live the overcoming life, before I can be of real service to my fellow-man.	1. He is the **Wise Servant**—Seen in Him selecting and setting others to work, I. 14 to 20, II. 13 and 14, III. 14 to 19, VI. 7 to 13. 2. He is the Servant **with authority.** He had power over demons, elements, and death, **and in teaching.** I. 21 to 28, IV. 35 to 41, V., VI. 47 to 51, IX. 14 to 29. 3. **His was a tender and loving ministry**, the outcome of compassion. I. 29 to 34, and 40 to 45, V. 41, VI. 34, VIII. 2, X. 13 to 16, X. 21. 4. His was a service the outcome of prayer, I. 35, VI. 46, XIV. 32 to 41. 5. His was a **bustling and active service** without fuss or fret, I. 36 to 39. 6. He was a servant, **never off duty**, ministering even in his own house, II. 1 to 12, 15 to 22. 7. His was a **costly service**, meaning much grief (III. 5) many sighs (VII. 34, VIII. 12), and death (VIII. 27 to 38). 8. His was a **self-denying service** (III. 20, VI. 31). 9. As a servant, **teaching divine truth in simple language** (IV., IX. 33 to 37, XII. 1 to 12, I. 22, see XII. 37). 10. He continued in His service, though despised and misunderstood (VI. 1-6). 11. A service which **took notice of the service of others** (IX. 38, 40, XII. 41-44). **Lesson:** He is the Pattern Servant. May our service be more like His!	1. Like the ox, He was ready either for service or sacrifice. He did both. 2. His dying was an invaluable service. He died for us! 3. Note XIV. 51 and 52 and the interesting supposition that this young man was Mark himself who witnessed all in Gethsemane.	1. He arose! And His resurrection can be viewed in the light of service. 2. Note the force and significance of "and Peter," in verse 7. 3. Observe by verse 20, He is still the Worker, working in co-operation with His servants.

THE GOSPEL ACCORDING TO St. LUKE

WRITER

Luke, the writer of this Gospel ,according to Eusebius, was a native of Antioch, in Syria. He was a Gentile. His name, an abbreviated form of Lucanus, is thought by some to prove he was a Greek. He was an educated man, and followed the profession of a physician. The first mention of him as fellow worker of St. Paul is in Acts XVI. 10.

PURPOSE

It was written for Greek readers—in the first instance sent to a personal friend—after exhaustive research, and was intended to stop the spread of spurious Gospels and false accounts of the Life of Lives. As Luke was companion to St. Paul, it is believed that he incorporated in this book the substance of that great apostle's preaching.

MESSAGE

(1) Renan, the sceptic, declared that this was "*the most beautiful book in the world.*" It is one that artists revel in. More pictures have been painted from it than from any of the others.

(2) That this book was intended for Greek readers is the clue to its message. The Grecian ideal of perfect manliness differed from that of the Roman. Whilst "*the Romans felt it to be their mission to govern, the Greeks felt it theirs to educate, elevate, and perfect man. The ideal of the Roman was military glory and governmental authority, but the Greek's was wisdom and beauty.*"

(3) *The portrait Luke draws of Jesus is that of the perfect Man, the One who more than meets the highest ideals of the Greeks.* Whilst he speaks of the Deity of Christ, the emphasis is placed upon the perfect manhood of Christ. His character as revealed in this Gospel is intensely human, as we shall see in the following study. He is "Son of Man" as well as the "Son of God."

(1) The Man "Made like unto His brethren."—Heb. II. 17. I. to III.	(2) The Man "Tempted like as we are,"—Heb. IV. 15. IV. 1 to 13.	(3) The Man "Touched with the feeling of our infirmities.—Heb. IV. 15. IV. 14 to XIX. 28.	(4) The Man As our kinsman, redeeming us, XIX. 28 to XXIII.	(5) The Man Still as Man in resurrection and ascension glory. XXIV.

1. One with us in His descent from Adam, the fountain head of humanity. III. 23. 38.
 	
2. One with us in common human relationships, with all its attendant duties and responsibilities, (first two chapters deal with the cousins of Mary.)
 	
3. One with us in our shame by the link of baptism, (in submitting to the rite of baptism He lost His character, that is, in the estimation of the Jewish world.)
 	
Note:
Here we have preserved the first precious germs of Christian hymnology. I. 68 to 79, I. 46, 55, II. 14, II. 29, 32.
	Luke views the temptation from the standpoint of man: "The Devil challenged the first Adam, the second Adam challanges the Devil, The Devil ruined the first man ; the Devil was spoiled by the Man Christ Jesus. The first Adam involved the race in his defeat ; the last Adam included the race in His victory."	**THE LORD JESUS AS:**
		
		1. **The Man of cosmopolitan interests.** This Gospel gives those incidents in the life of our Lord which shows His interest in the whole human race, and not merely the Jew, II. 10, II. 31 and 32, XVII. 18, XIX. 2.
		
		2. **The Man of Wisdom,** as shown in His teaching, IV. 14 and 15, 32. The Wisest of all Teachers, V. 30, 39, VI., X. 25 to 37, XX. 2 to 8.
		
		3 The Man of ability, IV. 33 to 37, V., VIII., IX. 37 to 43.
		
		4. **The Man full of human sympathy,**
		  1. For the fallen and despised, V. 27 to 39, VII. 36 and 37.
		  2. For the bereaved, VII. 11, VIII. 42, IX. 38, (Note "only.")
		  3. For the despondent, VII. 19.
		  4. For the diseased, IV. 38 to 41, V. 12, VII.
		    (Note the strong human element in all Luke's parables.)
		
		5. **The Man of Prayer :** Showing His absolute dependence upon God in all the great crises of His life, III. 21, V. 16, VI. 12, IX. 18 and 29, XI. 1 and 2, IX. 29
		
		6. **The Sociable Man,** VII. 36, XI. 37, XIV. 1, XIX. 7.
		
		7. **The Man of beauty and glory,** IX. 28 to 36.
			1. As the patriot, weeping over Jerusalem, XIX. 41.
			
			2. As Man, receiving angel's ministry, and that in answer to prayer, XXII. 43.
			
			3. As our kinsman, performing the kinsman's part (See Lev. XXV. 47 to 55, Ruth II., III. 10 to 18, IV. 1 to 10.
				1. The risen Lord still Man.
				
				2. As Man walking to Emmaus with two men.
				
				3. As Man, eating in the upper room, showing His still perfect humanity.
				
				4. Ascending in the act of blessing.
				
				Note :
				The Book begins and ends with rejoicing, and all in connection with Jesus.

WRITER

(1) John, the writer of this Gospel, was the son of a master-fisherman (his father had "hired servants, Mark I. 20) and of Salome, one of the women who ministered to the Lord of their substance (Matt. XXVII. 55 and 56, Luke VIII. 3); from this, and the fact that he had a home of his own in Jerusalem (John XIX. 27), it is quite evident he was in comfortable circumstances.

(2) Though of a contemplative character, he was of hasty and uncertain temper (called a "Son of Thunder") until grace took him in hand, and then the lion became a lamb. He became the apostle of love. Evidently he was the youngest of our Lord's apostles, and outlived all the others.

THE BOOK

(1) It is the last one of all the inspired writings, written quite fifty years after our Lord's ascension, and is the deepest and most profound of all.

(2) On the Continent it is called the "Bosom of Christ," because it reveals the very heart of Christ, the very Bosom of the Eternal.

PURPOSE

(1) According to the early Fathers it was *written and published at Ephesus, at the request of the Apostle Andrew and the Asiatic bishops,* to combat certain errors then prevalent concerning the Deity of Christ. This is important and worthy of notice.

(2) Its keyword is "Believe." *"In this Gospel, Jesus Christ is presented as the One whom we are to believe; in John's Epistles the One whom we are to love; and in the Revelation the One for whom we are to wait.* But believe what? The Deity of the Man Christ Jesus. Note XX, 31.

PECULIARITIES

Two peculiarities of this Gospel may be noted, 1. *The occurrence of the word "Jew." It is only found once in Matthew, twice in Mark, twice in Luke, but over sixty times in John.* 2. There are only eight miracles (or more properly "signs") recorded, all showing the power of Christ's Word, and of His Word alone.

PORTRAIT

The portrait drawn for us of Jesus is that of "the Only Begotten of the Father." John shows what it was that convinced men and women of all classes and positions that Jesus was God. The materials he uses in his Gospel are altogether fresh, kept in reserve by God.

(1) Jesus, the Son of God, BEFORE His Incarnation	(2) Jesus Revealed as Son of God by His Deeds and Words — John points out what convinced the people of His Deity	(3) The Son of God Revealing Himself More fully to His own	(4) The Son of God Slain	(5) His Claim to Deity Fully Established by His Resurrection.
I. 1 to 14.	I. 15 to XII.	XIII. to XVII.	XVIII. to XIX.	XX to XXI
1. God did not send Him into the world in order that He might become His Son; He is the Eternal Son. 2. This Gospel begins like the book of Genesis. 3. Gentiles would quite understand of Whom John speaks as the Word, for they used a similar phrase when speaking at times of their deities. 4. "In the beginning was the Word"—thus He was prior to all created things, therefore Jesus is no part of creation. 5. "Word was with God"—another Person, proving Jesus was not God alone.	1. John the Baptist discovered Jesus' Deity through baptism with the Holy Spirit, I. 33. 2. Nathaniel was convinced by His possession of omniscience, I. 48, 49. 3. His disciples were convinced of His Deity by His first miracle of turning water into wine, II. 11. 4. By His cleansing of the Temple, and the performance of many unrecorded miracles numbers of Jews acknowledged Him as Divine. II. 23. 5. Jesus reveals Himself to Nicodemus as Divine, III. 13 to 16. 6. John the Baptist's four remarkable testimonies, III, 25 to 36. 7. Jesus reveals Himself as Divine to the Samaritan woman, IV. 26. 8. The Samaritans accept Him as Divine, IV. 41, 42. 9. The nobleman was convinced that Jesus was Divine when he found His word was as effectual as His presence, IV. 53. 10. Opposition because He called God His Father, V. 17, 18. 11. Many convinced of His Deity by Miracle of loaves, VI. 14. 12. Note by VI. 35, VIII. 12, 58, X. 9, 11, XI. 25, XIV. 6, XV. 1, Jesus declares Himself to be the completed revelation of the great "I Am" of the Old Testament. 13. Jesus reveals Himself as the Divine One to the healed man, IX. 35 to 38. 14. Martha's confession, XI. 27, and the effect of the raising of Lazarus, XI. 45. 15. Jesus is at last acknowledged openly as Divine by Jew (XII, 12 to 19) and Gentile (XII. 20).	1. Finally and completely rejected by the representatives of the Jewish nation. (XI. 47 to 53). Jesus no longer openly declares himself to the World. (XI. 54). 2. Now He manifests Himself more fully to His disciples, so that their convictions as to His Deity were deepened and established.	1. Note the effect of one flash of His Divinity in XVIII. 6. 2. By XIX. 7 we see that He was slain not only because He declared Himself to be King, but because He claimed equality with God.	1. Read Rom. I. 4. 2. Surely no greater proof of His Divinity could have been given them by His resurrection. 3. Note (XX. 17), the first time the Lord called His disciples by the tender name "Brethren."

The ACTS OF THE APOSTLES

DEEDS OF CHRIST

(1) According to Daniel Crawford, the picturesque Bantu title for the book of the Acts of the Apostles is "*Words concerning Deeds.*"

(2) But whose deeds? Its present title is hardly correct, as it only deals really with two of the apostles, Peter and Paul. It was known in ancient times as the "Gospel of the Holy Spirit," and "Gospel of Resurrection." It has been called "The Acts of the Holy Spirit," and that is true; but its correct title is "The Acts of the Ascended and Glorified Lord." Chapter I. 1 gives the clue to its message. The Gospels record the life of Jesus in the flesh; the Acts record His life in the Spirit. In this book we see the risen and ascended Lord still living and working on by the Holy Spirit through His disciples. Luke, in his Gospel, told us what "Jesus *began* both to do and teach;" in this book we have a summary of what He *continued* to do, and is *still doing*.

ANALYSIS

(1) *This is the only unfinished book in the Bible.* Note how abruptly it closes. How else could it close? How can there be a complete account of a person's life and work so long as he lives! And the Lord Jesus still lives!

(2) *Yet in this incomplete book there is system and order.* I. 8 is the key to the analysis. The entire book records the fulfilment of that prophecy, showing how the work began in Jerusalem, then spreading "to all Judæa and Samaria," and eventually reached "the uttermost parts of the earth."

(3) The book opens with the preaching of the Gospel in Jerusalem, the great ecclesiastical centre of the Jewish nation, and closes with the preaching in Rome, the great centre of the world's power.

(4) Please note that at each of these widening circles of influence there is a marked outpouring of the Holy Spirit, and an act of Divine Judgment.

(A)	(B)	(C)
From Pentecost to Death of Stephen	Persecution by Paul, to his Conversion	Paul's Ministry, to Imprisonment
(1) **The Lord at Work in "Jerusalem"**	(2) **The Lord at Work in "Judæa and Samaria"**	(3) **The Lord at Work even unto "Uttermost Parts"**
I. to VII.	VIII. and IX.	X. to XXVIII.
1. Work at Jerusalem inaugurated by an outpouring of the Holy Spirit and judgment, II.1, and V. 1 to 11.	1. Work in this wider sphere inaugurated by an outpouring of the Spirit, VIII. 17, and threatened judgment, VIII. 22 to 24.	1. Work in this important section inaugurated by an outpouring of the Spirit and judgment, X. 44 to 48, XIII. 6 to 13.
2. Note (a) Ascension of our Lord, I. 1 to 11. (Out of sight, but not out of mind or touch; thank God!)	2. Note (a) Persecution under Saul, VIII. 1 to 4. (b) Ministry of Philip, VIII. 5 to 40.	2. Conversion of Cornelius, and sequel, X., XI. 18.
(b) Ten days waiting for the Spirit, 12 to 14.		3. The Church at Antioch, XI. 19 to 30.
(c) Appointment of an Apostle, 15 to 26.	3. Conversion of Saul, IX. 1 to 30.	4. Peter's arrest and deliverance, XII.
(d) Pentecost and founding of Church, II.	4. Further ministry of Peter, 32 to 43.	5. Paul's first missionary journey, XIII. to XV. 35.
(e) Lame man healed, and sequel, III.		6. Paul's second missionary journey, XV. 36 to XVIII. 22.
(f) First persecution, IV.		7. Paul's third missionary journey, XVIII. 22 to XXI. 17.
(g) Judgment, V. Deacons, VI. Stephen, VII.		8. Paul's imprisonment, XXI. 18 to end.

MESSAGE

We have stated that the Acts gives prominence to the Lord Jesus. *He* is *the* Worker. Let us trace this fact in the Book:

THE LORD JESUS

1. As the Commander and Instructor of His people ... ... I. 2 to 9.
2. As the great Hope of the Church ... ... I. 10 to 11.
3. As the Guide of His people in Church matters in times of perplexity I. 24, X. 13 to 16, XVI. 10, XXII. 18 to 21.
4. As the Bestower of the Holy Ghost ... ... II. 33.
5. As *the* Burden of all sermons and addresses, II. 22 to 36, III. 13 to 15, IV. 10 to 33, V. 30, VI. 14, VIII. 5, 35, X. 36, etc.
6. As the One who added to the Church ... ... II. 47.
7. As the only Hope for a perishing world ... ... IV. 12.
8. As the Active Partner in our service ... ... III. 16, 26, XVIII. 9, 10.
9. As the Personal Agent in the conversion of Saul ... ... IX. 3 to 6.
10. As the Encourager of His much tried ones ... ... VII. 55, 56, XXIII. 11.

THE EPISTLE

This epistle was written to the Christians of Rome in the month of February, A.D. 58, at Corinth, in the house of a wealthy Corinthian Christian, called Gaius (XVI. 23), by Paul, who had as amanuensis, Tertius (XVI. 22), and was taken to Rome by a well-to-do widow, named Phœbe, who went there on some private business (XVI. 1. 2).

OPINIONS

This epistle has ever been considered as St. Paul's masterpiece, whether judged from an intellectual or theological standpoint, and the greatest of men have ever valued it most highly. It is said that Chrysostom had this epistle read to him once a week; that Coleridge considered it to be " *the most profound work ever written:*" Calvin said "*it opened the door to all the treasures in the Scriptures*"; Luther pronounced it "*The chief book of the New Testament and the purest Gospel*"; and Melancthon, in order to become thoroughly acquainted with it, copied it twice with his own hand. Godet described it as " *the Cathedral of the Christian faith.*"

PURPOSE

This letter answers the query of the ages: " How should man be just with (or before) God !" (Job IX. 2.) No one can be just who is not adjusted with his Maker, This epistle reveals and expounds God's way of Justification. Its key verses are I. 16, 17. These two verses could be considered as the text and all the rest of the letter as the sermon.

ANALYSIS

It is in two sections. Like a wise preacher, Paul first gives the doctrine (I. to XI.), then makes the application (XII. to XVI.) The first section is subdivided into nine divisions.

(A) DOCTRINAL

(B) PRACTICAL

(1) Justification by faith revealed in the Gospel.	(2) The universal need of Justification by faith.	(3) How we are Justified.	(4) Justification by faith no new doctrine.	(5) Blessings that follow Justification.	(6) Justification by faith and the question of sin.	(7) The struggles and the groans of the Justified.	(8) Liberty and privileges for the Justified.	(9) Justification and the unbelieving Jew.	The Duties of the Justified
I. 1 to 17.	I. 18 to III. 20.	III. 21 to 31.	IV.	V.	VI.	VII.	VIII.	IX. to XI.	XII to XVI.
1. After the opening greeting, Paul stated that he desired to visit Rome (1) to satisfy the craving of his soul (2) to be the means of blessing to them (3) to discharge a debt, by preaching the Gospel there. 2. He then stated that this Gospel revealed God's methods of bestowing righteousness, God's way of Justifying the sinner. 3. This is the basal text, 16, 17.	1. In this section all mankind is shown to be in absolute need of God's Justifying Grace 2. He first shows how the Gentiles got away from God, and the awful results that followed, I. 18 to 32. 3. Then he proves in chap. II. that the Jew stands equally in need of that same grace 4. Justification by faith is only for those whose mouths have been stopped.	1. Its fountain is grace, verse 24. 2. Its ground is blood, verse 25 and V. 9. 3. Its channel is faith, verses 28, 26, 22. 4 The proof is resurrection of Christ, IV. 25. 5. Its evidence is works, (see James II. 14 to 26.) Note verse 23. All men are not sinners alike; yet all are alike sinners.	1. But is not this doctrine quite new? Is it not some new idea ? By no means. 2. Abraham was justified by faith 3. And even David described the blessedness of the Justified state. *This is a very important section.* Note R.V. of verse 19, where the negative is omitted, He deliberately faced the problem	Verse 1. Peace I. 2. Access, 2. 3. Joy, 2. 4. Glory in tribulation, 3. 5. Love of God in heart, 5. *NOTE.* 1. In verse 5 we have the first mention of Spirit in this epistle. 2 In the former part we are directed to Christ's work *for* us, before the Spirit's work *in* us.	Herein is shown that Justification by faith does not encourage continuance in sin On the contrary, we have died to it. Note R.V. of verse 2, "We who died to sin." For "Old man" 20th Century Version gives "old self."	Without doubt, we have here the experience of a regenerate person. though, of course, many an awakened, but unconverted one, has a similar experience. Here we witness the battle in progress between our old nature and the new.	In this chapter we have the Promised Land, flowing with milk and honey, for all to possess. What a contrast is this chapter to the previous one ! This chapter begins with "no condemnation," and ends with "no separation."	But what about Israel ? Chapter IX. " is devoted to vindicating the liberty of God to mould His plans according to His fore-knowledge ; in X. why Israel was rejected, and in XI. is shown that Israel's rejection is only partial, and, also, not permanent.	1. To God— Consecrate ourselves, XII. 1. No conformity to the world. 2. To ourselves— XII. 2. Not to be conceited, XII. 3. 3. To the Church— Use our gifts, XII. 4 to 8. 4. To other Christians— Love to be shown in various ways XII. 9 to 13. 5. To the enemy— "Avenge not," etc. XII. 14 to 21. 6. To the State— "Be subject to," etc. XIII. 1 to 7. 7. To neighbours— "Owe no man anything," etc., XIII. 8 to 14. 8. To weak brother— To be considered, XIV. to XV. 7. 9. To all— Observing the common courtesies of life, XV. 8 to XVI.

The FIRST EPISTLE TO THE CORINTHIANS

THE CHURCH

The Church at Corinth was founded by Paul, as the result of eighteen months' labour there. (1 Cor. IV. 15, with Acts XVIII).

ORIGIN OF EPISTLE

(1) After Paul's departure, grave disorders broke out. During his three years' stay at Ephesus (Acts XIX. and XX, 31) he must have rushed over to Corinth for a few days to put these abuses in order (first visit, Acts XVIII.; 1 Cor., and 2 Cor., were written towards the close of the third year's ministry in Ephesus, 1 Cor. XVI. 8, and yet in 2 Cor. XII. 14 and 2 Cor. XIII, 1, he speaks of paying his third visit.)

(2) On his return he wrote his first letter, now lost, (see 1 Cor. V. 9 and 11), thus making what we call the first, the second, and the second, the third.

(3) The arrival and report of some members of a well-known family (1 Cor. I. 11), and common reports from other travellers (1 Cor. V. 1, XI. 18) prove that in spite of all his efforts, the sad disorders continued. Presently a reply to his first letter came, with fresh enquiries (1 Cor. VII. 1), and to answer these questions, as well as to further unburden his soul about the disorders, he wrote this letter.

CLUE AND KEY

(1) The clue to the message and understanding of this epistle is the mental, moral and spiritual condition of the Corinthians.

(2) Though the members of the Corinthian Church were chiefly drawn from the lower classes (1 Cor. I. 26), they were not free from the *peculiar tendency of the Greek to intellectual pride.* "*Corinth was the rival of Athens. The Greeks were proud of their language, literature, learning and logic. Paul prepares this epistle to meet the Greek mind. He begins by renouncing wisdom* (1 Cor. I. 17, II. 1, etc.) *This epistle is throughout a rebuke to the princes of this world, confident in their worldly wisdom, but fools in God's sight. The world by wisdom knew not God* (1 Cor. I. 21). *The natural man does not, cannot receive the things of the Spirit; the highest truths are veiled to him* (1 Cor. II, 14)." (Dr. Pierson.)

(3) They were also addicted to immorality (1 Cor V. 1 to 11, VI. 15 to 18) and drunkenness 1 Cor. XI. 21), characteristic sins of their city.

TONE

This epistle is distinctly an epistle of reproof. Even the doctrine it contains is there by way of reproof and correction (see 1 Cor. XV. 12). It is intensely *practical* (even the glowing resurrection chapter is made an incentive to service), reproving and correcting abuses in the social and ecclesiastical life of the people; and though primarily intended only for the Christians at Corinth, the principles declared make it suitable and applicable to God's people of all time.

DIVISION

It falls naturally into two principal sections dealing with matters (1) reported *to* Paul (2) enquired *of* Paul.

I. Cor.	(A) Reported to Paul		(B) Enquired of Paul		I. Cor.
	(1) Church Disorders.	(2) Social Irregularities.	(3) Social Irregularities.	(4) Church Disorders.	
I. 1 to 9.	I. 10 to IV. 21.	V. to VI. 8.	VI. 9 to X.	XI. to XVI.	XVI. 5 to 24.
Introduction.	1. Party division denounced, I. 10 to 18 2. Worldly wisdom denounced, I. 19 to II. 16. 3. The true ministry (a) Hindrances, III. 1 to 4. (b) Source of success, III. 5 to 10. (c) Two kinds, 11 to 23. (d) Our Master, IV. 1 to 21.	1. Immorality denounced, V.¹ 2. Want of brotherly love strongly rebuked, VI. 1 to 8.	1. On marriage, celibacy and divorce, VI. 9 to VII. 2. On meat offered to idols, VIII. 3. Paul on his authority and example, IX. 4. Lesson from Israel, X. 1 to 15. 5. Law of love in relation to eating and drinking, X. 16 to 33.	1. Womanly modesty at Church, XI. 1 to 16. 2. Disorders at the Lord's table rebuked, XI. 17 to 34. 3. Spiritual gifts. XII. 4. On love, XIII. 5. Prophecy, the greatest gift, XIV. 6. The grand Resurrection chapter, XV. 7. "Concerning the Collection." XVI. 1 to 4.	Conclusion.

MESSAGE

A careful study of the New Testament reveals this fact, that our Lord's full title—Lord Jesus Christ—is never given to Him, *except when the writer is seeking to declare and emphasize the Lordship of Christ.* How significant, then, is it to find this title given to our Lord six times in the first ten verses (2, 3. 7, 8, 9, 10). The name "Lord" is very prominent (I. 31, II. 8, 16, III. 20, IV. 4, V. 4, 5, VI. 13, etc.) "There is deep significance in this, for all the disorders that had crept into their lives had arisen through failure to recognize Jesus Christ as Lord." Oh, crown Him Lord of *your* life!

CIRCUMSTANCES

After writing the first epistle to the Corinthians, and sending it by the hand of Titus, Paul left Ephesus, his departure, no doubt, being hastened by the tumult (see Acts XIX. 23 to 41), and slowly made his way to Troas (preaching en route) where he had arranged to meet Titus on his return from Corinth. Here Paul was much used of God. But the return of Titus was delayed. This greatly troubled Paul. So great was his anxiety to hear of the reception and result of his first letter, that, fearing the worst, he crossed the Ægean Sea, and went to meet him. Eventually they met at Philippi (2 Cor. II. 12, 13, VII. 5, 6). Paul was probably ill in body, too (2 Cor. I. 8 to 10).

PURPOSE

From Titus, Paul learned that his first letter had served its purpose, both the Church and the culprit being thoroughly repentant (2 Cor. VII. 7 to 16, II. 1 to 11). But the same messenger informed him of a fresh peril—Judaising teachers, armed with letters of introduction from the Church at Jerusalem, had arrived at Corinth, preaching another Gospel, and denouncing the apostleship of Paul—that the result of their labours was the rapid growth of a party hostile to him (III. 1 to 3. IV. 2, X. 10, XI. 1 to 4, 12, 13). Therefore, he wrote this second epistle (1) to explain why he had not as yet been able to visit them (I. 15 to 24, II. 1 to 3); (2) to praise them for obeying his first letter VII. 4, 15); (3) to urge the restoration of the repentant transgressor (II. 6 to 9); (4) to warn a few who were yet unrepentant (XII. 21, XIII. 2); (5) to warn them against the false teachers (XI. 3, 4, 13); (6) to vindicate his apostleship (XII. with XI.); and to urge them to pay their promised contribution for the poor saints at Jerusalem (VIII. 10, 11).

ANALYSIS

It is almost impossible to analyse this letter, as it is the least systematic of Paul's writings. It resembles an African river. For a time it flows smoothly on, and one is hopeful of a satisfactory analysis, then suddenly there comes a mighty cataract and a terrific upheaval, when the great depths of his heart are broken up. However, it falls roughly into three sections.

(1) EXPLANATION	(2) EXHORTATION	(3) VINDICATION
I. to VII.	VIII. and IX.	X. to XIII.
He explains the reason of his delay in visiting them, why he spoke so plainly and sternly in his first letter, why he was so concerned on their behalf, and gives an account of his sufferings.	He exhorts them to a prompt fulfilment of their promise to contribute for the relief of the needy brethren in Jerusalem, especially as he had boasted to the Macedonian churches of that promise.	A change in the Apostle's tone can be detected in this section—there is sternness, and irony, as he vindicates his apostleship, and proves his right to their love and respect.

REVELATION OF PAUL

This second epistle *contains more of Paul's personal history than any other of his epistles*. It is, in fact, a revelation of Paul himself. It certainly is a manifestation of the amazing *depth and strength of his love*, and the secret is V. 14. It shows that he suffered from *bodily weakness at times* (I. 8 to 10, XII. 7-9); and no wonder, when one remembers his labours, and notes his sufferings and hardships (XI. 23 to 33); do not X. 10 and XI. 6 give us a little knowledge of his personal appearance and speech? Chapter XII. reveals a secret Paul kept for fourteen years.

MESSAGE

The epistle contains many glowing and brilliant metaphors (II. 15 (Twentieth Century Version), III. 3, III. 18 (R.V.), IV. 7, V. 20, etc.) and most suggestive statements for preachers, but its special message is two-fold. The two words that are met with most frequently are "Comfort" and "Ministry," and the study of both these words forms helpful Bible readings, besides giving its message.

COMFORT.—Source, I. 3; purpose, I. 4; compensations, I. 5; Christian duty, II. 7; how God sometimes comforts, VII. 6, 7, 13; imperative command, XIII. 11.

MINISTRY.—Satan has his, XI. 15; God has His, VI. 4; Message, IV. 5, I. 19, II. 12; a spiritual, III. 6, and glorious ministry, III. 8, leads to the transformation of character, III. 3; helps us not to faint, IV. 1; is a ministry of reconciliation, V. 18; necessitates carefulness, VI. 3.

POINTS

This epistle is notable for many things. Often God is spoken of as Almighty in the Old Testament, but he is only referred to as such ten times in the New, nine of these being in Revelation, and the other in this epistle (2 Cor. VI. 18), but its most notable point is that *it provides us with the form of benediction now so general*, and with which most Christian gatherings are closed (see 2 Cor. XIII. 14).

GALATIA

Galatia, a broad strip of country in Asia Minor, was inhabited by a mixed race, with Gauls predominating. These Gauls left their own country now) known as France) 300 years B.C., and after a successful military campaign, settled here, and gave their name to the land. Even to-day, travellers are struck with "the fair hair and blue eyes that mark an affinity between the pastoral tribes of Galatia and the peasantry of western France."

CHURCH

Here Paul, delayed by illness (IV. 13) during his second missionary tour (Acts XVI. 6), preached the Gospel. It appears that the burden of his addresses was "Christ Crucified" (III. 1), that he was received as a heavenly messenger (IV. 14), that he was able to establish a Church there (I. 6), and that they lavished their love upon him (IV. 15).

PURPOSE

(1) But the Celtic temperament is very fickle, loving novelty and change, and when the Judaising teachers came that way, teaching salvation by works and the necessity of circumcision, etc., in unseemly haste (I. 6) they embraced their views

(2) Paul heard of their backslidden condition, and so urgent did the matter seem, that, though no amanuensis was near, he did, what he did not usually do, wrote the whole of the epistle himself (VI. 11).

PECULIARITIES

(1) Note (a) There is an unusual tone of severity about this epistle. (b) Paul begins without a word of praise or thanksgiving, which is most unusual of him. (c) There is no request for prayer in this epistle—how could they pray for others, backsliders as they were?

(2) This epistle has done more than any other book of the New Testament for the emancipation of the Christian from Judaism, Romanism, Ritualism, and every other form of externalism that has ever threatened the freedom and spirituality of the Gospel.

(3) This was Luther's favourite epistle, and played a very important part in the glorious Reformation under the Reformers.

(4) Galatians "takes up controversially what Romans puts systematically"; and it shows the Lord Jesus as the Deliverer.

(5) The doctrine of Justification by faith is stated here more emphatically than in any other of Paul's writings. Note the emphasis Paul places on the inward and spiritual nature of the Christian faith in contrast to the mere externalism of the other "isms," see I. 16, II. 20, IV. 6 and 19.

ANALYSIS

This epistle is in four parts, which are subdivided into eleven sections, as follows:

(A) Introduction.		(B) Paul's Apostolic Authority.		(C) Defence and Exposition of Salvation and Sanctification by Faith *alone*.					(D) Conclusion.	
(1) Paul's Cool **Greeting**	(2) Paul's Stern **Reproof.**	(3) Paul's Gospel received from the Lord by direct **Revelation.**	(4) With Peter and others, great **Contention.**	(5) **Justification** by faith alone.	(6) **Divine Union** by faith.	(7) Reception of the Spirit by faith.	(8) **Sonship** through faith.	(9) **Liberty** through faith.	(10) **Service** in compassion and faith.	(11) **Conclusion.**
I. 1 to 5.	I. 6 to 9.	I. 10 to 24.	II. 1 to 15.	II. 16 to 19.	II. 20, 21.	III. 23 to IV. 31.	III. 1 to 22.	V.	VI. 1 to 10.	VI. 11 to 18.
With the barest salutation, he introduces the atonement, a truth once so dear to them, but now practically rejected by them.	He expresses his great surprise that they should so soon have accepted another Gospel, which was no Gospel at all.	Here he proves that he received his Gospel direct from the Lord Himself, in the wilds of Arabia.	Paul herein shows how he had always resisted the Judaisers, even going to the length of openly correcting Peter.	As Jews, they had experienced the inability of the Law to save. But what the Law could not do, Grace had done. Justification is by faith, and faith alone.	Faith not only leads us into Justification, but also into identification with Christ, in His death and resurrection, and union of the soul with the Lord.	But we are not only Justified, but also Sanctified by faith. Here the Justified state leads to a state of sanctification, and that by faith.	Not only are we Justified by faith, but we also become the children of God, through faith, and are enabled to realize our sonship by the indwelling Spirit.	Christ leads into glorious freedom —a liberty we must preserve at all cost. But liberty does not mean license.	We must deal compassionately and sympathetically with each other, especially the erring ones.	What a magnificent conclusion this is! Note R. V. rendering of verse 17.

The Epistle to the EPHESIANS

THE CHURCH

Paul was the founder of the Church at Ephesus. His first visit, in the spring of A.D. 54. was very brief, as he had to be in Jerusalem by a certain date, to complete a vow (Acts XVIII. 19 to 21), but afterward he spent three years of whole-hearted and intensely active service there (Acts XIX. 8 to 10, XX. 31).

THE EPISTLE

This epistle was written during Paul's first imprisonment at Rome, ten years after he had established the Ephesian Church. It has been well said that "*this epistle surpasses all others in sublimity of style, and is pre-eminent, even amongst the apostle's writings, for the sustained majesty of its theme, and for a certain spiritual splendour, both in conception and language,*" Dr. Pierson has called it "*Paul's third heaven epistle,*" for in it "*he soars from the depths of ruin to the heights of redemption.*" It has also been called "*the Alps of the New Testament, for here we are bidden by God to mount, step by step, until we reach the highest possible point where man can stand, even the presence of God Himself.*"

ITS TEACHING

Its distinctive teaching is concerning the Church as the Body of Christ, and believers as members of that sacred Body. It proves that *the Father not only prepared a body for the Lord Jesus to suffer in, but also a body mystical, in which He should be glorified.* As we have two epistles on Justification (Romans and Galatians), so we have two concerning the Church—this and Colossians. Both the latter were written at the same time, and at first sight may seem alike; but on closer inspection, we find in Ephesians the emphasis laid upon the Church as the Body of Christ, whilst in Colossians, Christ as the Head of the Body is the prominent truth.

KEY WORDS

(1) This epistle abounds in key words—"In Christ Jesus," etc., (I, 1, 6, 7, 11, 13, II. 6, 10, 13, 21, 22, IV. 21), "Walk," (II. 2, 10, IV. 1, 17, V. 2, 8, 15,) "Together." (I. 10, II 5, 6, 21.) "Therefore," (II. 19, IV. 1, 17, V, 1, 7, 24.) "Wherefore," (I. 15, II. 11, III. 13, IV. 8, 25. V. 14, 17, VI. 13.) "According to," (I. 5, 9, 11, 19, II. 2. III. 7, 11, 16, 20.) "In Heavenly places," (I. 3, 20, II. 6, III. 10.) "Riches," (I. 7. 18, II. 7, III. 8, 16.) "Love," (I. 4, III. 17, IV. 2, 15, 16, V. 2.)

(2) This epistle gives three distinct figures of the Church of Christ: (1) Temple (II. 21, 22), (2) Human Body (I. 22, 23, IV. 15), (3) Bride (V. 25 to 32), but that of the Body is emphasised. and is the main teaching of Ephesians.

(A) Doctrinal Section I. to III. | (B) Practical Section IV. to VI.

(1) Greetings to Members of His Body.	(2) Blessings for Members of His Body.	(3) PRAYER on Behalf of Members of His Body.	(4) CHRIST the HEAD of His Body, the Church.	(5) How we are FITTED to be Members of His Body.	(6) A Close and Blessed Association is Membership of His Body.	(7) GENTILES have a Portion and Place in His Body.	(8) The UNITY of His Body.	(9) The UNIFYING POWERS of His Body.	(10) The EDIFYING of His Body.	(11) The DUTIES of Members of His Body.
I. 1 and 2.	I. 3 to 14.	I. 15 to 21.	I. 22 and 23.	II. 1 to 10.	II. 11 to 22.	III.	IV. 1 to 3.	IV. 4 to 6.	IV. 7 to 16.	IV. 17 to VI.
"In Christ Jesus" (as the body is joined to the head) is the key phrase of this epistle. "In" Him we are and have all.	These verses reveal to us the eternal counsels and purposes of God, the Father, "Gather together in one all things in Christ." Verse 10 is suggestive. Note the nine 'alls" in this first chapter,	There are two of Paul's prayers in this epistle, here, and in III. 14 to 21. In his first, he prays that they may have *light to know*, and in his second, *strength to know*.	What exalted teaching is this! Jesus exalted to be the Head of a new order, of a new Body, the Church. In Colossians this is more fully developed.	God's work is here seen in forming the body, the members of which were dead in sins, but had been forgiven, quickened, and seated with Christ.	"Remember"— "where the sweetness of forgiveness is, there is the sadness of remembrance." Compare "no more strangers" (19) with 1 Peter II. 11.	This teaching concerning the Gentiles was specially revealed to Paul by the Lord, and the preaching of it was the cause of his imprisonment (see verse 1).	The members of His Body must not only abstain from anything to break that unity, but do all they can to foster and strengthen it.	1, The unifying powers of the Body are here shown. 2. Observe, not only "above all" and "through all" but "in you all."	1. Various gifts for the edifying of the Body. 2. The word "perfecting" is a remarkable one, meaning "repairing" or "making good the damage."	1, Concerning "*Walk,*" IV.17 to V. 20. 2. Concerning the *home life,* V. 21 to VI. 4, 3. Concerning *employment,* VI. 5 to 9. 4. Concerning "*war fare,*" VI. 10 to 24.

THE EPISTLE

(1) This epistle ought to be greatly valued by Gentiles, because it was written to the first Church founded in Europe. (Acts XVI. 9 to 40).

(2) The Bishop of Durham calls this "*one of the fairest and dearest regions of the Book of God.*" Though not one of the most remarkable or deepest, it is yet one of the sweetest of Paul's writings. It is more in the nature of a love letter to the Philippians, who excelled all others in devoted attachment to St. Paul. Through this letter we get a glimpse into the apostle's heart.

NOTABLE POINTS

(a) There is not a solitary quotation from the Old Testament Scriptures in it.

(b) The word "joy" or "rejoice" is found in every chapter. I. 4, 18, 25, 26, II. 2, 16, 18, III 1, 3, IV. 1, 4, 10.

(c) Note the recurrence of the word "mind," I. 27, II. 2, 3, 5, III. 15, 19, IV. 2, 7.

(d) Only three times is the Spirit mentioned, but how significant is each passage: (1) Supply of Spirit, I. 19' (2) Fellowship of the Spirit, II. 1; (3) Worship by the Spirit. III. 3.

(e) Dr. Pierson calls this epistle "*the Disciple's Balance Sheet*," for here the apostle shows the renunciations and compensations of a disciple, and the excess in his favour, III. 4 to 14.

(f) This epistle contains less of censure and more of praise than any other.

THE CHURCH

The Philippian Church was noted for its generosity. Repeatedly had it ministered to the wants of Paul (IV. 15, 16). Hearing of the apostle's imprisonment in Rome, they sent help again by the hands of Epaphroditus (IV. 10, 18). who. however, was smitten down on his arrival by an almost fatal illness. Somehow news of this illness had reached Philippi, to their consternation; and on his recovery, Epaphroditus was anxious to reassure them in person (II. 25 to 28), so Paul wrote this letter for him to take.

OBJECT

(1) The object of this letter was two-fold. First, to thank them for their generous gift. But there was a more serious purpose. Through Epaphroditus, the apostle had learned that dissension had broken out there, threatening the peace and usefulness of the Church.

(2) Note (a) *Women, right from the first had an important place in that Church.* *Two of the leading women had fallen out* (IV. 2).
    (b) The subject of dissension was probably some phase of the doctrine of Christian perfection. Note the prominence given to this truth.
    (c) Apparently the Church had taken sides, and had split up into two divisions.

(3) Observe how Paul seeks to bring unity again :
    (a) He refuses to recognise two parties, hence is constantly using the word "all." Take your pencil and mark "all," and you will be surprised.
    (b) He did not lecture the women, indeed makes no reference to them until the letter is nearly ended. How wise this act was!
    (c) Instead, he seeks to fill their minds with our Lord's greatness, and yet His lowliness, meekness, and long-suffering.
    (d) Very pressing exhortations to unity. Ponder over I. 27, II. 1, 2, 3; III. 15, 16, IV. 2.

(4) Sometimes I have thought that this epistle ought to have succeeded, and not have divided, Ephesians and Colossians, with their wonderful Church teaching; but on further reflection one can only be thankful it is where it is. Ephesians speaks of the Church as the Body of Christ, and the mystic unity existing between HIM and the Church. This Philippian letter shows how that unity can be broken or maintained.

(1) Salutation to ALL.	(2) Prayer for ALL.	(3) Christ Glorified through Paul's imprisonment an encouragement to ALL.	(4) Christ's Lowliness and Humility an example to ALL.	(5) Warnings for ALL.	(6) Exhortations for ALL.	(7) Concluding Greeting from ALL and to ALL.
I. 1 and 2.	I. 3 to 11.	I. 12 to 30.	II.	III.	IV. 1 to 20.	IV. 21 to 23
1. Note how Paul goes out of his way to emphasise that he was writing to ALL 2. "At Philippi," but thank God "in Christ Jesus."	1. Paul's prayers make an interesting study. 2. He prayed for them : (a) With joy. (b) For more love. (:) Not a blind love. (l) Have good taste. (e) Sincere. (f) Filled with fruits.	1. His imprisonment led to wide dissemination of Gospel. 2. Many preached with unworthy motives. 3. Paul's love for the Lord, verse 21. 4. And their sufferings would also glorify the Lord, provided they were *one.*	1. As pride is foe of unity, he puts the humility of the Lord as an example for them to copy, 1 to 5. 2. His seven-fold humiliation and exaltation, 6 to 11. 3. The effect of this should be humility, and lowliness of heart and mind, the cure for spiritual pride.	1. Against false teachers, 1 to 3. 2. Against self-righteousness, 4 to 6. 3. Against absolute, instead of progressive perfection, 7 to 14 (with I. 6, 9, II. 12, 13). 4. Against false professors, 15 to 19	1. Unity, 1 to 3. 2. Rejoicing, 4. 3. Self control, 5. 4. Peace of God, 6, 7. 5. What to think, 8. 6. Contentment, and its source, 11 to 14.	1. "*Every* saint " saluted. 2. "*All* saints " send salutation. 3. Saints even in Cæsar's household.

THE EPISTLE To The COLOSSIANS

HERESY AT COLOSSE

(1) Paul had, as *fellow prisoner in Rome*, one by the name of Epaphras (Philemon 23). When this man was converted, we know not—probably during Paul's three years' ministry at Ephesus. As it is quite clear that the Apostle had not founded the Colossian Church (see I. 4, 7, 8, II. 1), it is thought that Epaphras had done so (I. 7, IV. 12).

(2) It was from Epaphras that Paul learned that heresy had broken out at Colosse. What its precise nature was is a matter of discussion. but, judging by the contents of the Epistle, we conclude that it was a curious mixture of Judaism, Gnosticism, and Asceticism, with angel worship, etc. One form of this heresy has been thus described: " Flesh is essentially evil, God is essentially holy; between the essentially holy and the essentially evil, there can be no communion. It is impossible, said the heresy, for the essentially holy to touch the essentially evil. There is an infinite gulf between the two, and the one cannot touch and be intimate with the other. The heresy then had to devise some means by which this gulf might be crossed, and by which the essentially holy God could come into communion with an essentially evil state in which mankind was dwelling. What did it do? It said that out of the essentially holy God there emanated a being slightly less holy, and then out of the second holy one, there emanated a third one less holy still, and then out of the third a fourth, and so on, with an increasing dilution of holiness, with divinity more and more impoverished, until One appeared (Jesus) who was so emptied of divinity, of holiness, so nearly like man, that He could touch man." (Jowett.)

(3) One thing is certain, as Bishop Moule points out, " It was a doctrine of God and of salvation which cast a cloud over the glory of of Jesus Christ—it put Jesus Christ into the background," This heresy, anyone can see, (1) destroyed the supreme lordship and sovereignty of Jesus Christ—it dethroned Him, emptying Him of divinity, and (2) destroyed the supreme mediatorship of Christ, making Him only one of a multitude of mediators.

PURPOSE

One could profitably study this Epistle by looking at its portrait of the Church (in which the Headship of Christ is emphasised, I. 18, II. 10, 19) of the Christian (I. 13, 14, etc.), and Christian worker (IV. 7 to 13, etc.), but the chief object and purpose of the letter is to draw a faithful portrait of the Lord Jesus in all His dignity, Deity, and glory.

ANALYSIS

It is in two main divisions, each of which is subdivided into three sections as follows :

(A) DOCTRINAL SECTION			(B) PRACTICAL SECTION		
(1) **Thanksgivings** on behalf of the Colossians	(2) **Intercession** on behalf of the Colossians	(3) THE SUPREME DIGNITY, GLORY, AND UNAPPROACHABLE PRE-EMINENCE OF THE LORD JESUS, VIEWED FROM EVERY STANDPOINT	(4) **Warnings** against Error and Heresy	(5) **Union with Christ** and Its Results	(6) **Greetings** to the Colossians
I. 1 to 8.	I. 9 to 14.	I. 15 to II. 3.	II. 4 to 23.	III. to IV. 6.	IV. 7 to end.
1. Note, faith first exercised before love manifested, 4.	1. Note the expression, "pray for you, *and to desire,*" 9.	This is the very heart of the Epistle. In no dictatorial manner, but in a hushed and awed mood, Paul gives a heart-moving and soul subduing affirmation of the glory of the Lord Jesus : *HERE CHRIST IS SEEN AS "ALL AND IN ALL."*	They are warned against : 1. Enticing words, 4.	As joined to our risen Lord, there must be :	What a rich collection of Christian workers we have here. Note the peculiarities of each.
2. In verse 8 we have the only mention of the Holy Spirit in the Epistle.	2. This prayer has no formal ending, but merges into " a worshipping and enraptured confession of the glory of the Christ of God."	1. In DEITY, equality with God—image of God, 15, abode of fulness, 19 and II. 9, and firstborn, 15, a title of dignity. 2. In CREATION, Creator of the universe—Wherein is shown that He is cause, Head and goal of the created universe. verse 16. 3. In PROVIDENCE, Sustainer of the universe—Verse 17, He, who by one creative act formed the universe, by continuous activity sustains it. 4. In CHURCH. In Ephesians we see what the body is to the Head, in Colossians what the Head is to the Body—Verse 18, whilst in Ephesians the emphasis is placed on the Church as body, in Colossians the emphasis is on Christ as its Head. 5. In REDEMPTION—20 to 23. He is the *only* Redeemer, and His redemption has wide extent. 6. In GOSPEL MYSTERY—24 to 29, the mystery is "Christ in you."	2. Vain Philosophy, 8. 3. Ritualism, 16, 17. 4. Angel worship, 18. 5. Empty and vain self humblings and denials, 20 to 23.	1. Heavenly mindedness, 1 to 3. 2. Holy living in home, service and all the walks of life, 4 to IV. 6.	

FIRST OF EPISTLES

This was the first of St. Paul's Epistles, and was written by him from Corinth, probably about the year 53 A.D.

THE CHURCH

The Church at Thessalonica was planted by St. Paul in the course of his second missionary journey (Acts XVII. 1 to 9), after his memorable visit to Philippi. Though St. Paul could only have spent about a month there, yet he laboured so strenuously and faithfully, that a Church was not only founded, but firmly established. Like the man in Acts III. 7 to 9, these young converts dispensed with the customary crawling and creeping stage, walking briskly right away: and they made such rapid growth that the Apostle could immediately begin to feed them with strong meat. *i.e.*, "Election," I. 4; "Holy Spirit," verse 6; "Trinity," verses 1 and 6; "Second coming of Christ," I. 10; "Holiness," IV. 1 to 3; truths and doctrines now, alas, only considered suitable for those who have been long on the Heavenly way.

PURPOSE OF EPISTLE

(1) By chapter III. 6 to 8, we learn that this first Epistle was written on the return of Timothy, whom Paul had sent from Athens (III. 1, 2). He was greatly cheered by the report of their vigorous and healthy state, but *hastened to correct some erroneous views they held concerning the Lord's coming.* For instance, they were in sorrow concerning some who had died, thinking that they would have no part in the glory of the second advent of the Lord; and others were so overwhelmed by the thought of the imminence of the Lord's return that they had ceased to work, IV. 13 to 18, and 11, 12.

(2) The teaching concerning our Lord's coming *for* His own was not known until the Lord revealed it to Paul (note " by the word of the Lord," IV. 15).

(3) Our Lord's coming is mentioned 318 times in the 260 chapters of the New Testament, occupying one in every twenty verses from Matthew to Revelation. Surely this should be sufficient to show its importance.

ANALYSIS

This short Epistle is in five sections, four of which end with statements concerning His coming, which admirably sums up previous teaching.

(1) Conversion and the Second Advent	(2) Service and the Second Advent	(3) Purity of Heart and Life and the Second Advent	(4) Bereavement and the Second Advent	(5) Alertness and the Second Advent
The Lord's Coming: **AN INSPIRING HOPE** for the YOUNG CONVERT	The Lord's Coming: **AN ENCOURAGING HOPE** for the FAITHFUL SERVANT	The Lord's Coming: **A PURIFYING HOPE** for the BELIEVER	The Lord's Coming: **A COMFORTING HOPE** for the BEREAVED	The Lord's Coming: **A ROUSING HOPE** for the SLEEPY CHRISTIAN
Chapter I.	Chapter II.	Chapter III to IV. 12.	Chapter IV. 13 to 18.	Chapter V.
1. Salutation - - Verse 1. 2. Thanksgiving because of (Verses 2 to 8) (a) Their splendid service. (b) Their patience of hope. (c) Their election. (d) Their acceptance of Gospel. (e) Their noble example (f) Their activity in preaching. 3. In their conversion (Verses 9 and 10) (a) they turned to God from idols (not from idols to God.) (b) To a life of service. (c) And to a life of expectancy, waiting for their Lord.	A remarkable summary of the nature of Paul's service: 1. Not in vain, verse 1. 2. Bold in spite of much opposition, verse 2. 3. Frank and open, verse 3. 4. Only for God's glory, 4 to 6. 5. Was gentle, 7 to 9. 6. Backed up by his holy living, 10 to 12. 7. Was successful, 13 to 18. 8. His greatest reward at the Lord's coming, next to seeing the Lord himself, would be the sight of his converts sharing in that great event, verses 19, 20.	1. Paul's anxiety, III. 1 to 4. 2. Paul felt he could not live if they did not stand fast, verse 8. 3. The coming of the Lord an incentive to (a) Holiness, III. 13. (b) Consistent walk, IV. 1. (c) Purity, IV. 3 to 8. (d) Brotherly love, IV. 9, 10. 4. Looking for His glorious appearing, does not mean a life of idleness, IV. 11, 12.	1. Our loved ones who have died in Him shall rise first. 2. And will accompany our Lord as He comes for us. *NOTE:* " I shall go to him but he shall not return to me," was all the broken-hearted David could utter concerning his dead child (2 Samuel XII. 23); but we who look for a Saviour, can say more than this, since " them also which sleep in Jesus, *will God bring with Him.*" *Our loved ones will* come to us.	1. Our Lord's coming will be " as a thief in the night," *i.e.* swiftly, quietly, suddenly, unexpectedly. 2. But He will not come " as a thief in the night " to those who are looking for Him, for we " are not in the darkness " (see verse 4), and He will not surprise us, for we are expecting Him. 3. This necessitates watchfulness on our part.

WHY THIS EPISTLE WAS WRITTEN

Not very long after writing and forwarding his first letter to the Christians at Thessalonica, St. Paul found it necessary to write again. The reason for this was that it had been reported to him that, owing to a forged letter and a false verbal message, both supposed to have come from the Apostle, with imaginary revelations of the Spirit (II. 2) given through some member or members of the Thessalonian Church, they were distressed at the thought that they were now passing through the great Tribulation, that the great and dreadful " Day of the Lord " had come.

TEACHING OF THE EPISTLE

(1) In this Epistle, he sets their minds at rest by declaring that certain events must take place before the " Day of the Lord " be ushered in, viz.: (1) A great falling away from the faith. (2) The coming of Christ *for* His people. (3) The coming into public view of the " Man of Sin," and his open and awful campaign against the Lord. (4) *Then* the coming of the Lord with His people in terrible judgment. (See II. 1 to 4 in the R.V.)

(2) In the first letter, Paul taught that the saints who had fallen asleep in Christ would share the coming of the Lord ; in his second he shows that the saints who are alive shall not be overtaken by the judgments of the " Day of the Lord " ; in his first, he taught the Lord's coming would be *sudden*, but in the second, he points out that " *sudden*" *does not mean* " *immediate*."

ANALYSIS

(1) Persecution and the Lord's Coming. The Coming of the Lord: ## A Comfort to the Persecuted I. 1 to 7.	(2) The Impenitent and the Lord's Coming. The Coming of the Lord: ## A Terror to the Unconverted I. 7 to 12.	(3) The Apostasy and the Lord's Coming. The Coming of the Lord : *For* His people leads to the Revealing of } THE MAN *With* His people means the Destruction of } OF SIN II. 1 to 12.	(4) Service and the Lord's Coming. The Delay of the Lord's coming means : ## Unique Opportunities for Service III. with II. 13 to 17.
1. *SALUTATION*, verses 1, 2. 2. *COMMENDATION*, verses 3, 4. If we look we shall often find something to commend in those whom we denounce or reprove. 3. *INSPIRATION*, verses 4 to 7. The fact of the Lord's second advent :— (*a*) Inspired them to a noble piety, leading to a growth in faith, and a deepening of love, verse 3; and (*b*) Inspired them to great patience and trustfulness in persecution, verse 4. (*c*) For on His arrival glaring wrongs would be righted and vengeance meted out to all their oppressors, verses 5 to 7.	1. These verses destroy the view that He will not come until the world is converted. 2. The world has never seen our Lord Jesus since it crucified Him. Like Joash (2 Chron. XXII., XXIII.) He is hidden in the Sanctuary; but now He will be publicly made known to the whole world. 3. What a vivid contrast there is between this and 1 Thess. IV. 14 to 18. (*a*) There He comes attended by *one* angel, here by many. (*b*) Then only seen by His own, here by all (Rev. I. 7). (*c*) Then "for," now "with" His saints (Jude 14). (*d*) Then He came for a peaceable object, now for Judgment (Jude 15).	1. It is important to note the R.V. renderings of verses 1 and 2, in order to understand this chapter aright. 2. This section contains one of the most important prophecies in the New Testament—the great Pauline prediction of Antichrist. 3. "Man of Sin" is a Hebrewism, meaning "a man of eminent wickedness." 4. Many hold the theory that the "Man of Sin" has already been revealed in the Pope. Whilst there are remarkable points here which harmonise with a just description of the character and history of the Papacy, we cannot but arrive at the conclusion, that *he is yet to come.* *NOTE :* 1. "The sin of man has its final outcome and fruition in the 'Man of Sin.' " (*Mauro*). 2. "Not until the Lord has caught up His own will the Lawless One come into public view." (*Mauro*). 3. "The mystery of godliness is God humbling Himself to become man; the mystery of iniquity is man exalting himself to become God." (*A. J. Gordon*).	1. With what relief Paul turned from this awful subject to the Believers, II. 13, 14. 2. Our Lord's delay gives us unique opportunities: First—Of loyalty to Him, II. 15 Second – Of evangelising the world, III. 1. Third—Of praying for His servants, III. 1, 2 Fourth - Of patient waiting for Him, III. 5. Fifth—Of living the separated life, III. 6 to 14. Sixth - Of tenderness towards the erring, III. 15.

First Epistle to TIMOTHY

TIMOTHY

Timothy was the son of a Greek father and a Jewish mother. He was converted at the age of fifteen, during Paul's ministry at Lystra (Acts XIV., 1 Timothy I. 2). Seven years afterwards he had so advanced in grace that he was "well reported," and became Paul's companion (Acts XVI.), and there then began one of those beautiful friendships between an older and a younger man, which are usually so helpful to both (Philippians II. 22).

CIRCUMSTANCES

Immediately on his release from his first imprisonment before he visited Spain (Romans XV. 24, Philemon 22), Paul probably visited Macedonia, Ephesus, etc. Not being able to stay long at Ephesus, he left Timothy to take charge of the work. This parting was a sore trial to Timothy (1 Timothy I. 3, 2 Timothy I. 4). To encourage and instruct Timothy (who was sensitive and timid, and not strong, V 23), Paul wrote and forwarded this letter from Corinth.

CHARACTER

The two letters to Timothy and the one to Titus are known as Pastoral Epistles. They were addressed to individuals, and not to congregations. Paul was about seventy when he wrote them, consequently we have in them the farewell words of the great Apostle to ministers and Christian workers. In them we have the mellow wisdom of old age. All Christian workers have, for centuries, found these letters a source of encouragement and help. One prominent minister declared that he read them every Sabbath evening for his own soul's welfare.

PECULIARITIES

There are several phrases only found in these Pastoral Epistles. (1) "God, my Saviour," a phrase common enough in the Old Testament, with one exception (Luke I. 47) is only found in the new Testament in the Pastoral Epistles (1 Timothy I. 1, II. 3, IV. 10, Titus I. 3, II. 10, 13, III. 4); (2) "Godliness" is another of the peculiar phrases confined entirely to these letters, with the exception of 2 Peter I. 3, 6, 7, III. 11 (1 Timothy II. 2, 10, III. 16, IV. 7, 8, VI. 3, 5, 6, 11, 2 Timothy III. 5, Titus I. 1); (3) "Sound" (healthful, R.V.), a medical metaphor Paul probably borrowed from Luke, the beloved physician, is only found here, ("mind," 2 Timothy I. 7, "words," 2 Timothy I. 13, "Doctrine, 1 Timothy I. 10, 2 Timothy IV. 3, Titus I. 9, II. 1, "Faith," Titus I. 13, "Speech." Titus II. 8); (4) "Man of God," often met with in the Old Testament, is only found twice in the New Testament, and then only in the Pastoral Epistles (1 Timothy VI. 11. 2 Timothy III. 17); (5) Remembering Timothy's sensitiveness, and the meaning of "Mercy" (see Luke X, 37. Genesis XXXIX. 21), it is most suggestive to find, only in the Pastoral Epistles, that "Mercy" is added to the usual couplet of "Grace and Peace" (see 1 Timothy I. 2, 2 Timothy I. 2, Titus I. 4, and the beginnings of other Epistles); (6) and only in the Pastoral Epistles do we find the "faithful sayings," *i.e.* Christian household proverbs (1 Timothy I. 15, III. 1, IV. 9, 10, 2 Timothy II. 11 to 13, Titus III. 8).

DIVISION

The purpose of the Epistle is admirably given in 1 Timothy III. 15, and the whole of the contents are designed to enable the young worker to rise to the height of 1 Timothy IV. 12.

(1) On the Imperative Need of **Sound Doctrine**	(2) On the Nature and Order of **Public Prayer**	(3) On the Qualifications Necessary for **Spiritual Oversight**	(4) The Christian Pastor's and Worker's **Spiritual Duties**
I.	II. 1 to 8.	II. 9 to III.	IV. to VI.

1. Introduction, 1, 2.
2. Why left, 3, 4.
3. Practical godliness, 5, 6.
4. The Law—its use and abuse, 7 to 11.
5. Personal testimony, 13 to 17.
6. A solemn charge, 18 to 20.
	1. What to pray for, 1 to 3.
	2. How to pray, 8.
	3. God's
	   (a) Pleasure, 3.
	   (b) Desire, 4.
	   (c) Provision, 5 to 7.
	   (d) Condition. IV. 10.
		1. The scope of the ministry, and adornment of women, II. 9 to 15.
		2. Qualifications necessary: Irreproachable in
		   (a) Family life, III. 2, 4, 5, 11, 12.
		   (b) Personal life, 2, 3, 6, 8.
		   (c) Public life, 7.
		   (d) Spiritual belief, 9.
			1. To warn others, IV. 1 to 6.
			2. To exercise oneself, IV. 7, 8, 9 to 16,
			3. How to treat others, V.
			4. Duty of servants. VI. 1, 2.
			5. Sundry exhortations, 3 to end.

STRIKING R.V. RENDERINGS

There are several striking and suggestive renderings in the R.V. of this Epistle :
(1) "Gospel of the Glory," I. 11, suggesting, not what the Gospel is, but what it is about.
(2) "His longsuffering," I. 16, *i.e.* He gives the necessary grace, and enables us to suffer long and patiently.
(3) "Which thou has followed until now," R.V. of IV. 6.
(4) "Ready to sympathise," VI. 18, R.V. *marg.*
(5) The finest definition of eternal life is VI. 19. *i.e.* "the life which is life indeed."

ANALYSIS No. 55

KEY WORD, "Ashamed." I. 8, 12, 16, II. 15.

MESSAGE — Loyalty to the Lord and Truth, in View of Persecution and Apostasy

Second Epistle to TIMOTHY

PAUL'S SECOND IMPRISONMENT

After writing his first Epistle to Timothy, Paul left Corinth, and set sail with Titus for Crete, where he left him to set the Church in order (Titus I. 5). On returning to the mainland, he wrote to Titus. On his way to Nicopolis, where he intended to winter (Titus III. 12), Trophimus was left at Miletum sick, and Erastus at Corinth (2 Timothy IV. 20). Probably, whilst at Nicopolis, he rushed over on a short visit to Troas, but was arrested in the house of Carpus, and hurried to Rome. His arrest was so sudden that he had no time to gather up his precious books and parchments, or even to wrap his cloak around him (2 Timothy IV. 13). This second imprisonment was very different from the former one : (1) Then he had his own hired house, now he is kept in close confinement ; (2) then he was accessible to all, now, even Onesiphorus could only find him with difficulty and at great risk (I, 16, 17) ; (3) then he was the centre of a large circle of friends, now, almost alone (IV 10 to 12) ; (4) then, he hoped for speedy liberation, now, he was expecting to die (IV, 6).

PAUL'S OBJECT IN WRITING

Paul had appeared before Nero once, but his case had been adjourned (IV. 16, 17). He expected to appear again in the winter, and wrote urging Timothy (who had been liberated, Hebrews XIII. 23), to come at once with Mark and the things that were left, (IV. 9, 11, 13, 21). But, uncertain whether Timothy would arrive in time (he did not, for the trial and death took place long before winter—in June), he desired to give a last warning as to heresies, and encouragement to zeal, courage, and patience.

CHARACTERISTICS OF EPISTLE

This was the *last Epistle* ever written by Paul. The *personal nature* of the Epistle is remarkable, for there are references to twenty-three individuals, and one of them (Claudia) is believed to have been a British princess. *Its style* is abrupt, without plan or method, strongly emotional, with a vivid remembrance of the past, and anxious thoughts for the future. Paul, like his beloved Lord, though bearing the burden of loneliness, and the consciousness of approaching death, *forgot himself* in thoughts of others. The Bishop of Durham writes : "I have often found it difficult deliberately to read these short chapters through, without finding something like a mist gathering in the eyes. The writer's heart beats in the writing." Only in this Epistle are we informed of the names of Timothy's relatives, and Moses' opponents." (See I. 5 and III. 8).

KEY. MESSAGE. AND ANALYSIS

Its key-word is "Ashamed." I must not be ashamed of my Lord, His Gospel, or His suffering saints (I.); How I can become a workman that "needeth not to be ashamed" (II. and III.) ! and then the Lord will not be ashamed to own and stand by me (IV).

(1) Loyalty to the Lord, His Truth, and Servants in spite of SUFFERING	(2) Loyalty to the Lord in Devoted SERVICE	(3) Loyalty to the Lord and His Truth in spite of APOSTASY	(4) The Lord standing by His Loyal Servant in DESERTION
I.	II.	III. to IV. 5.	IV. 6 to end.
1. Paul's — 1. Preaching - 1. / 2. Prayers - 3. / 3. Service - 3. / 4. Desires - 4. / 5. Thoughts - 5.	1 Five miniature parables on Christian service : (a) Restored invalid, 1. (b) Faithful steward, 2. (c) Hardy soldier, 3, 4. (d) An athlete, 5. (e) A Farmer, 6.	1. A saddening catalogue of Twentieth Century vices, 1 to 9.	1. The Christian Life under three metaphors. He speaks (IV. 7, 8) : (a) As a Soldier, likening life to a fight. (b) As an Athlete, likening life to a race. (c) As a Trustee, likening life to a sacred trust
2. Timothy's — 1. Early Days - 5. / 2. Beloved by Paul 2. / 3 Remembered by Paul 3,5. / 4. Desired by Paul 4.	2. The Christian worker's chief (a) Remembrance, 8. (b) Encouragement, 9. (c) Support, 13. (d) Study, 15.	2. The Holy Scriptures, 10 to 17. / 3. Two things Timothy knew : (a) The book of Paul's life and character, 10. (b) The inspired Book of God, 15.	2. Paul, the *man*, seen in his : (a) Sigh over loneliness, 9 to 12, 21. (b) Desire for bodily comfort, 13, 21. (c) Suffering through an enemy, 14, 15. (d) His plaintive lament over lack of legal aid, 16
3. Why even the most timid should not be ashamed of the Gospel, 6 to 14.	3. The Unmoved Foundation, 16 to 19.	4. What a Christian preacher must do in perilous times, IV. 1 to 6.	3. Paul, the *saint*, seen in his : (a) Exulting testimony concerning the Lord, 17. (b) Bold witness for the Lord, 17. (c) Confidence in the Lord, 18.
4. A sad statement, 15 to 18.	4. The great house and its vessels, 20 to 22. / 5. The power of gentleness, 23 to 26.	5. Paul's three "Readies" : Ready for (a) Service, Romans I. 15. (b) Suffering, Acts XXI. 13. (c) Sacrifice, 2 Timothy, IV. 6.	

SOME STRIKING R.V. RENDERINGS

(1) "Stir into flame," (I. 6), (2) " I know *Him*," (I. 12), (3) "The good deposit," (I. 14), (4) " Be strengthened," (II. 1), (5) "Take thy part in suffering," (II. 3.) (6) " Remember Jesus Christ," (II. 8), (7) " Handling aright," (II. 15,) (8) "I have fought *the* good fight," (IV. 7.)

FIVE OBJECTS OF LOVE

(1) Money (1 Timothy VI. 10), (2) Self (2 Timothy III. 2), (3) Pleasure (2 Timothy III. 4), (4) World (2 Timothy IV. 10), (5) The cure for all these is the fifth—His appearing (2 Timothy IV. 8).

The Epistle to TITUS

WRITER

Without doubt Paul wrote this Epistle. Some have thought that because of its *strong emphasis on works* (I. 16, II. 7, 14, III. 1, 8, 14), Paul did not write it; but III. 5 is a sufficient answer to that objection. It was *written about the same time,* and at the same place as 1 Timothy.

TITUS

It is quite clear that Titus was *one of Paul's converts* (I. 4). He must have been converted in the early years of Paul's ministry, for he accompanied Paul and Barnabas to Jerusalem at the conclusion of their first Missionary journey, seventeen years after Paul's conversion. (See Gal. II. 1.) Titus differed from Timothy in many respects. Whilst Timothy had been brought up as a Jew, and was circumcised by Paul, *Titus was a pure Gentile,* and was not circumcised, (Gal. II. 3.) He must have been *older than Timothy in years and grace;* and certainly was a *much stronger man physically and morally,* for Paul seems less anxious about the conduct of Titus, and the way others might treat him, than he was about Timothy.

CRETIANS.

Paul does *not give the Cretians a very good character.* (I. 12, 13.) "The Cretians are said to have been a turbulent race—or rather a group of turbulent races—neither peaceable among themselves, nor very patient of foreign dominion. Previous to their conquest by the Romans in B.C. 67, they had been accustomed to democratic forms of government, and therefore would be likely to feel the change to the Roman yoke more acutely. For all these reasons, Paul must have known that he was charging Titus (in III. 1) to give instructions which would be very unwelcome, even to the Cretian converts." Recognising the difficulties, Paul (who had great faith in the wisdom and ability of Titus, and had entrusted to him delicate missions *e.g.* to the Corinthians, 2 Cor. II. 13, VII. 6, 7,) on leaving Crete after a visit, left Titus to put things in order. (I. 5.)

NOTABLE POINTS

(1) This Epistle contains *two of the most comprehensive statements of Christian truth* to be found in the New Testament, (II. 11 to 14, III. 4 to 7.)
(2) The only time Paul calls himself a "bondman of God," is in this epistle, (see I. 1, R.V.)
(3) Paul is the only New Testament writer who *quotes from Heathen writers.* He does so three times; (1) In this epistle (I. 12), (2) Acts XVII. 28, and (3) 1 Cor. XV. 33).
(4) This Epistle enables us to see that Christ's personal and pre-millenial coming, of which Paul wrote so fully to the Thessalonians thirteen years before, *was still to him in his old age a blessed hope* (II. 13.)

ANALYSIS

(1) Emphasis in this section is on CHURCH ORDER. Key—I. 5.	(2) Emphasis in this section is on DOCTRINE. Key—II. 1, 2, 7, 10.	(3) Emphasis in this section is on WORKS. Key—III. 1, 8, 14.
AN ORDERLY CHURCH	**A SOUND CHURCH**	**A PRACTICAL CHURCH**
I.	II.	III.
1. Paul's loving and suggestive greeting, 1 to 4. (Note - Verse 2 is a striking contrast to the lying character of the Cretians, see verse 12.) 2. Object in leaving Titus, 5. 3. Qualifications for eldership, 6 to 9. 4. Unruly character of Cretians, 10 to 16. 5. Note that suggestive statement in verse 15: "Unto the pure all things are pure."	1. A message for (a) Titus, verses 1, 7, 8, 15, (b) Aged, verses 2, 3. (c) Young, verses 4 to 6. (d) Slaves, verses 9, 10. 2. Backed up by Paul giving, in a sentence, all the Gospel—past, present, and future, 11 to 14.	Verses. 1. Practical citizenship - 1 2. Practical godliness - 2 3. A sad retrospect - 3 4. What led to our transformation- 4 to 7 5. Need for practical piety - 8 6. What to avoid - 9 7. Whom to avoid ; 10, 11 8. Conclusion - 12 to 15

MESSAGE

(1) God's ideal for a Church: Orderly organization, soundness in faith and morals, and practical works of piety and philanthropy.
(2) God's ideal for a Christian worker: A love of order and method, a healthy and living orthodoxy, a sober mien, and chastened speech.

PAUL'S PRIVATE CORRESPONDENCE

Some time ago, that famous editor and literary authority, the Rev. Sir W. Robertson Nicoll, wrote: "If I were to covet any honour of authorship, it would be this: That some letters of mine might be found in the desks of my friends when their life struggle is ended." Whether Paul coveted this honour or no, one private letter of his was cherished. Of all Paul's *private* correspondence, this is the only example that has been preserved. It is the briefest of all Paul's Epistles. It is a gem.

THE STORY IN THE EPISTLE

A slave of Philemon (who was an important member of the Church at Colosse), Onesimus by name, had absconded, and made his way to Rome, apparently with the aid of money stolen from his master. There he was providentially brought under the influence of Paul, was converted, and endeared himself to the Apostle by his grateful and devoted service. But he was Philemon's lawful slave, and Paul could not think of retaining him permanently in his service, as he could not use the servant, and benefit by his labours, without his master's knowledge.

PAUL'S PROBLEM

(1) He wished to save the runaway slave from the severe and cruel punishment he merited according to Roman law.

(2) And he wanted to conciliate Philemon, without humiliating Onesimus; to commend the wrongdoer without extenuating his offence. How was this to be done? That was the problem confronting the aged Apostle.

PAUL'S STRATEGY

(1) He feels the slave must not encounter his outraged master alone, so secures a mediator in Tychicus, who was on his way there.

(2) He wrote this personal letter to Philemon, for Onesimus to take with him, a letter which is a model of tact and courtesy.

(3) And then, to make it more difficult for Philemon *not* to pardon and restore the culprit, he commends him to the whole Church (see Col. IV. 9).

ITS DIVISION AND KEY-WORD

(1) It falls naturally into four divisions. **Greeting** (1 to 3), (2) **splendid character of Philemon commended** (4 to 7), (3) **Intercession for Onesimus** (8 to 21), (4) **Salutation and conclusion** (22 to 25).

(2) Its key-word is '' Receive." Note how in verses 12, 15, 17, he strikes a louder note and a higher key each time he repeats it.

THE EPISTLE IS OF VALUE

First—As a Revelation of Paul's character. We learn more accurately the real character of a man from his private letters than from his public correspondence Whilst a person shines in the latter, he often shows himself in his true colours in the former. Yet we find by a study of this brief Epistle, the consistency of Paul's character—he is the same courteous (it has been called "the courteous Epistle"), lovable, humble, holy, unselfish man.

Second—As an example of Paul's Tact and Wisdom. It is a masterpiece, and a model of graceful, tactful, and delicate pleading.

(1) Desiring to touch a chord of tenderness in Philemon's heart, he mentions several times the fact that he was a prisoner (1, 9, etc).

(2) He cordially acknowledges Philemon's excellencies, thus making it most difficult for him not to exercise them in forgiving Onesimus (4 to 7).

(3) By delaying to mention the name of Onesimus, until he had thus carefully paved the way.

(4) By refusing to command with the authority of an Apostle, but pleading as a bosom friend (verses 8, 9, 20).

(5) By *earnest* entreaty (note "beseech"), referring to Onesimus as "my son" (10), and assuming Philemon would do as asked (verse 21)

(6) By frank acknowledgment of the wrong done (11), and promise to make good any loss (verses 18, 19).

(7) Though once unprofitable (11), Paul could vouch now of a thorough change that had taken place, and could guarantee the same (13).

(8) By his genial play upon words (2, 11), and touching upon the Providential aspect of the question (15).

(9) By his careful choice of words. He says "departed," not "fled" or "escaped." He would use no word that might awaken resentful feelings in the master, and he therefore chooses one that describes, not the quality of the servant's act, but simply its external aspect. "For a *season*"—only a short while (15).

(10) By mentioning the hope he had of soon being liberated and seeing him (22), and how could he face Paul if he did not do as requested?

Third—As an illustration of the Gospel Method of Social Reform. This Epistle has been appealed to by the friends and advocates of slavery, as furnishing a support or apology for that institution. Could slavery exist long if verses 16 and 17 were put into practice? It is a good illustration of the reforming influence of the Gospel, which seeks to gain its end by persuasion, rather than by compulsion; by gentleness, rather than by dynamite. It seeks to overthrow by a process of sapping.

Fourth—As an Analogy of our Redemption. "The sinner is God's property, and he has not only run away from his Master, but robbed Him. The Law affords him no right of Asylum, but Grace concedes him the right of appeal. He flees for refuge to Jesus, whom God counts as Partner. In Him he is begotten anew, as a son, and finds both an Intercessor and a Father; he returns to God, and is received, not as a slave, but as Christ Himself, and all the debt is put to Christ's account."

The Epistle to the HEBREWS

AUTHORSIHP

The writer of this Epistle is unknown. Eusebius tells us that Pantœnus of Alexandria (second century) assigned the authorship to Paul, Tertullian of Carthage (third century) declared Barnabas was the writer, Luther thought that Apollus had written it, Dr. Campbell Morgan thinks it bears traces of Paul's *thinking* and Luke's *writing*, and Dr. Schofield believes that we have preserved in this Epistle some of Paul's synagogue addresses. It must have been written about A.D. 64, as the Temple is referred to as still standing.

OBJECT

Owing to bitter persecution, the Jewish Christians were beginning to think they had lost everything (altar, priests, etc,) by espousing the cause of Christ. They had begun to undervalue Christian privileges, were getting absorbed with their sufferings, and were generally in a backsliding condition. The Apostle (for no donbt Paul wrote it) sent this letter to rectify these errors.

SKILL

Note the writer's skill in dealing with these despondent and despairing Christians: (1) First he fills their minds with the glory of the Person, and the grandeur of the work of the Lord Jesus, (2) he shows that, instead of losing all, they had gained all, (note " We have," in IV. 14, VI. 19, VIII. 1, X. 34, XIII. 10, 14,) and their Christianity was superior to Judaism; (3) and then he shows they had not yet suffered as much as others. Coleridge has beautifully pointed out that, whilst the Romans Epistle proved the *necessity* of the Chris ian religion, the object of Hebrews was to prove the *superiority* of the Christian religion, and this the writer does, *not by slighting the old*, but by showing the new as the fulfilment of the old. They had good things in the old system, but they now have everything " better." This Epistle has been called " the Fifth Gospel"—the other four speak of His work on earth, this speaks of that, and also His work in Heaven.

TOPICAL STUDY

No book lends itself so readily for topical study as this, as follows : (*a*) *"Perfect,"* (II. 10, V. 9, 14, R.V. Marg, VII. 11, 19, 28, R.V., IX. 9, 11, X. 14 XI. 40, XII. 2, R.V,) (*b*) *" Heavenly,"* (I. 10, III. 1, IV. 14, VI. 4. VII. 26, VIII. 1, 5, IX. 23, 24, X. 34, XI, 16, XII. 22, 23, 25, 26.) (*c*) *" Eternal,"* (I. 8, V. 6, 9. VI. 20. VII. 17, 21, 24, 28, IX. 12, 14, 15, XIII. 8, 20, 21.) (*d*) *:" Sat down,"* (I. 3, VIII. 1, X. 11, 12, XII. 2.) (*e*) *" Once,"* (VII. 27, IX. 12, 26,, 27, 28, X, 2, 10.) (*f*) *" Better,"* (I. 4, VI. 9, VII, 7, 19, 22, VIII. 6, IX. 23, X, 34, XI. 6, 35, 40, XII. 24.)

ANALYSIS

(A) THE ARGUMENT. Chapter I. to X.. 18					(B) THE APPLICATION. X. 19 to end
THE GLORY OF THE PERSON AND WORK OF CHRIST					**THE LIFE *WE* SHOULD LIVE BECAUSE OF HIS LIFE AND WORK**
(1) The Lord Jesus **Greater than Prophets**	(2) The Lord Jesus **Greater than Angels**	(3) The Lord Jesus **Greater than Moses**	(4) The Lord Jesus **Greater than Joshua**	(5) The Lord Jesus **Greater than Aaron**	Like a wise preacher, the writer did not leave the application until the end, but repeatedly drove home the lesson, as II. 1 to 4, III. 7 to 19, VI. 1 to 12. But the application proper begins here, and is remarkable for the repetition of the phrase, "Let us."
I. 1 to 3.	I. 4 to II	III.	IV. 1 to 13.	IV. 14 so X. 18.	**LET US :**
1. The prophets were great, but the Son is greater, because whilst God spake *"by"* the prophets, He speaks *"in"* His Son. Jesus is God's last word. 2. Observe the phrase "sat down," in verse 3. This is one of the characteristic utterances of Hebrews suggestive of a work perfectly finished.	1. Angels are great beings, but the Lord Jesus is greater, for (1) He is Son of God. (2) Begotten of God, (3) God never said to them what He says to the Lord Jesus, "Thy throne O God." 2. "The oil of gladness above Thy fellows," verse 9, proves that our Lord was not onl *"The* Man of Sorrows" but also *"The* Man of gladness."	1. How great Moses was ! But Jesus is greater. Moses was a faithful *servant,* but Jesus is a loyal Son over His own house. 2. This statement would fall with tremendous weight on the Jews of those days, as indeed it does even in our day.	1. Joshua was a great leader, yet he failed ; Jesus is a greater, for He alone can give and lead to real rest. 2. Is "the Word of God" in verse 12 the Lord Jesus ? Certainly He is the Word of God, and is alive (quick) and powerful, and the All-wise and All-knowing One.	Aaron and his successors were great, but Jesus is better, for : 1. He was sinless, whilst they were sinful, IV. 15. 2. He was Priest after a higher order than the Aaronic, V. 6. 3. He is our Fore-runner—Aaron never was, VI. 20. 4. Abraham acknowledged Melchisedec greater, VII. 4. 5. The order of Melchisedec is an *everlasting* one, VII. 16. 17. 6. Aaron served the shadows, Jesus the realities, VIII. 1-5 7, He is the medium of a better Covenant, VIII 6-13. 8. He ministers in a better sanctuary, IX. 1 to 25. 9. And ministers as offering a better sacrifice, IX. 25-28.	1. "Be borne along" (literal rendering) - VI. 1. 2. "Draw near" - X. 19 to 22. 3. "Hold fast" - X, 23. 4. "Consider one another"- X. 24, 25. 5. Persevere - X. 26 to XI. 6. "Lay aside every weight and sin" - XII. 1. 7. "Run with patience" - XII. 1, 2. 8. "Endure manfully" - XII. 3 to 29. 9. "Let brotherly love continue" - XIII. 1 to 4. 10. "Let your conversation be without covetousness" - XIII. 5. 11. "Go forth" - XIII. 13. 12. "Offer the sacrifice of praise" - XIII. 15.

AUTHOR

(1) Without doubt. *James, the brother of our Lord, was its writer.* Three men bearing the name of James are mentioned in the New Testament : (1) The son of Zebedee, (2) The son of Alphæus, (3) James, the Just, our Lord's brother, the writer of this letter.

(2) He was bitterly opposed to our Lord during His earthly ministry, but was converted by a special and private interview with the Risen One (1 Cor. XV. 7), became a man of prayer, was made Bishop of the Jerusalem Church (Acts XV. 13 to 21, Gal. II. 9), and was slain by Jews, A.D. 62.

STYLE

(1) It was *written by a Jew to Jewish Christians*, and there is a great deal that is distinctly Jewish in its style and spirit.

(2) *One clue to the Epistle is the character of James himself.* He was stern and severe, much like the Old Testament prophets. His style is curt, bold, rapid ; he was a wonderful man for metaphors (I. 6, 10, 17, 18, 21, 23, V. 5).

TIME

By internal evidence, authorities are more and more coming to agree that we have in James the *first* of the New Testament Epistles. It must have been written between A.D. 45 and A.D. 53. This is of vast importance. Many have imagined that James wrote his Epistle to combat the Pauline view of Justification by faith, as unfolded in Romans, whereas it was written some years *before* Romans.

PURPOSE

(1) Jewish Christians were passing through severe trials and temptations, and he writes to comfort and encourage them.

(2) There were grave disorders in the early Jewish Christian assemblies, and he writes to correct same.

(3) There was a tendency to divorce faith and works. *"A right strawy Epistle,"* says Luther, referring, presumably, to the "stubble" of 1 Cor. III. 12—" Having no true evangelical character." He was unable, through hasty views of the Epistle, to reconcile it with the grand doctrine which he felt called upon to champion ; but years afterwards he saw differently, that, in fact, James is really the complement to Paul. The proof that I am justified by faith is seen in my works.

CONTENTS

(1) There is little doctrine here, but much of practice, and much of morals. James was exceedingly practical. He lived what he preached. This is a book of Holy Living.

(2) Its key verse is II. 26. *It is, in reality, a very practical treatise on Faith, its nature and work.* It seems almost as fragmentary and disconnected as Proverbs, but on closer inspection beautiful order is discerned.

(1) Greeting	(2) Faith Tested and Shown by our Temptations	(3) Faith Shown by our Works	(4) Faith Shown by our Words	(5) Faith Shown by lives of Unworldliness	(6) Faith Shown by our Patience under Cruel Wrong	(7) Faith Shown by our Believing and Effectual Prayers
I. 1.	I. 2 to 21.	I. 22 to II.	III.	IV.	V. 1 to 12.	V. 13 to 20.
1. Note his humility in making no reference to his relationship to Jesus. 2. Only mentions Jesus twice, but see how reverently and devotedly he refers to Him. This is worthy of our attention, for, alas, usually familiarity breeds contempt.	1. Count the testing a glorious opportunity of proving our faith (2 to 4). 2. For wisdom to behave wisely in time of trial, when wronged and insulted, ask God (5 to 11). 3. The man who does not escape, but survives and conquers temptation, is blessed (12). 4. Temptations to evil do not come from God (13 to 18). 5. Under trial, be slow to speak (19 to 21).	1. Do not be deceived about God (16 R.V.), ourselves (22), or religion (26). 2. Respect of persons is not only a breach of good manners, and discourteous to the poor, but sin (II. 1 to 13). 3. From II. 14 to 26 we have the very heart of the Epistle, showing that real living faith is always known by its fruits.	1. "It is quite apparent from this letter that there was a great deal of ill-considered, ill-natured, self-assertive, and violent speech amongst Jewish Christians ; a great deal of angry debating and bitter strife. 2. Here he shows that one proof of our justified state is seen in our *Words*— our speech will reveal what, and whose, we are.	1. "The world is that order of things about us, or that spirit in us, which is blind and deaf to the value and reality of spiritual things, and careless to the Will of God." 2. Unworldliness is here shown to be an infallible proof that we stand amongst the justified, that we have real and saving faith in Christ Jesus. 3. Observe "Submit" to God before attempting to "resist the Devil"	1. Evidently many of the humble folk amongst the Christian Jews were oppressed by the wealthy, and defrauded of their hard earnings. 2. Faith in Christ and His Coming will lead us to a patient sufferance of evils we cannot avoid. 3. This has application to-day. 4. "The Just One." is R.V. of verse 6.	1. The tradition concerning James is that his knees were worn hard as a camel's through his constant habit of prayer. 2. What he practised he preached. 3. Note how abruptly the Epistle closes. There is no leave-taking. It could not close with a more impressive note. 4. Specially note, the "Weymouth" rendering of verse 16.

First Epistle of PETER

FOR WHOM?

(1) This letter was written by St. Peter towards the close of his life (A.D. 60), whilst he was staying at Babylon (V. 13), where a Christian Church had been established, and was sent by the hand of Silas (V. 12), one of Paul's companions, now free for this work, as Paul was a prisoner.

(2) It was intended principally, though not exclusively, for Hebrew Christians (Jews—I. 1, R.V.; Gentiles—II. 9, 10).

PURPOSE

Evidently it was written for a two-fold purpose: First—Many of the primitive Christians had begun to think that St. Paul and St. Peter held diverse views on the fundamentals of our Christian faith. It is thought that Peter wrote this Epistle, and sent it, by the hand of Paul's companion, to the Asiatic Churches planted by Paul, to demolish that error. Second—It was also *intended to strengthen and encourage the converted Jews who were passing through sore trial and bitter persecution*, and thus perform the ministry our Lord had bade him exercise, (see Luke XXII. 31, 32.)

PETER TRANSFIGURED

The portrait of Peter in the Gospels and his own writings are amazingly and gloriously different. In the former, Peter saw his Lord transfigured; in the latter, we see Peter transfigured by the boundless grace of God. In the former, we see Peter impetuous, courageous, restless, buoyant, quick to meet personal slight, and ambitious of earthly power; but in the latter, we see him patient, restful, forbearing, trustful, loving, and with the old buoyancy and courage purified and ennobled. It provides a telling illustration of the transforming power of the grace of God.

KEY WORDS

(1) The word "precious" was evidently a favourite with Peter. Seven precious things are mentioned—1 Peter I. 7; 19, II. 4, 6, 7, III. 4. 2 Peter I. 1, 4.

(2) Peter was radiantly buoyant, therefore it need not surprise us to find that "Hope" was another of his favourites. (I. 3, 13, 21, III. 15.) Whilst Paul has been called the "Apostle of Faith," and John, "the Apostle of Love," Peter is called "the Apostle of Hope."

(3) Peter is great on Election (I. 2); Foreknowledge (I. 20); Trinity (I. 2); Vicarious death of Christ (I. 2, 18, 19, II. 21, 24, III. 18, IV. 1).

(4) Peter was most teachable, and never forgot his lesson. He learned, I. 17, in Acts X. 15, 34; II. 4 to 8, in Matthew XVI. 18; II. 25, in John X. 1; IV. 19, in Luke XXIII. 46; V. 2, at John XXI. 15, 17; V. 5. in John XIII. 4, 5.

(5) But *the* key word is "Suffering." This word, and its equivalent, is found twenty-one times in this short Epistle, and gives the message of the book. The sufferings of Christ are referred to in every chapter, though never once in the second Epistle.

(1) Key—I. Verse 6.	(2) Key—II. 12, 19, 20. III. 1, 17 (with IV. 15, 16).	(3) Key—IV. 13.	(4) Key—V. 1, (with I. 11, 13 and V. 10.)	(5) Key—V. 9.
Able to Rejoice in suffering because of **SALVATION** I. 1 to 13.	That we should Suffer Innocently and to the Glory of God. **HOLINESS** is Essential. I. 14 to III.	In thus Suffering, we have **FELLOWSHIP** with our Lord. IV.	In Suffering, Never Forget the **GLORY** which shall follow. V. 1 to 4.	Remember, Suffering is **COMMON** to All. V. 5 to end.
1. "Peter," the name Jesus gave him. 2. Note the force of the word, "Wherein," in verse 6. 3. This glorious salvation which is ours through grace, enables us, through suffering and trial, "to rejoice with joy unspeakable." 4. And with great hope (13).	1. The imperative need and necessity for holiness of heart and life underlies all that Peter writes in this section. 2. He is anxious that none should, by careless and sinful conduct, merit persecution and suffering. 3. Loose living exposes us to the scorn of the enemies of the Cross.	1. Note, "they think it strange," (verse 4), and "think it not strange" (12). 2. The thought Peter gives here is that, provided the life is right, in suffering we are in blessed fellowship with our Lord. 3. There is a covering of sin which is legitimate (8) provided it be the sin of others and not our own.	1. One blessed comfort in sorrow and trial is the thought of the future. 2. This short section is full of "the glory that should follow." 3. "Be clothed with humility" (5) is literally "Put on humility like a slave's apron."	1. It is not good to imagine that none suffer as we. 2. The fact is, as we have it in verse 9, that suffering and sorrow are experiences common to all. None are exempt. 3. "Humble yourselves" (6), else He will be compelled to humiliate you.

Second Epistle of PETER

AUTHOR

There is hardly a book in the New Testament the authorship of which has been so called into question as this. Usually four objections are given why we should not believe that Peter wrote it, but these objections can be satisfactorily dealt with :

(a) Doubts were raised as to the Petrine authorship as far back as the third century. Answer: Objections concerning other books were held in the third century, but proofs have been discovered in our own time showing how groundless these objections were.

(b) It could not have been written in Peter's lifetime, as "all" Paul's epistles had not then been written (see III. 16). Answer: But surely the plain sense of III. 16 is " all his epistles " then written !

(c) The style and language are different from that of 1 Peter. Answer : Surely the fact that it was written for a different purpose settles this?

(d) Chapter II. is evidently a copy of Jude, and surely no one dare charge the great Apostle with plagarism. Answer: Neither Peter copied from Jude, nor did Jude copy from Peter. Peter, in chapter II., prophesies (note future tense in II. 1, "shall be "); Jude, in Jude 4, 12, 16, 17, shows that Peter's prophecy has now come to pass (note present tense " there are ").

Note—(a) the writer was an apostle (III. 2) ; and (b) an apostle who had been one of the privileged three on the Mount of Transfiguration (I. 18) ; (c) and had written an epistle prior to this to the same people (III. 1) ; (d) therefore the claim of I. 1 is the only logical possibility.

CONTENTS

This letter contains a touching reference to Peter's old age and impending death (I. 14), and to his experience on Transfiguration Mount (I. 17, 18), is remarkable for its description of the Christian graces (I. 5 to 8), the last days (III. 4 to 11), and eulogy of Paul's epistles III. 16.

KEY WORDS

There are four words frequently met with in this Epistle, and they are characteristic of the book : (a) Peter, who knew his Lord so well, speaks frequently of the value of such a *knowledge of the Lord*, (I. 2, 3, 5, 8, III 18, II. 20) ; (b) he was energetic, and thought highly of *diligence* (I. 5, 10, III. 14) ; (c) he had suffered much from forgetfulness, therefore he is great on *remembrance* (I. 12, 13, 15, III. 1, 2) ; (a) and he has much to say on *corruption* and pollution (I. 4, II. 12, 19, 20).

PURPOSE

This second epistle was written for an altogether different purpose from that of 1 Peter. The first was designed to encourage and support Christians under trial and persecution. but *the second one was intended to warn them against false teachers and their corrupt and corrupting doctrines.* This is why the Lord's sufferings are never once mentioned in the second Epistle. In the first, enemies are met with ; in the second, darkness is mentioned, and the need of the Lamp of Truth (I. 19). The first was written to console, the second to warn ; in the first, we have much about suffering, in the second, much about error.

ANALYSIS

It falls into three divisions, as follows : (Note each section has its Key, Cure, and Safeguard.)

(1) Moral Corruption	(2) Doctrinal Corruption	(3) Steadfastness — In View of this Corruption.
Key—I. 4. Cure—The Divine Nature. Safeguard—Remembrance, I. 12, 13.	Key—II. 1, 2. Cure—Scriptures, I. 19. Safeguard—Remembrance, 1, 15.	Key—III. 17. Cure and Safeguard—Remembrance, III. 1, 2.
I. 1 to 14.	I. 15 to end of II.	III.
HOW 1. Precious faith is obtained, verse 1. 2. To gain more peace and grace, verse 2. 3. To receive all things necessary for life and godliness, 3. 4. To escape moral corruption, verse 4. 5. To avoid spiritual shortsightedness, verses 5 to 9. 6. Not to fall, verse 10. 7. To have an abundant entrance, 11.	1. Christian Faith no fable, I. 16. 2. Divine origin of Scriptures, I. 17 to 21. 3. *False teachers*, II. 1. 4. Their large following, II. 2, 5. And their severe judgment, II. 3 to 9. 6. Their presumption, II. 10 to 11. 7. Corrupt doctrine produces corrupt practices, II. 12 to 22.	1. Even pure minds need prompting, verse 1. 2. One fruit of false teaching is rejection of second advent truths, verses 3 to 9. 3. Certainty of the Day of the Lord, verse 10. 4. Fruit of belief in His coming is holiness of heart and life, verses 11 to 17. 5. The importance of spiritual growth, verse 18.

First Epistle of JOHN

WRITER

This Epistle, written by the aged Apostle John about the year 90 A.D., probably at Ephesus, was not addressed to any particular Church or individual, but to all Christians, see II. 12 to 14.

PURPOSE

(1) Soon after the Christian Church was founded, error crept into its teaching. The converts from Judaism and Paganism sought to impregnate the Christian faith with the theories of their former beliefs. This led to heresy and apostasy, culminating eventually in Gnosticism. This sect, whilst admitting the Deity of Jesus, denied His humanity, and held other heretical views. They styled themselves Gnostics (knowing ones), posed as " the aristocracy of knowledge," boasted that they alone had the true knowledge, and looked down with pity and contempt upon all who were old fashioned enough to adhere to the apostolic faith.

(2) Without doubt, St. John had this heresy in mind when he wrote this epistle: (a) In I. 1, 2, he declares the humanity of Christ, affirming that they had not only heard, but seen and handled Him. (b) Denounced those who denied that humanity (IV. 2, 3). (c) Emphasized the fact that the Gnostics had not a monopoly of knowledge, but the Christian, the orthodox believer, had a knowledge not derived, as theirs, from speculation, but from revelation. (See I. 5, II. 20 and 27.) The word "know" and its equivalent is met with thirty-two times in this Epistle. See section (4) in Analysis below.

TOPICAL STUDY

The topical method of study is valuable in enabling one to grasp the teaching of this letter. For instance, let us take three topics:

(a) LOVE. (1) God's love to sinners (IV. 9, 10); (2) the outcome of that love is adoption (III. 1); (3) Why we ought to love one another (IV. 11 with III. 11 and 23); (4) What the fact that we love proves (III. 14); (5) Love—Its absence or presence is the difference between a child of God and a child of the Devil (III. 10); (6) Why we love God (IV. 19); (7) What loving the world proves (II. 15); (8) in whom the love of God is matured (II. 5): (9) the result of that mature love (IV. 18); (10) and the great fact of all that God is not only " Light " (I. 5), but " Love " (IV. 16).

(b) SIN. (1) Its universality (I. 8, 10); (2) Two definitions of sin (III. 4, V. 17); (3) Why our Lord came (II. 2, III. 5, IV. 10); (4) There is cleansing from sin (I. 7); (5) for those who confess (I. 9); (6) We may know that our sins are forgiven (II. 12); (7) No need to be continually slipping into sin (II. 1, also see III. 8, 9); (8) Secret of overcoming sin is "abiding" (III. 6), and "being kept" (V. 18 R.V.)

(c) NEW BIRTH. Its evidences and results: (1) Doth not continue in sin (III. 9); (2) Love (IV. 7); (3) Faith (V. 1); (4) Overcomes (V. 4); (5) the begotten one is kept by the only Begotten of the Father (V. 18, R.V.); (6) Holy Living (II. 29.)

JOHN'S FOUR REASONS

John, himself, gives four reasons for the writing of this Epistle, and all are the fruits of living in fellowship with God.

(1)	(2)	(3)	(4)
John Wrote: (1) "That your joy may be full." I. 4.	John Wrote: (2) That they might know there was no necessity for sinning, II. 1·	John Wrote: (3) That they might be put on guard against error, II. 26 R.V.	John Wrote: "That ye may know."
The Life of Fellowship **Is the Joyful Life**	The Life of Fellowship **Is the Victorious Life**	The Life of Fellowship **Is the Guarded Life**	The Life of Fellowship **Is the Life of Knowledge**
I.	II. 1 to 17.	II. 18 to IV. 6.	IV. 7 to end of V.
1. These Christians to whom John wrote, had joy (the joy of forgiveness), but not fulness of joy (the joy of fellowship).	1. The life of fellowship means victory, therefore there is no need to go on in bondage to sin, no necessity for sinning, but alas we do sin (1).	1. Heresy already at work, II. 18, 19.	1. A knowledge that rests upon the testimony of God's Word and God's Spirit, V. 6 to 12.
2. He points out that fulness of joy is the outcome of fellowship (a) with the Father, (b) Jesus Christ, and (c) with our fellow-believers.	2. And *for us there is an Advocate through Whom our fellowship can be maintained !* and pray note that the atonement is by no means a limited one (1, 2).	2. But believers were safe—guarded by the Holy anointing (II. 20 to 27).	2. For what we know, consider the following Passages:
3. He notes that this close and blessed fellowship is conditional on :	3. Fellowship with God means, and is dependent upon (a) obedience (verses 3 to 6) (b) not loving the world (15 to 17), (c) but our brethren (7 to 11).	3. *The Gnostics talked a great deal, and lived badly,* not so the Christians (III. 11 to 24).	II. 3, 5, 13, 14, 20, 21. 29. III. 2, 5, 14, 15, 19, 24. IV. 2, 6, 13, 16. V, 2, 13, 15, 18, 19, 20,
(a) Walking in the light. (b) Confession of sin. (c) Forgiveness of sin. (d) Cleansing from sin.		4. Why the world hates us (III. 1). 5. The marks of the false teachers (IV. 1 to 6).	

Second Epistle of JOHN

NATURE

(1) This Epistle is notable as being *the only one in the New Testament exclusively addressed to a lady.*

(2) It is *a private, personal letter*, addressed to an unknown Christian woman and her family, and is a charming example of the private correspondence of the apostles, and of the early Christian Church.

(3) Who the "lady" was is not known. Some consider that the words "elect lady" constitute a title, proving that the individual was one who was well-to-do, and moved in high society. There is a tradition that *the person addressed was Martha of Bethany.* Bengel says that the Greek "kyria" (lady) answers to the Hebrew "Martha." If this be true, the "Sister" referred to in verse 13 would be Mary.

AUTHOR

(1) Owing to the absence of a name in the introduction, the authorship of this Epistle has been much disputed.

(2) There is every evidence that John wrote it. It resembles his first Epistle very closely—eight of its thirteen verses may be found in the first Epistle, either in sense or expression. John must have been a very old man when he wrote it. He calls himself "Elder." He must have been at least ninety years of age.

PURPOSE

(1) The word "love" occurs four times in this short Epistle (1, 3, 5. 6), "truth" five times (1 (*twice*), 2, 3, 4).

(2) It appears to have been *written to warn a benevolent lady against entertaining some false teachers* (10).

KEY

(1) Without doubt, Truth must be considered the key-word of this Epistle, and as providing its message.

(2) That word is used in three senses: (1) for the body of Christian teaching (1 and 4); (2) for Christ, Himself; and (3) for "truly."

(3) Thus it provides us with *a little homily on truth, giving us its nature, test, fruit, character, and defence.*

(1) LOVE In the TRUTH	(2) FORSAKE Of the TRUTH	(3) SALUTATION In the TRUTH	(4) WALKING In the TRUTH	(5) THE TEST Of the TRUTH	(6) DEFENCE Of the TRUTH
Verse 1	Verse 2.	Verse 3.	Verses 4 to 6.	Verses 7 to 9.	Verses 10 to 13.
1. John did not scruple to give this lady her own title of honour. 2. Truth as the: (a) Source of love (See R.V.) (b) Nature of love (no pretence of love). (c) Reasons for love (her loyalty to truth). 3. Not only John, but all who knew her and her family, loved them.	1. Can we not spell Truth here with a capital "T"? He *is* Truth. 2. He, as Truth, is: (a) Within us, (b) With us, (c) and for His sake we love and do.	1. A most unusual form of salutation, only found in the pastoral epistles. 2. We need both. (a) Grace, (b) Mercy, (c) and Peace. 3. Note the combination of Divine names.	1. "Certain of" is R.V. of verse 4. 2. Truth is given to walk in (4). 3. We must love (5). 4. And love manifests itself in ready obedience (6).	1. Denying the reality of Christ's humanity. (a) In His earthly life, (b) and in His second advent (see R.V.) is one mark of Antichrist and false teachers. 2. Don't be crownless (verse 8).	1. There is a false charity. 2. In defence of the truth, we must not entertain or bid godspeed to false teachers. 3. An affectionate ending (verses 12, 13).

Third Epistle of JOHN

MESSAGE
1. The duty of Hospitality in the Church.
2. The Peril of Domineering Leadership.

FOR WHOM

(1) This letter was written "unto the well-beloved Gaius," (verse 1,) by the apostle John when an aged man.

(2) There are five individuals referred to by this name: (1) Gaius of Macedonia, Acts XIX. 29; (2) Gaius of Derbe, Acts XX. 4; (3) one whom Paul baptised, 1 Cor. I. 14; (4) one of Paul's hosts, Romans XVI. 23; (5) and the one John wrote to. Probably the last three were one and the same.

(3) Therefore we learn that Gaius was converted through John (verse 4), baptised by Paul, and was a wealthy and hospitable member of the Church at Corinth.

PURPOSE

(1) Many of the early Christians were called to a life of itinerant evangelism, without fee or earthly reward (verse 7), consequently they were dependent upon the hospitality of the Christians settled in the various towns, villages, or cities they passed through.

(2) A man called Diotrephes had secured almost absolute control over this Church, and in a domineering and autocratic manner, refused to entertain or allow these evangelists to minister there, and excommunicated the hospitable church members who did receive them (verse 10). John had written to the Church about the matter (one of the many lost epistles), but Diotrephes had rejected it, and would not acknowledge John's apostolic authority (verse 9).

(3) The aged apostle now wrote to generous and warm-hearted Gaius, commending him for past kindnesses shown, and urging him to continue his most God-like work of entertaining the Lord's servants in spite of Diotrephes (verses 5, 6, 8), promising to deal drastically with this usurper when he next visited that church (verse 10).

CONTRAST

A striking contrast is seen in the three persons mentioned in this short epistle: (1) Gaius, the kind, generous, and hospitable; (2) Diotrephes, the arrogant church official; and (3) Demetrius, who was praised by all,

CONTRIBUTION

Though this letter contains no important doctrinal teaching, it is yet of great value, as giving us the beginning of arrogant, autocratic, and domineering leadership, which has been such a curse to the Christian Church, both in the days of the past, as well as the present. Even an apostle's authority was called into question.

TRUTH

As in the second epistle, the word " Truth " is frequently referred to. Truth is viewed: (1) as the source and nature of the Apostle's love, verse 1; (2) as an inward presence and power, verse 3; (3) manifesting itself in outward practice, verses 3 and 4. We are exhorted to use Truth as our weapon in Christian service and warfare—see R.V. of 8, and as our companion and partner, verse 8 A.V. Truth will then give its testimony in our favour, verse 12.

ANALYSIS

(A) Introduction and Salutation.			(B) The Purpose of the Epistle.		(C) Conclusion.	
(1) The Apostle's LOVE	(2) The Apostle's PRAYER	(3) The Apostle's REJOICING	(1) The Apostle's Commendation and EXHORTATION	(5) The Apostle's DENUNCIATION	(6) The Apostle's COMMENDATION	(6) The Apostle's EXPLANATION
Verse 1.	Verse 2.	Verses 3 and 4.	Verses 5 to 8.	Verses 9 to 11.	Verse 12.	Verses 13 and 14.
1. Note the strong affection of the Apostle. 2. His love was (a) Sincere, (R.V.) (b) Rooted in truth. (c) On account of the truth.	1. Not merely a wish, but, as R.V. shows, was a prayer. 2. Was Gaius ill and weak in body? 3. He was well in soul. 4. Look well at R.V.	1. Truth was to Gaius, (a) Indwelling power. (b) Road he walked on. (c) Atmosphere he breathed. 2. Note what John rejoiced over.	1. By "brethren and strangers," John means converted Jews and Gentiles. 2. One can hardly tell where John's commendation ends and exhortation begins. 3. Read verses 7 and 8 in R.V.	1. This letter is lost, 9. 2. Diotrephes (a) Loved to be in front (b) Rejected John's letter. (c) Backbited John. (d) Was inhospitable. (e) Commended inhospitality. (f) Cast out hospitable.	1. Was this the same Demetrius as Acts XIX. 24? If so, what a change! 2. He had good opinion of (a) All men (b) Of Truth itself. (c) Of Apostle. (d) Of other Christians.	1. Here John explains why he wrote so brief a letter. 2. The Apostle valued friendship.

The Epistle of JUDE

AUTHOR

(1) Jude, (another form of Judas), brother to our Lord and to James, (Matthew XIII. 55, Mark VI. 3,) was the author of this letter.

(2) Like James, he was not an apostle, but an ordinary disciple. *"He was a plain man, but of fiery spirit, and filled with prophetic zeal"* ; yet, behind all that austerity beat a warm and loving heart—note occurrence of the term, "Beloved" (3, 17, 20).

TO WHOM?

(1) It must have been written about A D. 69, as he refers to the prophecy in 2 Peter, and that was not written until A.D. 66. His brother James had died a martyr a few years before he wrote this letter.

(2) It was not written to any particular church or people, but to all Christians everywhere, hence called a " General Epistle.'

WHY WRITTEN

(1) By verse 3 it appears he was about to write a treatise on Salvation, when he was constrained by the Spirit to change its theme. *Already the primitive Church was in dire peril through traitors within it, through many who had deliberately rejected the faith, though still retaining their membership. He writes to warn them, and to put them on their guard.*

(2) *Jude's epistle is one of the most solemn in the Bible.* It gives a history of apostasy from before time to the end of time, dealing with the ambitious angels, self-righteous Cain, depraved Sodomites. rebellious Israel, greedy Balaam, presumptuous Korah, and the apostasy of his day and ours; in all, three judgments on *corporate* wickedness, and three on *individual*.

NOTE

(1) It is the only book in the Bible which records the strife over the body of Moses (9), and Enoch's prophecy (14, 15).

(2) Three eternal things are mentioned : (1) life, verse 21 ; (2) chains, verse 6 ; (5) fire, verse 7.

(3) Its key words are " keep " and " kept," mentioned five times, 1 and 6, R.V., 21 and 24 A,V, Its divisions are six, as follows :

(1) To whom written ?	(2) Why it was written	(3) Past Instances of Apostasy	(4) A Vivid Description of the Character of the then Apostates.	(5) The Necessity of Keeping in Love, as well as in the Faith.	(6) A Remarkable and Beautiful Doxology
To the Lord's people who were **Kept by God** for the **Lord Jesus**	To Exhort the Lord's People to Contend for and to **Keep the Faith**	Those who Kept not to the paths of truth and obedience are **Kept Unto Judgment**	Disastrous deterioration of Character through **Not Keeping the Faith**	The Lord's people to see that they are **Kept in the Love of God**	The Lord's people to be **Kept from Stumbling**
Verses 1 and 2.	Verses 3 and 4.	Verses 5 to 7.	Verses 8 to 19.	Verses 20 to 23.	Verses 24 and 25.
1. R.V. for "preserved" is "kept for Jesus Christ." 2. It is written to those who are (as R.V.); (a) Called ones. (b) Beloved of God. (s) Preserved through union with Christ. (d) and "kept for Jesus Christ," as a precious gift to be presented to Him by God, the Father.	1. Note the RV. rendering of verse 3, which shows the Holy Spirit constrained him to change his theme. 2. "*Common* salvation" does not mean a salvation that is cheap and of little value, but a salvation available for all, as our village commons. 3. "*Once* delivered" means that it needs no further commendation, and is incapable of improvement.	1. As a warning they were reminded of well known instances of apostasy, upon whom the severe judgment of God fell, even in this life, with the certainty of judgment in the future. 2. Those who "kept not" are "kept" (R. V. *i.e.* reserved unto judgment).	To forsake the faith leads to terrible deterioration in character as shown here: (a) Loose morals, 19, 18. (b) Corrupt thoughts, 8, 10. (c) Impatient of control, 8, 16. (d) Mocking spirit, 8. 18. (e) Boastful words, 8, 10, 16. (f) Outwardly religious, but mere shams, 12, 13, 19. (g) Indeed, act as "hidden rocks," (verse 12 R.V.) (h) Always complaining (note Weymouth on 16).	1. It is possible to be loyal to truth and yet lack love. 2. Note, there must be on our part: (a) Building, 20. (b) Praying, 20. (c) Keeping, 21. (d) Looking, 21. (e) Pitying, 22- (f) Saving, 23. (g) Hating, 23.	1. This is a strikingly beautiful doxology. 2. How glorious it is to learn that He is able to keep us from even "stumbling." (R. V. for "falling.") Stumbling is that which precedes falling.

ANALYSIS No. 66

Key Verse, I. 19. Key Phrase, 'The Revelation of Jesus Christ.' The Book OF THE REVELATION

MESSAGE

Jesus, the Gloriously Triumphant One

DIFFICULT BOOK.

This is confessedly *the* book of the Bible most difficult of interpretation; and because of this, though a special blessing is promised to its readers (I. 3), it is very much neglected. We cannot but think that Satan has something to do with this neglect, because it has so much to say about his final downfall. Why should we pass the book by because it is so mysterious and difficult? Do men of science leave scientific problems alone because they happen to be difficult to fathom and comprehend?

SPLENDID FINISH TO BIBLE

It makes a splendid finish to the Divine library. The Rev. Archibald G. Brown points out the striking balance which exists *between* Genesis and Revelation. " In Genesis I see earth created; in Revelation I see it passing away. In Genesis Sun and Moon appear; in Revelation I read they have no need of the Sun or Moon. In Genesis there is a garden, which is the home for man; in Revelation there is a city, the home for the nations. In Genesis there is the marriage of the first Adam; in Revelation there is the marriage of the second Adam. In Genesis there is the first grim appearance of that great enemy Satan; in Revelation there is his final doom. In Genesis there is the inauguration of sorrow and suffering, you hear the first sob, you see the first tear; in Revelation there is no more sorrow, and no more pain, and all tears are wiped away. In Genesis we hear the mutter of the curse, which falls because of sin; in Revelation we read 'there shall be no more curse.' In Genesis we see man driven out from the garden with the tree of life; in Revelation we see him welcomed back, with the tree of life at his disposal."

CLUES

In order to a right understanding of the book, several facts must be noted, and constantly kept in mind:

(1) It gives a glowing portrait of the Lord Jesus as the Triumphant One. The key phrase is "The Revelation of Jesus Christ." It unveils the Lord Jesus. "*Whoever sets upon the study of the book to find out what it says about the Lord Jesus, will find it a marvellous revelation,*" No less than twenty-six times do we find in it Christ's sacrificial title " Lamb." It is full of Him!

(2) After the end of Chapter III. the Church is never represented as on the earth in this book. Between Chapters III. and IV. the removal of the Church must have taken place. Chapter IV. and onward has to do with the awful tribulation and last things.

(3) The law of recurrence (to be observed in other books of the Bible, notably that of Genesis) must be noted. After reviewing some great procession or national event, on returning home we usually give an account to our loved ones of what we have seen. After completing our story, we may return to the subject again and again to give additional particulars. This is the law of recurrence. This is precisely what John does. After giving an account of the beginning of the Judgments on the earth, and the final victory of the Lord Jesus in Chapters IV. to XI. 18 (see Division C, Section 1, of Analysis), he returns again to the subject in Chapters XI. 19 to XVI., and again in XVII. to XXII. It is most important to keep this law of recurrence in mind when reading Revelation.

ANALYSIS

Chapter I. verse 19 gives the three-fold division, the last again falling into three sub-sections.

(A) "The things which thou hast seen."	(B) " The things which are."	(C) "The things which shall be hereafter."		
(1) THE LORD JESUS AS THE **GLORIFIED ONE**	(2) THE LORD JESUS AS THE **HEAD OVER THE CHURCH**	(3) THE LORD JESUS AS (4) **THE TRIUMPHANT ONE**		(5)
I.	II. and III.	IV. to XI. 18.	XI. 19 to XVI.	XVII. to XXII.
1. Revelation, not revelations. 2. Of Jesus, and not of John. 3. Blessing for readers and hearers, verse 3. 4. Glowing vision of the Lord Jesus. 5. Observe, that the R.V. of verse 5 gives love in the present tense, He did love us, but, blessed be His Name, He still loves.	1. The Lord's striking message to the seven Churches of Asia. 2. of They are applicable to the Churches to-day. 3. Before the vision of the Father in IV. 3, we have the vision and words of the Son in I. to III. I must get to know the Son before I can savingly know the Father. He is the way to God.	1. Scene shifts from earth to Heaven, to the audience chamber of the Most High, IV. 2. The book in chapter V. is not the book of life, but of Judgment. 3. The day of tribulation begins with the opening of the seals, VI. 4. The plagues increase in intensity and severity in succeeding chapters. 5. Chapter VII. must be considered in the light of a parenthesis, a welcome break to get a view of the Lord preserving His own. 6. At last we see the final and complete victory of our Divine and ever-blessed Lord.	1. The former division had more to do with secular evils and wickedness, having for its standpoint the Throne: this division has more to do with spiritual wickedness, and its standpoint is the Temple. 2. In former divisions we began with Christ as the Glorified One; here we are taken further back, even to His birth, and shown the Devil's hatred of Jesus, and attempts to get rid of Him 3. We get the rise and progress of the awful trinity of evil. 4. Then the sight of Christ as Conqueror, the defeat of the allied forces of evil, and the fall of Babylon.	1. We are again introduced to the last things, in order to get further particulars about, (a) Fall of Babylon, XVII. XVIII. (b) Advent of Christ the Conqueror, and marriage of the Lamb, XIX. (c) Satan's fall, imprisonment, final overthrow and end, XX. (d) New heavens and earth, XXI. (e) Garden City, and last words of Jesus, XXII. 2. Note, there are four woes and four alleluias all in chapter XIX.; there are nine references to woe, yet ten songs.